Navigation Essentials:

An introductory guide to learning to navigate on land or at sea

by
Scott H. Fraser

ISBN (978-0-692-50572-4)

*This book is dedicated to my wife Stephanie
and to our children Riley and Wren.
May you always follow your own compass.*

Table of Contents

Introduction

This book is written for the purpose of providing to the novice navigator some basic and essential tools and knowledge for the purpose of being able to navigate on land or sea. The material in this text represents the results of over 20 years of personal and professional navigation as an outdoor educator and guide. It is in no way a complete collection of the body of navigational knowledge. Instead, this book contains the most basic building blocks for becoming proficient at staying found.

Written as a text for a basic navigation course, this book contains activities at the end of each chapter that will allow the reader to demonstrate understanding of key principles introduced in that chapter. I have tried to approach each concept with the intention of providing the reader with an understanding of each principle, rather than require a memorization of specific steps. I believe firmly that if a learner truly understands the theory behind a process, there will be no need to memorize anything.

However, I have also provided step-by-step guides for most of the major processes introduced into this book, mainly to be used as a reminder or to provide a systematic application of the theory, rather than suggest the reader memorize the steps.

This book is written as a guide, not a novel. I don't recommend sitting down and reading it cover to cover. Rather, follow through each chapter sequentially. Navigation is an active process - you must get out and "*do navigation*" to become good at it. Apply the concepts discussed in each chapter by getting outside and trying them out. Practice the processes and attempt to understand *why they work*.

Notice that I have not included methods that involve electronic navigation, such as GPS and other technologies. In this age of high-tech gadgetry, I believe that understanding the basic manual skills discussed in this book is fundamental and can provide a level of confidence and proficiency in navigating that will enhance your use of technology later on.

As you become more proficient, be aware that there is always more to learn about navigating in the outdoors. There are numerous resources available to help you build your skills far beyond those introduced in this text. Seek out these other resources and find various methods that will compliment those I have presented in this book.

In this vein, I have included QR codes that provide links to online resources that will hopefully help the reader to better understand the concept or theory. These codes can be scanned by using a smart phone or other capable digital device with the appropriate application installed. All of these codes provided accurate and updated links at the time of publication. It is entirely possible that these links could change over time and no longer work. If you find this to be the case, please contact me and let me know so that I may update them.

Also feel free to contact me if you have any questions or comments regarding anything else printed in this book.

Scott Fraser
Perry, Maine

Part 1

Navigation
on
Land

Chapter 1
The Topographic Map
The Foundation of Navigation

Chapter Objectives:
- Demonstrate understanding of the relationship between contour lines and 3-dimensional topography
- Demonstrate the ability to accurately measure distance on a map
- Demonstrate knowledge of basic topographic map symbols

It could be argued that the ability to read a map is the most important technical outdoor skill. Even in today's world of sophisticated electronic navigation devices, understanding and interpreting a paper map forms the foundation of all navigation skills. Navigation, in turn, forms the foundation of all of our other technical skills. Whatever decision-making model we employ will at some point take in to consideration our environment. "Where are we?", "What is the terrain like?", and "Where do we want to be or *not* be?" are all data that can be collected from a map and fed into our decision-making process.

A map is a 2-dimensional drawing of a 3-dimensional surface; the earth's surface is spherical. Early on, maps were drawn by hand using measurements and mathematical calculations. Later, maps were made from photographs taken from specialized cameras mounted in low-flying aircraft. Today, most maps are created using satellite technology and a combination of aerial photographs, computer models, mathematical formulas, and measurements made by surveyors in the field.

Maps are created for a variety of purposes. For navigational purposes on land in the recreation industry, we rely specifically on ***topographic*** maps. These maps include specific information, such as elevation, that are useful for traveling through wilderness areas.

The standard source for topographic maps for use in the recreation industry is the ***United States Geological Survey (USGS)***, an agency of the US Department of the Interior.

USGS Topo Map Downloader

The USGS publishes their maps in several series based upon the amount of area each map covers. The most popular series of

What do you think is the difference between a ***planimetric*** and a ***topographic*** map?

maps for recreational use is the *7.5 minute series* as each map in the series covers a reasonably large area, yet still contains recognizable features that we might want to use for navigation,

The USGS has two types of topographic maps that will most likely be of interest to the recreational user: *US Topo*, and the *Historical Topographic Map Collection (HTMC)*. Both are available for free download via their "Map Locator and Downloader" application on their website at https://store. usgs.gov/map-locator.

Until 2006, The USGS had printed its maps and distributed them to the public through retailers such as outdoor stores, hardware stores, or through their website. These maps are static, in that once they are printed, they are not updated by the USGS. The Historical Topographic Map Collection (HTMC) includes all of these maps that were originally printed between 1884-2006. Many of these paper maps have been scanned into the computer and are now available as a download from the USGS. However, they still remain static in that they haven't been updated.

However, in 2009, the USGS launched the "US Topo" project, which included the advanced, new generation of topographic maps. These maps are modeled after the HTMC maps, but are only available as downloadable *pdf*, or portable document files, from their website. This new breed of map contains various layers of information and allow the USGS to keep the maps updated.

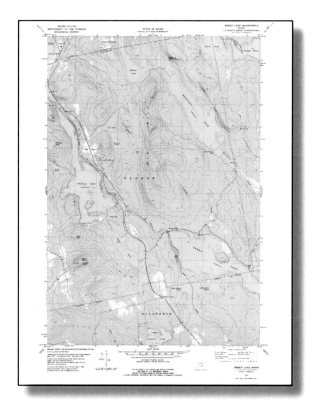

USGS Historical Topographic Map Collection (HTMC) maps may be downloaded as pdf files or may be ordered printed on paper from the USGS

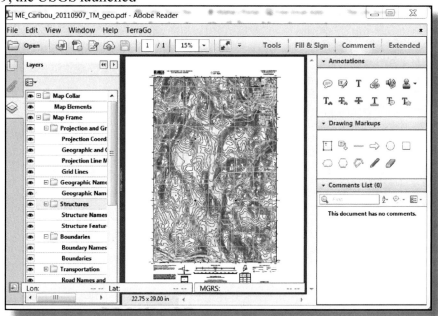

US Topo maps are available as pdf downloads and can be viewed and customized using Adobe Acrobat Reader

USGS Topo Map Margin Information

The following list explains some of the most relevant features included in the map margin at the bottom and sides of a USGS topographic map:

1. State plane coordinate system - in this case, this point is 290,000 feet north of the origin within the state plane grid system.

2. Latitude marking - the bottom edge of this map is 44 degrees, 37 minutes, and 30 seconds north of the equator.

3. Longitude marking - the left side of this map is 68 degrees, 37 minutes, and 30 seconds west of the Prime Meridian, which runs through Greenwich, England.

4. Credit Legend - this block contains critical information about when the map was made and edited, what datum was used (important for using with a gps), what UTM Zone, and what projection was used to build the map.

5. Magnetic Declination - on this map, magnetic north is 19 degrees west of true north.

6. Magnetic North Arrow - this arrow points to magnetic north.

7. True North Arrow - this arrow points to the true north pole (also known as rotational or geographic north pole).

8. Grid North Arrow - this arrow points to grid north, or the north direction of the UTM grid at the center of the map.

9. Grid Declination - on this map, UTM grid north is 18 minutes to the east of true north (see Chapter 4 for UTM info)

10. Adjoining Map Name - the name of the map that adjoins this map to the south.

11. Map Scale - this map is drawn 1/24,000th the size of the real world. In other words, 1 inch on the map equals 24,000 inches (or 2000 feet) in the real world.

12. Map Bar Scale - this scale can be used to measure distances on the map in miles, feet, or kilometers.

13. UTM Easting Marking - On this map, this point is 530,000 meters east of western side of the UTM zone (zone 19). Note that the last three zeros are omitted in an effort to declutter the map.

14. Map Reference Code - unique identifier code that can be used to reference this map. "N44337.5" references the latitude at the bottom of the map. The second part "W6830" references the longitude at the right side of the map, and the "7.5" denotes that the map is drawn to cover 7.5 minutes of latitude (or is drawn at 1:24,000 scale).

15. Map Date - indicates the date the map was drawn or last revised.

16. Map Name - this is the name given to the map quadrangle. The name usually references the prominent feature within the quadrangle.

17. Adjoining Map Name - the name of the map that adjoins this map to the southeast.

18. UTM Northing Marking - This value is the distance in meters north of the equator. Notice that the last three zeros on some markings are eliminated in an effort to declutter the map.

USGS Topo Map Bottom Margin Information

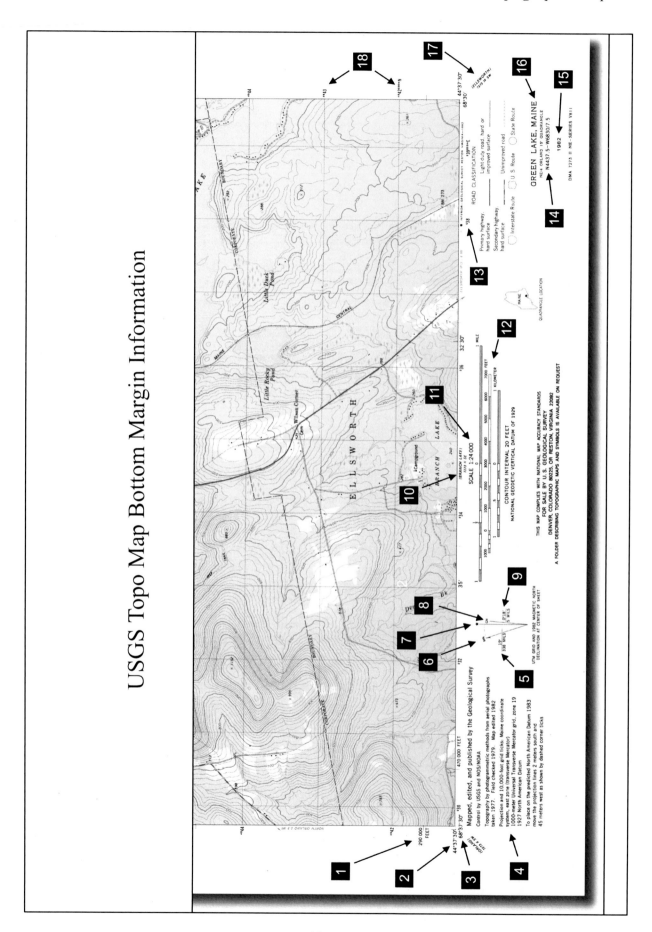

One new feature of the US Topo maps is the ability to turn on or off various layers on the map, such as roads, map margin information, and rivers, lakes, and streams. In addition, the maps contain layers not found on previous versions of the maps, such as satellite imagery.

This new functionality allows the user to customize the topographic map for the user's specific purpose. The user may then print out the custom map on his own printer, and thus contain more up-to-date information than maps that were printed years ago and have been sitting on a shelf somewhere waiting for someone to purchase them.

Topographic Map General Information

Scale - The scale is really a *ratio* – a comparison of two numbers. In this case, the scale is a comparison of a measurement on the map and a measurement in the "real world". It is a measure of how many times the world has been shrunk down to fit on a piece of paper.

Most of the time, the most appropriate scale for us to use for recreational navigation purposes is 1:24,000 (read "one to twenty four thousand"). This means that the world has been shrunk down 24,000 times to fit on the paper. In other words, a measurement of one inch on the map equals a distance of 24,000 inches (or 2000 feet) in the real world.

Dates - Maps contain several dates such as:
- **Horizontal Datum** - the date that the features other than the elevation were collected
- **Vertical Datum** - the date that the elevation data was collected.
- **Photorevised Date** - the date that the map was most recently updated using an aerial photograph
- **Aerial Photo Date** - the date that the aerial photograph was taken

to update or make the map
- **Field Checked Date** - the date that the field survey data was collected

These dates are important to the map user as the accuracy of information on a map is directly connected to the date the information used to build the map was collected. As can be seen from the image below of a USGS topo, it is not unusual for the data used to build today's topographic maps to be decades old.

Mapped, edited, and published by the Geological Survey

Control by USGS and NOS/NOAA

Topography by photogrammetric methods from aerial photographs taken 1977. Field checked 1979. Map edited 1982

Projection and 10,000-foot grid ticks: Maine coordinate system, east zone (transverse Mercator)
1000-meter Universal Transverse Mercator grid, zone 19
1927 North American Datum

To place on the predicted North American Datum 1983 move the projection lines 2 meters south and 45 meters west as shown by dashed corner ticks

It is not unusual for the data used to build today's topographic maps to be decades old.

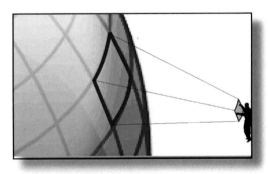

The scale of a map is the amount that it is shrunk down to fit on a piece of paper and is given as a ratio.

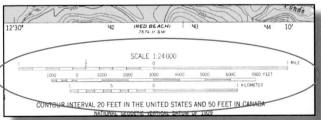

The map's bar scale can be used to measure distances on the map

12

Scale Calculation Examples

There are several ways to measure distance on a map. The scale bar (previous page, bottom right) may be used (see p. 12) or if we know a map's scale we can use it as a ratio to calculate distances on the map. For example, a 1:24000 scale map means that one inch on the map equals 24,000 inches in the real world. If we measure a distance of 1.75 inches on the map, we can set up a ratio to calculate how far this would be in the real world, like so...

$$\frac{1 \text{ in. on map}}{1.75 \text{ inches on map}} = \frac{24{,}000 \text{ in. in the field}}{D \text{ inches in the real word}}$$

When we solve this, we end up with: D = 42000 inches

Next. we'll divide by 12 to convert this to feet:

$$\frac{42000}{12} = 3500 \text{ feet}$$

And divide again by 5280 to convert to miles:

$$\frac{3500}{5280} = .66 \text{ miles}$$

So 1.75 inches on the map equals 3500 feet or .66 miles.

To convert miles to feet, we can do the process above in reverse and *multiply* by 5280.

And to covert feet in the real world to inches on the map, we'll *multiply* feet by 12 to convert to inches, and then *divide* that by 24,000 to convert to the scale on the map.

Map Projection

In our attempt to draw the 3-dimensional surface of the earth on 2-dimensional paper, some distortion occurs. To demonstrate this, peel an orange taking care to take the peel off in one piece. Now try to flatten the peel and you will notice that it will rip in places where it is stretched as you lay it flat. This is exactly the type of "stretching" or distortion that occurs when a map is made.

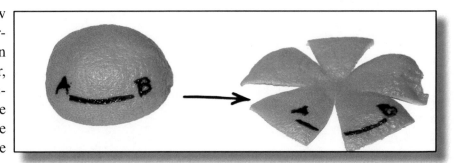

The stretching or distortion that occurs when a flat map is made from a curved surface is a result of its "projection".

The process of converting the 3-dimensional surface of the earth to a piece of paper is called **projection**. There are several types of projections, each distorting the earth's surface in a different way. Most maps created by the USGS that we use for navigation are created using the **Polyconic Projection**. Other common types of projection include the **Planar** and **Mercator Projection**.

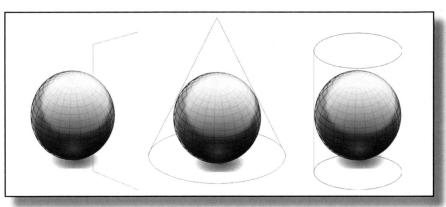

Planar, Conic, and Mercator Projections

About Map Projections

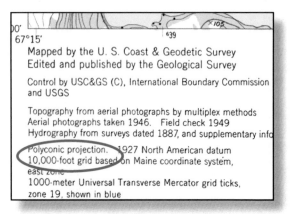

00'
67°15'   ⁶39
Mapped by the U. S. Coast & Geodetic Survey
Edited and published by the Geological Survey

Control by USC&GS (C), International Boundary Commission and USGS

Topography from aerial photographs by multiplex methods
Aerial photographs taken 1946.   Field check 1949
Hydrography from surveys dated 1887, and supplementary info

Polyconic projection.   1927 North American datum
10,000-foot grid based on Maine coordinate system,
east zone
1000-meter Universal Transverse Mercator grid ticks,
zone 19, shown in blue

The projection that is used to make the map is noted in the credit legend

What happens to the distance between A & B when the orange peel above is flattened? What happens to the direction you would be travelling if you were walking from A to B?

Contour Lines

Topographic maps by definition represent a 3-dimensional landscape in 2 dimensions. This is accomplished with the use of *contour lines.*

Contour lines are drawn in brown. They give us enough information to be able to "build' a 3-dimensional landscape in our brain and visualize what the land should look like. Contour lines represent the theoretical edge of the land if it were sliced at even vertical intervals. To envision this, imagine making a landscape wedding cake that has several cake layers each of the same thickness. The edge of each layer would appear as a contour line as it is drawn from the view above (see below, right). The values of each contour line indicate its elevation above the average sea level of the nearest ocean.

The thickness of each layer of cake is analogous to the *contour interval* on a map. The contour interval for a given map is indicated in the title block at the bottom of the map.

The relationship between contour lines describes the shape of the landscape and reveals specific features that we can utilize to help us relate the map to the landscape. Notice that the closer the lines are together, the steeper the slope. Also notice that each line forms a loop, and that every position along that line/loop is exactly the same elevation. Finally, see that as these concentric loops get smaller and smaller in size, the elevation increases until we reach the inner loop, which denotes a *summit* or *peak* of a hill or mountain.

The next page includes some common landscape features and what they might look like on a topographic map.

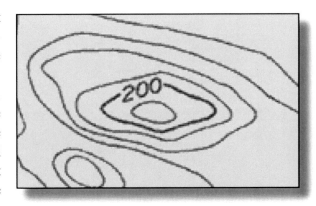

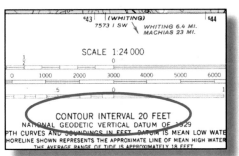

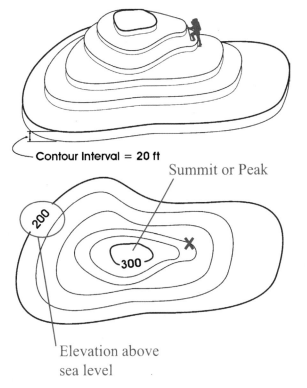

Contour Interval = 20 ft

Summit or Peak

Elevation above sea level

What is your elevation if you are standing at the red "X" in the drawing above?

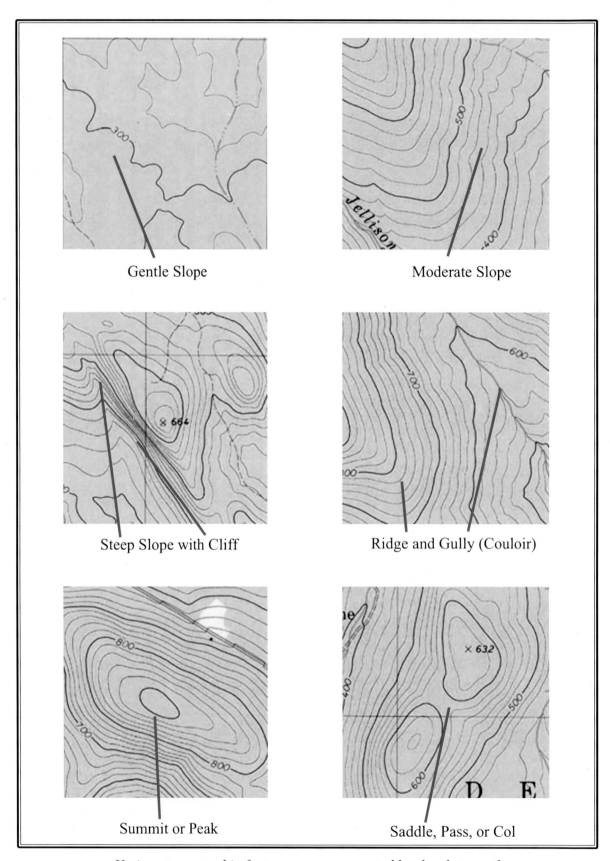

Gentle Slope

Moderate Slope

Steep Slope with Cliff

Ridge and Gully (Couloir)

Summit or Peak

Saddle, Pass, or Col

*Various topographic features are represented by the shapes of
contour lines and the spatial relationships among them*

Two of the features that many people have trouble distinguishing from one another are ridges and gullies. From the images on the previous page, locate the one block that shows both a ridge and a gully. Notice that the contour lines for both of these features form a "V" or show a fairly sharp bend in them. Also notice that the point of the "V" "points" toward an area of higher elevation in a gully, and toward an area of lower elevation on a ridge.

This can best be demonstrated using your hands. Stack one hand on top of another taking care to line up your fingers as shown in the photo below. Offset your hands so that your fingers on your lower hand extend beyond the end of your fingers on your top hand. Now note that your fingertips will form a "V" shape that will "point" away from you and toward an area of lower elevation. Similarly, note the "V" or "U" shape formed by the base of your fingers. See how the "V's" "point" toward an area of higher elevation like the top of your hand?

Calculating Slope

The slope of a landscape can be thought of as an angle of elevation measured in degrees. This angle can be calculated using either a slope gauge or by doing mathematical calculation.

A slope gauge (see Appendix B) can be placed on the map so that the index lines on the gauge match with the contour spacing on the map. Then by reading the slope angle on gauge.

Alternatively, slope can be calculated mathematically, using the following formula:

$$\text{Tangent (a)} = \text{rise/run}$$

where (a) is the slope angle, the rise is the elevation change of the run, which is the distance over which you measure the elevation change.

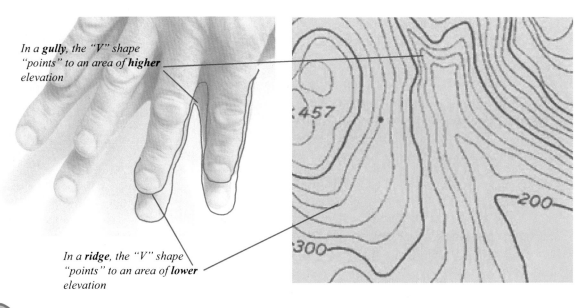

In a **gully**, the "V" shape "points" to an area of **higher** elevation

In a **ridge**, the "V" shape "points" to an area of **lower** elevation

In the topo map above, draw in where a stream would be likely to form in the event of a heavy rain. What would be the direction of flow? Are the "V's" pointing upstream or downstream?

Measuring Distance on a Map

Let's say you want to know how far it is in miles from Wilson's Corner heading west to the first "T" in the road on the Green Lake, Maine topo. Using the bar scale on your map, you can easily measure that distance.

First, using a piece of scrap paper (or fold over an edge of your map), line up the edge of the paper along the distance you are trying to measure. Then make a pencil mark on the paper at each end of the distance you are trying to measure.

Next, align the two marks along the scale bar at the bottom margin of the map. Notice that there are three separate units of measurement each represented by a separate bar: miles, feet, and kilometers. Find the "Zero" point in the middle of the bar that measures distance in miles (usually the top one), and then align one of the marks at the zero mark, and the other to the left of zero if the distance is less than one mile. This distance measures .55 miles.

This method works great for straight-line measurements. However, if we want to measure the distance along a winding road or trail, we can either break the trail into smaller, straight sections and measure each one separately, adding up the distances, or we can use a string. Simply line up the string along the trail or road.

Then straighten out the string and align it with the bar scale just as you did with the marks on the piece of paper.

Some compasses have a scale measurement tool on their baseplates. These can be useful for measuring straight-line distances as well. Note that the scale should be consistent with the scale of the map that you are using.

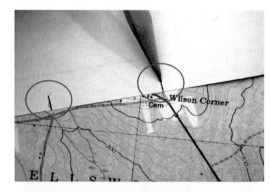

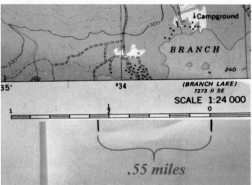

.55 miles

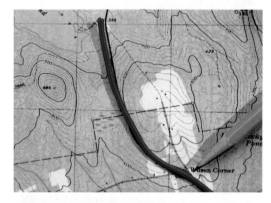

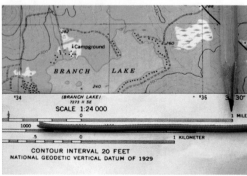

What is the measurement in miles of the string in the photo above?
In feet?
In kilometers?:

18

Distance Unit Conversions

The ability to convert between units of measurement in the field is a skill that is often overlooked by beginning navigators. For instance, being able to convert from miles to feet, or miles to kilometers can make the difference between getting to your destination on time and arriving after dark.

The following are common equivalencies that are useful enough to commit them to memory:

> *1 mile = 5280 feet*
> *1 mile = 1.6 kilometers*

If we want to convert .55 miles to feet, we simply multiply by 5280:

.55 X 5280 = 2904 feet

Likewise, if we want to convert .55 miles to kilometers, we multiply by 1.6:

.55 X 1.6 - .88 kilometers

Of course, if we want to convert from feet to miles, we would simply divide the number of feet by 5280:

2904 feet / 5280 = .55 miles

Similarly, if we want to convert kilometers back to miles, we would divide the number of kilometers by 1.6:

.88 kilometers / 1.6 = .55 miles

If this type of math is confusing to you, you will need to work on this until it becomes easy for you. Practice this until you can do these conversions quickly, with confidence, under pressure.

USGS Topographic Map Symbols

Most of the features on a topographic map are represented using a collection of symbols. These symbols have been developed to be intuitive in that may of them actually look like the feature they represent.

Not only does the shape of the symbol carry meaning, but its color also denotes the type of feature it represents:

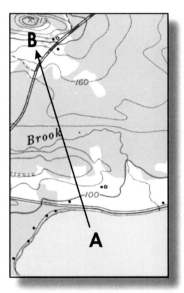

Map colors each have meaning

- **Black** – man made objects such as buildings, roads, and political boundaries
- **Blue** – water (lakes, rivers, streams, ocean, swamps)
- **Green** – vegetation over 6' in height
- **Brown** – elevation (see contour lines on pp. 15-17)
- **White** – open areas with vegetation less than 6 feet high
- **Red** – major roads and highways

Based solely on colors, describe what you would encounter as you travelled from point "A" to point "B".

Contours and Elevation Profiles Exercise

Draw in each box the profile of the landscape that is described with the contour line drawing.

Measuring and Converting Distances on a Topographic Map

Measure the distances between the following points on the Green Lake, Maine topographic map number N4437.5-W6830/7.5. Measure using the boxed unit and then convert to the other two for each distance.

FROM	TO	Miles	Feet	Kilometers
1. Summit of Bald Mtn.	Summit of Oak Hill	☐	____	____
2. Summit of Oak Hill	Outlet of Goose Pond	____	☐	____
3. Outlet of Goose Pond	Summit of Bald Mtn.	____	____	☐
4. Outlet of Mountainy Pond	Highest summit of Big Hill	☐	____	____
5. Highest summit of Big Hill	Northernmost inlet of Mountainy Pond	____	☐	____
6. Northernmost inlet of Mountainy Pond	Outlet of Mountainy Pond	____	____	☐
7. Southernmost occupied dwelling on Little Rocky Pond	Cemetery near Wilson Corner	☐	____	____
8. Cemetery near Wilson Corner	Campground north of Branch Lake	____	☐	____
9. **Distance by road** from the southernmost occupied dwelling on Little Rocky Lake	Campground north of Branch Lake	____	____	☐

10. Which is the ***easier*** route from the southernmost occupied dwelling on Little Rocky Lake to the Campground north of Branch Lake (#7 + #8, or #9 above)? Why?

Topographic Map Symbols

Find the following symbols on a topographic map and draw the symbol on this sheet.

Occupied Dwelling   _____

Unoccupied Dwelling   _____

School   _____

Gravel pit   _____

Trail   _____

Cemetery   _____

Open area (veg. under 6')   _____

Vegetation over 6'   _____

Improved roads   _____

Unimproved roads   _____

Railroad Tracks   _____

Church   _____

Marsh   _____

Topographic Model and Map

Interpreting map topography is an important skill and critical to wilderness navigation. Using the classroom lecture notes, activities, and your texts, you will demonstrate your understanding of the relationship between contour lines and three-dimensional topography by creating a 3-D model and 2-D topographic map.

1. Build a 3-dimensional model of terrain that includes the following:
    - Gentle Slope
    - Moderate Slope
    - Steep Slope
    - Summit
    - Saddle
    - Couloir
    - Cliff
    - Ridge

2. Apply contour lines to your 3-D model using an appropriate contour interval.

3. Draw a 2-D topographic map of your model that includes contour lines and appropriate symbols and colors.

Chapter 2
The Magnetic Compass
Finding Direction and Distance in the Field

> **Chapter Objectives:**
> - Demonstrate understanding of Earth's magnetic field
> - Identify parts of the baseplate compass
> - Demonstrate the ability to accurately measure (+/-3°) magnetic bearings in the field
> - Demonstrate the ability to follow magnetic bearings in the field
> - Identify the 16 cardinal points and relate them to numeric bearings
> - Demonstrate the ability to calculate one's pace and use pacing to measure distance in the field

The Chinese are credited with discovering that the earth has an invisible magnetic field. They also reportedly first came up with a means of utilizing this field and its lines of flux for detecting direction. By floating an iron-rich stone on a piece of wood on water, they noticed that the stone would align itself to always point halfway between

Magnetic North Pole

Lines of Flux

N

S

Magnetic South Pole

The lines of flux that result from a magnetic field can be seen when iron filings are placed around a magnet. Notice how the lines of flux originate from the north and south poles.

where the sun rose and set every day.

Most middle-school students today learn about the basic concepts of magnetism in their earth science class. If you reach back in your distant eighth-grade memory, you may recall that a magnet has a north and a south pole, and between them exists an invisible magnetic field. You may also recall that ferrous metals are influenced by this field, and will align along the magnetic lines of flux that connect the poles. These lines of flux can be demonstrated by placing a magnet amidst a pile of iron shavings (left).

The earth's magnetic field exists between its magnetic north and south poles, which are not the same as its rotational (or true) north and south poles. In fact, earth's magnetic north pole is near Ellsmore Island in the Arctic Ocean in Northern Canada. You can think of the location as a point directly north of central Minnesota.

If we take a closer look a the earth's magnetic field, we will notice that the lines of flux are not as perfect as those created by the single magnet we played with in eighth grade. Notice results of the irregular lines of flux indicated on the map on the next page. The earth's magnetic field is quite complex, as it is influenced by various deposits of iron ore under the earth's surface.

The earth's magnetic field is also constantly changing, as is the location of the magnetic poles. In fact, the magnetic north pole wanders as much as 25 miles each year. The resulting changes in the earth's magnetic field are updated on newer maps, another reason to pay attention to the date your map was printed.

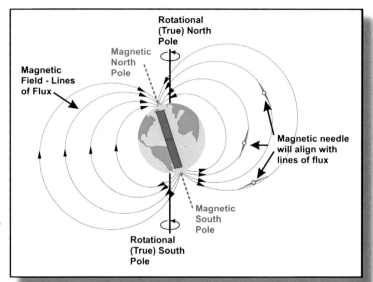

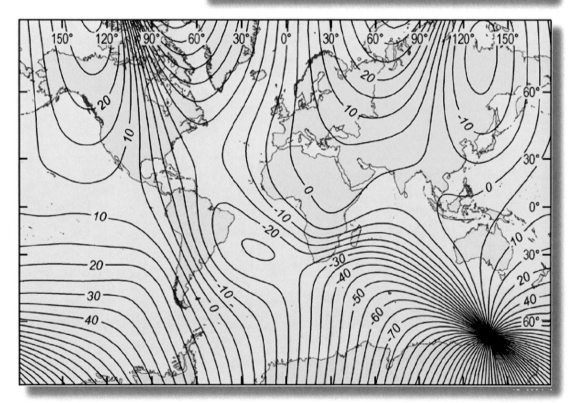

The variability of magnetic declination can be represented on a map. The numbers represent the number of degrees of magnetic declination - the angle difference between magnetic north and true (rotational) north.

On the map above, identify the magnetic north and south poles. Also identify the true north and south poles. Then, draw in the direction a magnetic needle will point in various parts of the world. Will the needle always point toward the magnetic north pole?

Baseplate Compass Anatomy

The modern baseplate compass is a simple tool that allows us to utilize the earth's magnetic field to determine direction. It has several specially designed features to make it extremely accurate as a navigation tool both on land and on water. Although there are several variations of the baseplate compass, the **Silva Type 7** and the **Suunto A10** are two that are similar in design, include all the necessary tools for effectively navigating, and are quite inexpensive to purchase. Let's take a look at the components of this tool:

Scale: This can be used to measure distance on the map. Notice that the Suunto A10 has a scale rule for a 1:24000 map, whereas the Silva contains an inch ruler.

Direction of Travel Arrow: points in the direction you will travel, or toward the object you are measuring a bearing to.

Index Line: This is the white line under the dial bezel that does not move when you rotate the dial bezel. This is where you will read your bearing.

Bearing Readings: the numbers arranged around the dial bezel. These will read from 0 to 360 and represent the bearing in degrees that you are measuring. Notice that the tic marks represent 2° increments, with labels every 20°.

Orienting Arrow: Also referred to as "the shed", this arrow will rotate with the dial bezel, and will always point at "0" or "N" on the dial.

Declination Scale: Can be used to automatically account for magnetic declination.

Magnetic Needle: This is the pivoting magnetized needle that will align itself with the lines of flux from a magnetic field. Notice that this will only be used to measure magnetic bearings, or angles measured from magnetic north.

Dial Bezel: This dial will rotate separate from the baseplate.

Baseplate: the flat base into which the dial bezel is mounted.

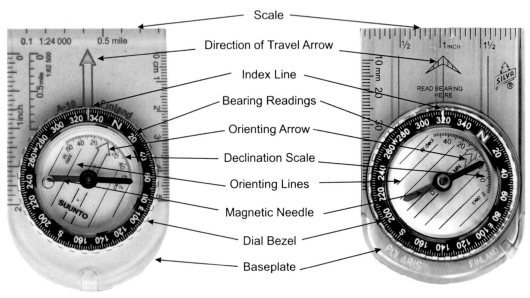

Scale — Direction of Travel Arrow — Index Line — Bearing Readings — Orienting Arrow — Declination Scale — Orienting Lines — Magnetic Needle — Dial Bezel — Baseplate

Suunto A-10 compass   *Silva Type 7 compass*

Finding Direction Using a Compass

Now that we have a basic understanding of the earth's magnetic field, let's think about how we could use this invisible tool to find our direction. Just as the Chinese discovered back in the year A.D. 80, we know that a pivoting magnetic needle will align itself with the lines of flux from the earth's magnetic field. Our baseplate compass is really nothing more than a protractor that will allow us to measure an angle (called a bearing or azimuth) away from those lines of flux.

If we want to measure the angle (bearing) of an object from magnetic lines of flux, we will need to follow three simple steps outlined in the sidebar to the right. As we follow this process, keep in mind that because we are using the earth's magnetic lines of flux to measure from, we are measuring **magnetic bearings.** This is significant, because in the next chapter we will learn how to measure true bearings; these are measurements from **true north**, rather than from **magnetic north.**

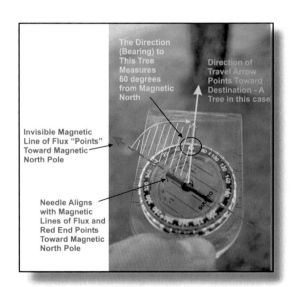

The concept behind using a compass to measure magnetic bearings is simple. The diagram above demonstrates that the compass is simply measuring the angle between the direction of travel arrow and the magnetic needle.

3-Step Process for Measuring Magnetic Bearings in the Field

This is the process if you see an object in the distance and want to know what bearing it is from magnetic north

S*tep 1 – "Sight In" Your Bearing* – holding the compass in front of you, look across the top of the compass and beyond the *direction of travel arrow* to the desired object.

Step 2 – "*Box the Needle*" – WITHOUT MOVING THE BASEPLATE, rotate the *dial bezel* until the *magnetic needle* is completely aligned with the *orienting arrow* in the *dial bezel.*

Step 3 – *Read the Magnetic Bearing* – Read the bearing where the numbers on the *dial bezel* align with the *index line.*

This bearing would read **104° Magnetic or 104°M.**

27

3-Step Process for Following Magnetic Bearings in the Field

Step 1 – Dial in the Magnetic Bearing – rotate the *dial bezel* until the desired magnetic bearing is aligned with the *index line*.

This bearing is **206 degrees.**

Rotate Dial Bezel Until...

The desired Magnetic Bearing appears in line with the *index line*.

Rotate entire body and compass until...

Step 2 – Box the Needle – rotate your body and the compass until the red *magnetic needle* is completely within and aligned with the *orienting arrow* in the *dial bezel*.

Magnetic needle is within and aligned with the Orienting Arrow. AKA *"Put Red in the Shed"*

Step 3 – Sight in Your Bearing – look across the top of the compass and beyond the *direction of travel arrow* to an object in the distance. The magnetic bearing from you to that object is the bearing that you dialed in Step 1.

The Direction of Travel Arrow will point in the direction of the desired Magnetic Bearing.

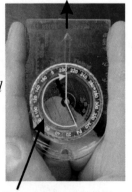

We have just measured 206 degrees from Magnetic North. This is a magnetic bearing of 206° or "206°M"

Compass Directions

The image below contains a compass rose, a diagram that has been used for thousands of years to reference navigational directions measured from north.

If you stand facing magnetic north (position "A" below), your magnetic bearing or azimuth to magnetic north is zero, because magnetic north is the starting point for measuring magnetic bearings. If you turn to the right as in position "B" in the diagram below, you are facing magnetic east, or 90 degrees from magnetic north. As we continue all the way around, we can see that position "C" is magnetic south, at 180 degrees from magnetic north, and position "D" is magnetic west, or 270 degrees from magnetic north. When we rotate back to position "A", we have rotated 360 degrees, or back to zero.

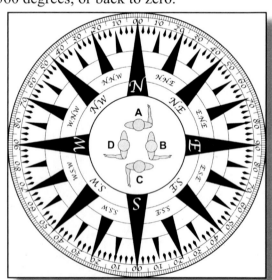

Look closely and see that 45 degrees is halfway between north and east, and is therefore referred to as "northeast" or "NE". Likewise, halfway between east and south is "southeast" or "SE", and so on.

Finally, notice that halfway between north and northeast (22.5 degrees) is north-northeast or "NNE". Similarly, halfway between NE and E is ENE. These bearings that are referred as specific directional points are called ***cardinal points***.

28

Image you were walking at a bearing of 270 degrees, or due West. If you wanted to turn around and walk back to where you came from, you would be heading at 090 or due East. Note the difference between these is 180 degrees. This is called a **back bearing**, and is always 180 degrees from the forward bearing. Note that if your front bearing is less than 180 degrees, you will want to add 180, and if your front bearing is more than 180 degrees, you will want to subtract 180 to arrive at your back bearing.

Measuring Distance in the Field

In Chapter 1, we have already discussed how to measure distances on a map using the bar scale printed in the bottom margin of the map. However, if we wanted to measure distance in the field, we will want some additional basic techniques.

Both techniques discussed in this text are based upon one's **pace**, or rate of stepping. We can measure our pace using either distance or time. Whether we choose distance or time as a measurement depends upon the situation.

First, if we want to measure shorter distances, such as a few hundred feet, we might choose to measure distance by measuring how far we can cover in one step, count the number of steps, and then calculate how far we have walked. To accomplish this, first measure out 100 feet using a long tape measure. It is also possible to do this using 12" square floor tiles in a long hallway. Then, simply walk with a normal gate from one end to the other, counting how many times your right foot touches the ground. By counting only your right foot, you will be counting every other step, which will make your pace easier to count in the field. When you reach the 100 foot mark, turn around and walk back, again counting the number of times your right

foot touches the ground. These should be the same, or very close.

This number represents how many paces it takes you to cover 100 feet. If we divide the number of paces into 100, we will end up with the number of feet we cover in each pace. For example, if it takes me 20 pac-

---

$$100 \text{ ft} \div 5 \text{ ft per pace} = 20 \text{ paces per } 100 \text{ ft}$$

---

es to cover 100 feet, the number of feet I cover with each pace (each time my right foot hits the ground) is 5 feet. We can use this number to calculate how many paces it will take you to cover any distance by walking.

Once you know the length of your average pace, you can easily calculate how many paces it will take you to cover any distance. Let's say you want to cover 250 feet. If you simply divide 250 by 5, you will find that you need to count off 51 paces. Remember that we defined a pace as a double-step, or each time our right foot touches the ground.

$$250 \text{ ft} \div 5 \text{ ft per pace} = 51 \text{ paces}$$

We can also use the number to calculate how far we have travelled in the field. Let's say we just paced off 88 paces. To find out how far we travelled, we simply multiply 88 time 5 to find that we walked 440 feet.

$$88 \text{ paces} \times 5 \text{ ft per pace} = 440 \text{ ft}$$

Alternatively, we could also measure the amount of time it takes us to travel a certain distance. This method works better for longer distances, such as hiking several miles in the desert where there may not be other recognizable features we could find on the map. To use this method, first measure out a set distance on a section of trail, such as a half mile

(2640 ft). Then time yourself walking this distance at a normal pace. Multiply this time by 2 to calculate how much time it takes you to cover one mile. Let's say you walked a half mile in 12 minutes and 30 seconds. When we double this number, we get 25 minutes to walk one mile. You can then use this pace in a similar way to counting paces in order to calculate distance in the field using time.

Compass Care and Maintenance

Your compass is a sensitive, accurate instrument. Because you rely on it to navigate, you should take care to make sure that it is kept in fine working order. There are a few things you can do to ensure its accuracy:

- keep it stored away from ferrous metals or magnetized objects
- keep away from electronic devices such as cell phones, radios, computers, etc that give off an electromagnetic field.
- rinse after being exposed to salt water
- Avoid dropping or bumping on hard surfaces.
- Check its accuracy against another compass

Distance Conversion Exercises

Using your known pace per 100 feet and your knowledge of converting miles to feet and back from chapter 1, calculate the missing variables below.

My number of paces per 100 feet is _____

Paces	Feet	Miles
__21____	_____	_____
_____	__230___	_____
_____	_____	____1____
____68__	_____	_____
_____	____655__	_____
_____	____220__	_____
__95____	_____	_____
_____	_____	____.75___

Cardinal Point/Bearing Conversion Exercises

Find the missing values for cardinal points and bearings.

Cardinal Point	Bearing in Degrees	Back Bearing in Degrees	Back Bearing Cardinal Point
N	_____	_____	_____
S	_____	_____	_____
E	_____	_____	_____
_____	270°	_____	_____
SW	_____	_____	_____
NE	_____	_____	_____
_____	315°	_____	_____
SE	_____	_____	_____
WSW	_____	_____	_____
ESE	_____	_____	_____
_____	157.5°	_____	_____
NNE	_____	_____	_____
SSW	_____	_____	_____
_____	337.5°	_____	_____
WNW	_____	_____	_____
ENE	_____	_____	_____

Orienteering

Using the form below, create an orienteering course for someone else to follow. Start by selecting an object such as a tree, rock, etc. Write this object down as the landmark for your starting point. Then, using your compass, sight in another object in the distance such as another tree, rock, etc. Write down the magnetic bearing to this next landmark. Pace off the distance to that next landmark, and write down the bearing, distance, and name of the landmark on your form below. Continue this process. Make your last landmark the same as your starting point. Find a partner with whom to swap your bearings and distances. Read your bearings and distances to each landmark *without giving them your landmarks*. Follow each other's course and fill in the landmarks that you find. Last, compare your courses with each other to find if you correctly followed their course.

Complete this section for yourself…

Heading/Bearing   Distance (in ft)   Landmark

……… STARTING POINT   _____

_____   _____   _____

_____   _____   _____

_____   _____   _____

_____   _____   _____

Only fill in Heading/Bearing and Distance on this section…

Heading/Bearing   Distance (in ft)   Landmark

……… STARTING POINT   _____

_____   _____   _____

_____   _____   _____

_____   _____   _____

_____   _____   _____

Chapter 3
Map & Compass Together
Tools to Navigate Accurately and Efficiently

> **Chapter Objectives:**
> - Demonstrate understanding of magnetic declination
> - Accurately measure (+/- 3 degrees) true bearings from a map
> - Accurately orient a map
> - Accurately measure (+/- 3 degrees) magnetic bearings from a map
> - Convert between magnetic and true bearings

So far, we have discussed how to interpret the topographic map and how to follow and measure magnetic bearings in the field. This chapter discusses methods and strategies to utilize both the map and compass together in order to navigate in the outdoors accurately and efficiently.

Measuring Bearings on a Map

In the last chapter, we learned how to use the magnetic needle of our compass to measure a direction in degrees relative to magnetic north. We understand that this direction is called a magnetic bearing because it is measured from magnetic north.

We can also measure a direction on a map. However, the process is quite different. If we look at the sides of our map, we'll notice that they are formed by *longitude lines*. If we follow these lines north off the page, we will eventually end up at the *true north* pole. Because of this, we can say that our USGS topo maps are drawn referencing true north, not magnetic north. Therefore, the bearings we take from our map will be true bearings, rather than magnetic bearings. We'll revisit this again later in this chapter, but just keep in

mind that we'll be referencing true north on our map, and magnetic north in the field.

If we take a look at the north and grid arrows on the bottom margin of the map, we can see that true north (the star) is straight

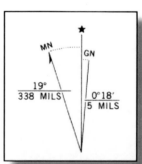

"up" on the map. We'll also see that the UTM grid north (GN) is aligned 18 minutes to the east of true north on this map (see chapter 4 for more on UTM). This is about 1/4 of

For recreational navigation, the difference between grid north and true north in most locations are negligible.

a degree, and therefore negligible for recreational navigation purposes. Therefore, we'll use the grid lines as true north lines (or longitude lines) and assume that the are parallel with the longitude lines at the sides of the map and accept the 1/4 degree error that will result.

This is advantageous, because we now have a grid aligned (within 1/4 degree) with true north overlaying our map that we can use to measure any bearing from.

For example, let's say that you are positioned at the intersection shown on the map to the right. You want to travel to the occupied dwelling that lies on the hilltop to your east. You could simply draw a bearing line from your location to the dwelling and measure the angle of that bearing line from the UTM grid lines (true north). If we used a protractor, we can easily see that the angle is 100 degrees. This represents a true bearing and we would refer to it as "*100 degrees true*", and may write it as "*100 True*" or "*100T*".

Now might be the best time to begin building good habits related to communicating bearings. The preferred method of referring bearings verbally would be to sound out each numeral in the number followed by the word "true", such as "*one zero zero true*". This helps alleviate any confusion in the bearing reading that could occur between numbers. This becomes important when trying to communicate numbers that sound similar, such as "*fourteen*" and "*forty*". In this example, if each numeral is sounded out, "*one four true*" sounds much different than "*four zero true*", and therefore eliminates confusion when trying to communicate the information, particularly in an emergency situation.

In addition, it is advisable to drop the degree symbol ° altogether from your bearings. This will eliminate any confusion of the symbol with the number "*0*". For example, if you are writing the bearing *10°T* and are a little messy with your handwriting, it could easily be confused with *100T*.

Looking at the example to the right, it is easy to see how measuring a bearing on a map is quite straight forward using a protractor. However, if we want to use this method in the field, we may not always have a protractor. Lucky for us, our baseplate compass can be utilized as a protractor for measuring true bearings off a map as well as for measuring magnetic bearings in the field.

The four-step process for using your compass as a protractor is outlined on the next

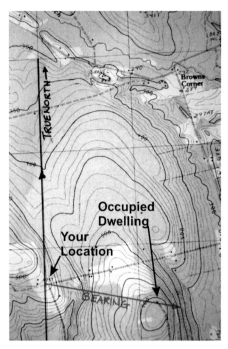

Drawing a bearing on the map identifies where we are (A) and where we want to go (B)

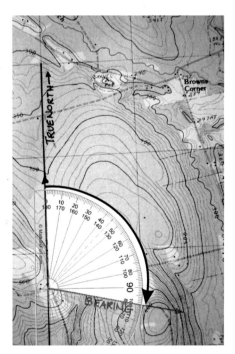

Measuring a true bearing is really nothing more than measuring the angle between the bearing and the direction to the true north pole

4-Step Process for Measuring True Bearings from a Map

Step 1 - Draw bearing line - using a straight-edge, draw a line on the map starting where you are (Letter "A") through the point where you want to measure the bearing (Letter "B"). Draw an arrow on the end of the line that points to where you want to be.

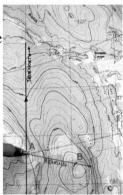

Step 2 – Align compass edge – Place the compass on the map with the edge of the Baseplate aligned with the bearing line drawn on the map. Be sure the Direction of Travel Arrow is pointing toward the direction of the bearing. Be sure the Orienting Lines in the Dial Bezel intersect a longitude line.

Direction of Travel Arrow points same direction as arrow you drew in Step 1

UTM grid line intersects with Orienting Lines in Bezel

Step 3 – Measure Bearing Angle from True North – Holding the baseplate and map still, rotate the Bezel until the Orienting Lines are parallel with a longitude line, making sure the Orienting Arrow is pointing toward True North.

Without moving the Baseplate...

Rotate Bezel Until...

Orienting Lines are parallel with UTM grid line

Note that the Magnetic Needle is completely ignored using this method, as you are NOT measuring a Magnetic bearing

Step 4 – Read the True Bearing – Lift the compass off the map and read the bearing where the dial bezel intersects the index line. This is your TRUE BEARING because it is measured from True North.

Read Bearing Here at Index Line

page. Notice how the bezel is essentially a protractor that measures the angle between the **orienting arrow** and the **direction of travel arrow**. Also notice that the **direction of travel arrow** is parallel to the side edges of the **baseplate**, which makes them interchangeable when measuring angles.

In the example above, what is the **true bearing**?
What is the **magnetic bearing** if the magnetic declination is 018W?
Why would you need to know both?

Magnetic Declination

If you were to stand on the earth and point toward the true (rotational) north pole with one hand, and then point toward the magnetic north pole with our other hand, our arms would create an angle. This angle represents the difference in degrees between magnetic north and true north from where we stand. This difference is called ***magnetic declination***.

Looking at the diagram to the right, if we are standing at position "1" and we pointed to the true north pole with our right hand and the magnetic north pole with our left hand, our declination would be ***west***, as the magnetic north is to the ***west*** of true north. If we then measured the angle created by our left and right arms, in this case 20 degrees. Our declination at position "1" would be 20 degrees west, or ***20°W***.

At position "2", our left hand would be pointed to true north, and our right hand at magnetic north. In this case, magnetic north is east of true north. Therefore, our magnetic declination at point "2" would be ***20°E***.

Finally, at position "3", both of our arms are pointed in the same direction, as magnetic north and true north are aligned. In this case, our magnetic declination would be zero. If we draw a line on the earth starting at true north and continuing through magnetic north, we form a line on which magnetic declination will always be zero, as our arms

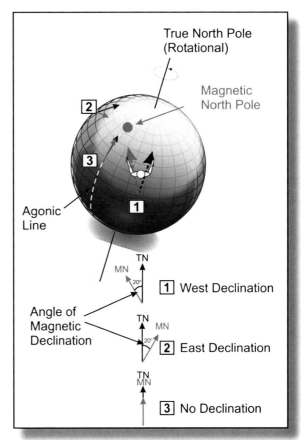

Magnetic declination is the angle difference between magnetic north and true north

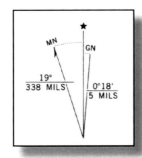

The magnetic declination of an area can often be found on the north arrow diagram on the bottom margin of the map.

will always be pointing the same direction. This line is called the ***Agonic Line.*** It is worth noting that the agonic line runs through central Canada and the United States.

It is important to understand the earth's magnetic lines of flux do not run parallel to the earth's surface. They actually pass in and out of the ground at different angles. As a result, the "pull" they exert on a compass's magnetic needle could be in an upward (away from the earth) or downward (toward the earth) direction as well as toward an object in the distance. This upward/downward force is called "***dip***". In order to account for this dip, compass manufacturers counterweight the magnetic needle so that it will "float" properly in the bezel.

On the map on p. 25, identify the ***Agonic Line***.

37

Converting True to Magnetic Bearings

Now that we're familiar with how to take a true bearing off a map, let's think about how we could take that bearing and follow it in the field.

So far, we understand how to take a **true bearing** off a map and how to follow a **magnetic bearing** in the field. How do we put these together so that we can take a bearing off a map and follow it in the field? The answer is that we need to convert our true bearings from the map to a magnetic bearing that we can measure them in the field.

In the example on the previous page, if we're standing at point "A" and wanted to hike toward the occupied building on top of the hill at point "B", we will need one more step beyond what we already know.

If you recall from the previous page, **magnetic declination** is the difference in degrees between the direction to the true north pole and the direction to the magnetic north pole. So, if we want to convert a true bearing to a magnetic bearing, all we need to do is account for declination. But how?

In the diagram to the right, notice that the direction of travel (your bearing) is measured in degrees from either true north (a true bearing) or from magnetic north (a magnetic bearing). Also notice that mag-netic north in this example is to the west of true north. Therefore, if we want our direction of travel to be measured from magnetic north, we will need to add our magnetic declination to our true bearing when our declination is west.

Of course if our declination is east, we would then subtract declination from our true bearing to get to calculate our magnetic bearing. Hence the saying "***West is best, East is least,***" meaning west declination is best (positive, so add), east declination is least (negative, so subtract). Another helpful way to remember this is "<u>**M**</u>agnetic is always <u>**M**</u>ore," meaning that magnetic bearings will always be more than true bearings (when declination is west.

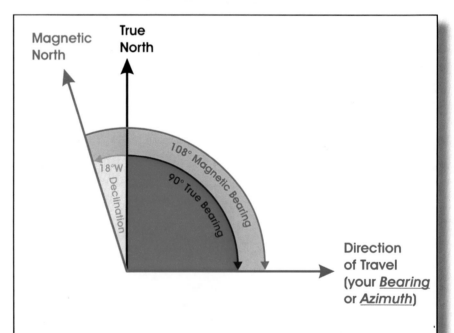

Declination is the angle measurement in degrees East or West of True North to Magnetic North along Earth's magnetic lines of flux.

When Magnetic North appears West of True North, Declination is West.
When Magnetic North appears East of True North, Declination is East.

A *Magnetic Bearing* or Azimuth is the angle measurement you are traveling from Magnetic North. A *True Bearing* or Azimuth is the angle measurement you are traveling from True North.

A *Magnetic Bearing* or Azimuth of 108° is exactly the same *direction* as a *True Bearing* or Azimuth of 90°... 108°T = 90° M

When Declination is West, <u>**M**</u>agnetic Bearings are always <u>**M**</u>ore than True Bearings.

Magnetic/True Bearing Conversion Exercises

Declination	True Bearing	Magnetic Bearing
21°W	090	
5°W	230	
11°W		001
05°W	182	
09°W	355	
18°W	220	
07°E		355
90°W		005
22°E	355	
08°W		005
10°E		355
16°W	348	

Measuring Magnetic Bearings Directly from the Map

From what we have learned so far, we are able to measure a true bearing from a map, convert it to a magnetic bearing, and then follow that magnetic bearing in the field. It is also possible to measure magnetic bearings directly from the map and skip the process of having to convert from a true bearing.

There are actually a couple of ways we can accomplish this. The first involves orienting the map first and then measuring the magnetic bearing from the map, as outlined on the next page. The major disadvantage of this process is that its accuracy is reliant upon some very important variables. Be-

3-Step Process for Orienting the Map

Another useful technique for helping to navigate is to orient your map. This process involves rotating the map so that features on the map are aligned with those in the "real world". This can be accomplished in three steps.

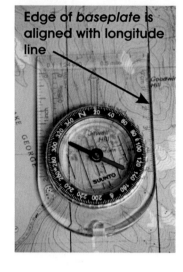

Edge of *baseplate* is aligned with longitude line

Step 2 - Align the Baseplate with True North - Align the edge of the Baseplate with a longitude line, the edge of the map, the North Arrow at the bottom of the map, or any other line pointing to True North.

Step 1 - Dial in the Magnetic Declination - Rotate the dial bezel until the desired declination is in line with the index line. West Declination will be positive, and East Declination will be negative on your dial bezel ("West is Best, East is Least"). Declination in this example is 18°W.

Rotate Dial Bezel Until...

Desired declination appears on the index line.

Step 3 - Rotate the Map and the Compass together and Box the Needle - Carefully rotate both the map and the compass together until the Magnetic Needle is aligned with and within the Orienting Arrow ("Put Red in the Shed").

Rotate map and compass together until...

The magnetic needle is aligned with the orienting arrow. "Put Red in the Shed".

Your map is now oriented with objects in the field. Check to make sure it is accurate by locating objects in the field and confirming they line up with objects on your oriented map. At the end of every navigational procedure, always ask the question - does this make sense?"

cause we are relying on an oriented map to take the bearing, we will need to make sure that the map does not become "un-oriented" throughout our process. This means that we can't be moving (like in a canoe or kayak, for example) in order for this process to work. In addition, we are relying on the integrity of the magnetic field present when we take the bearing. This means I will likely not want to use this method when I am inside sitting at my desk, where local magnetic disturbances from the iron in my desk and the electro-magnetic field from nearby lights or electronics may skew the accuracy of my measurement.

5-Step Process for Measuring Magnetic Bearings Directly from the Map

Step 1 - Draw bearing line - using a straight-edge, draw a line on the map starting where you are (Letter "A") through the point where you want to measure the bearing (Letter "B"). Draw an arrow on the end of the line that points to where you want to be.

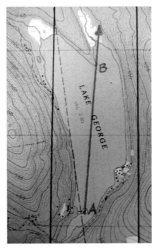

Step 4 – Measure Bearing Angle from Magnetic North – Rotate the Dial Bezel until the Magnetic Needle is aligned with and within the Orienting Arrow ("Put Red in the Shed")

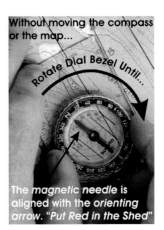

Without moving the compass or the map...

Rotate Dial Bezel Until...

The magnetic needle is aligned with the *orienting arrow. "Put Red in the Shed"*

Step 2 - Orient the Map - see the 3-step process on the previous page.

Step 3 – Align compass edge – After the map is oriented, pick up the compass without moving the map. Place the compass on the map with the edge of the Baseplate aligned with the bearing line drawn on the map. Be sure the Direction of Travel Arrow is pointing toward the direction of the bearing you want to measure.

Direction of Travel Arrow points same direction as arrow you drew in Step 1

Longitude Line intersects with Orienting Lines in Dial Bezel.

Step 5 – Read the Magnetic Bearing – Without moving the compass or the map, read the bearing where the dial bezel intersects the index line. This is your MAGNETIC BEARING because it is measured from Magnetic North.

This bearing is 22° Magnetic.

Map & Compass Bearing Exercises

Using Canaan, Maine map 44069-G5-TF-024, measure the following:

A.   From the summit of Jewell Hill to the schoolhouse west of Canaan village:

_____   True Front Azimuth   _____   True Back Azimuth

_____   Magnetic Front Azimuth   _____   Magnetic Back Azimuth

_____   Distance

B.   From the outlet of Oaks Pond to the inlet of Round Pond:

_____   True Front Azimuth   _____   Magnetic Front Azimuth

_____   True Back Azimuth   _____   Magnetic Back Azimuth

C.   From the outlet of Oaks Pond to the peak of Jewell Hill:

_____   True Front Azimuth   _____   Magnetic Front Azimuth

_____   Distance

D.   From the schoolhouse to the occupied dwelling in The Notch near Whittemore hill:

_____   True Back Azimuth   _____   Magnetic Back Azimuth

_____   Magnetic Front Azimuth   _____   True Front Azimuth

_____   Distance

E.   From the occupied dwelling in The Notch to the northernmost occupied dwelling on Lake George:

_____   Magnetic Front Azimuth   _____   True Front Azimuth

_____   Distance

Map & Compass Bearing Exercises

Using the USGS Solon, Maine map 44069-H7-TF-024, measure the following:

A.   From the southernmost point on Gray Island to the footbridge across Michael stream.

_____   Magnetic Front Azimuth   _____   True Front Azimuth

_____   Magnetic Back Azimuth   _____   True Back Azimuth

_____   Distance

B.   From the footbridge to the peak of Robbins Hill.

_____   Magnetic Front Azimuth   _____   True Front Azimuth

_____   Magnetic Back Azimuth   _____   True Back Azimuth

_____   Distance

C.   From the peak of Robbins Hill to Bench Mark #374 in Embden.

_____   Magnetic Front Azimuth   _____   True Front Azimuth

_____   Magnetic Back Azimuth   _____   True Back Azimuth

_____   Distance

D.   From the Bench Mark to the Campground above the rapids of the Kennebec River.

_____   Magnetic Front Azimuth   _____   True Front Azimuth

_____   Magnetic Back Azimuth   _____   True Back Azimuth

_____   Distance

Chapter 4

Coordinate Systems

Pinpointing Your Location

Chapter Objectives:
- Demonstrate understanding of the Latitude and Longitude and the UTM coordinate systems
- Calculate and communicate a position using the latitude and longitude and UTM coordinate systems
- Plot a position on a map when given a UTM or Latitude and Longitude coordinate

---

If you were standing at the corner of 3rd street and 9th Avenue, how would you communicate your position to someone else?

If you were in the middle of the wilderness, however, it might not be so simple to communicate your position. That is, unless you used a *coordinate* system. The word coordinate literally means "two numbers". Just like using the two references "3rd Street" and "9th Avenue" in town, we can use a system of two numbers to pinpoint your location anywhere on Earth. For thousands of years, we have used a coordinate system called ***Latitude and Longitude*** that is based upon angles, rather than distance or blocks like city streets.

Coordinate systems are analogous to streets in a city. One street by itself is linear and not specific. Two intersecting streets pinpoint one location.

Latitude lines run east-west along the earth's surface, but they measure distance in degrees north or south of the Equator.

Latitude lines are analogous to rungs on a ladder. The rungs are essentially lines that run horizontally (east-west), but can be used to measure how high you are (north-south).

Longitude is a series of lines that run along the earth's surface from the North Pole to the South Pole.

Latitude and Longitude

Latitude is a series of lines formed by the intersection of earth's surface and angles measured from the earth's core measured in degrees North or South of the Equator.

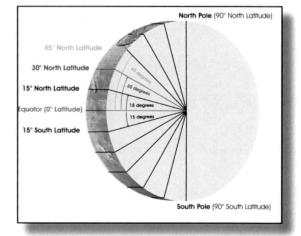

Latitude lines run east-west parallel to the equator and are measured in degrees north or south of the equator

Longitude lines are also called "***Meridians***" and are analogous to the lines formed by the segments of a peeled orange.

Longitude is measured in degrees East or West of the ***Prime Meridian*** – an arbitrary line that runs from pole to pole and passes through Greenwich, England. No matter where we are on Earth, our location can be described as being on a ***line of position*** that is a certain number of degrees east or west of the Prime Meridian.

When latitude and longitude are used together, we are able to pinpoint a unique location on the surface of

Longitude lines run between the True North and True South poles. However, they measure distance in degrees east or west of the prime meridian

the earth. Latitude is always listed first, followed by latitude. For example 44°N, 66°W would be read "Forty four degrees North (latitude), sixty six degrees West (longitude)".

Measuring Angles Using Degrees, Minutes, and Seconds

Angles are measured using degrees. One degree is defined as 1/360th of a circle. Because of the way in which they are measured, latitude will never be more than 90°N or 90°S, and longitude will never be more than 180°E or 180°W.

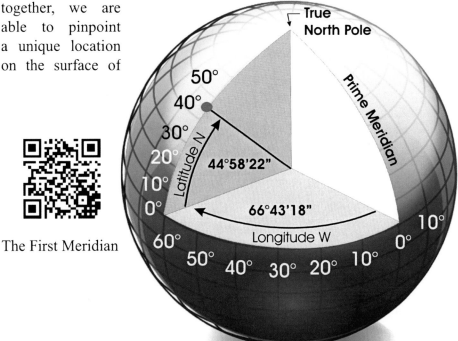

The First Meridian

Latitude and Longitude Explained

What is your latitude if you are standing at the red "X" in the drawing on the previous page?

To ensure accuracy, each degree can be broken down further into 60 sub-units called minutes (no reference to time) abbreviated with the apostrophe symbol. For example, 60.5°W can be written 60°30'W. To get even more accurate, every minute can be broken down into 60 seconds (again, no reference to time) and is abbreviated using the quotation symbol. For example, 60°30.5'W can be written 60°30'30"W.

There may be times when you want to convert decimal degrees to degrees and minutes. To do this, simply multiply the decimal by 60. For example, 30.75° can be converted to degrees and minutes by multiplying .75 times 60 (because there are 60 minutes in a degree). 60 X .75 = 45. This means there are 45 minutes in .75 degrees. Thus, 30.75° can be written as 30°45'.

The same process can be used to convert decimal minutes to seconds. For example, 45°28.25' can be converted to degrees, minutes, and seconds by multiplying .25 times 60 (because there are 60 seconds in a minute). 60 X .25 = 15. This means there are 15 seconds in .25 minutes. Thus, 45°28.25' can be writ-

ten as 45°28'15". Similarly, the conversion from seconds to decimal minutes would be accomplished by dividing the seconds by 60 to find decimal minutes. For example, 63°18'30" can be converted to degrees and minutes by dividing 30 by 60. 30/60 = .5. This means there are .5 minutes in 30 seconds. Thus, 63°18'30" can be written as 63°18.5'.

Although this may seem confusing at first, the ability to convert between decimal degrees, minutes and seconds is extremely useful and worth spending time practicing.

44.5° or 44°30'

Degree units of measurement can be subdivided into either decimal units (10ths or 100ths) or into minutes (60ths).

Minutes/Seconds Converter

More on Degree, Minutes, Seconds conversions

How would you write 28.25°N in degrees and minutes?

How would you write 67°33.75'W in degrees, minutes, and seconds?

Finding Latitude on the Map

Just like using street names to identify which corner your are standing on, Latitude and Longitude can be used together to identify your location both in the field and on a map.

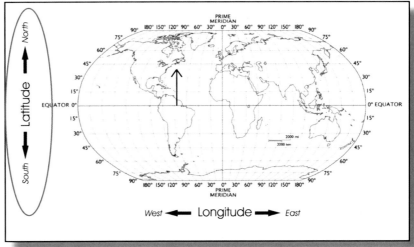

Latitude and longitude scales can be found along the margins of your USGS topographic map. Remember that latitude lines run east-to-west, but measure how far north or south you are from the equator.

To locate the latitude scale on a map, look for the numbers with degree, minute, and second notations in side margins of the map. If you follow the margins up to the top corner, you'll easily find the latitude along the top edge of the map. In the image to the right, the latitude along the top of this map is 44°45' North (read forty-four degrees, forty-five minutes north). We understand this to mean that if you are located anywhere along the top edge of this map, you are 44°45' north of the equator.

Now look at the latitude at the bottom edge of the map. Notice that it is 44°37'30" (read forty-four degrees, thirty-seven minutes, 30 seconds). Notice that the latitude at the bottom of the map is less than the latitude at the top of the map because it is less distant from the equator.

As you continue to look along the side margins, you'll find latitude notations approximately every 2.5 minutes (2 minutes 30 seconds).

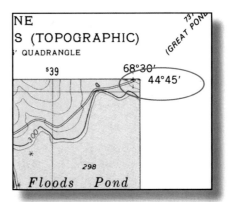

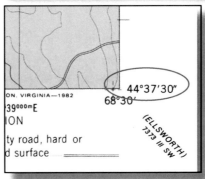

Latitude is found in the margins on the sides of the map and on each corner

Subtract the latitude at the bottom of the map from the latitude at the top of the map.

Why is the 1:24,000 scale map also referred to as the 7.5 minute series map?

47

Finding Longitude in the Map

Just as latitude lines run east-west and measure distance north or south of the equator, longitude lines run north-south and measure distance east or west of the prime meridian.

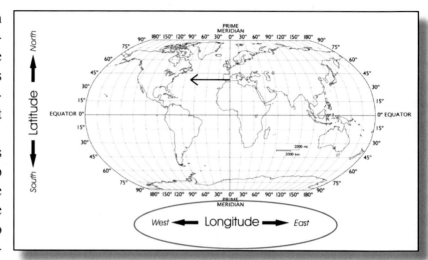

Longitude lines can be found along the top and bottom margins of the map. Find the longitude notations along the top two corners of the map. Compare the two longitude readings and notice that as one travels west along the map, the longitude increases. In other words, the longitude at the upper left corner of the map is greater that the longitude at the upper right corner of the map. This is consistent with our understanding that longitude is measuring distance in degrees from the prime meridian

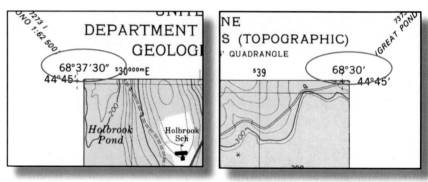

Longitude is found in the margins on the top and bottom of the map and on each corner

which runs through Greenwich, England.

If we reference the map at the top of this page, we can see that we are indeed to the west of the prime meridian, and therefore our longitude readings would increase as we travel farther west from the prime meridian.

Notice that the entire right edge of the map is all the same longitude, as every point along that edge is the same distance from the prime meridian. Likewise, every point along

the top of the map has all the same latitude, as every point along that edge is the same distance from the equator.

Notice that the longitude readings on the map do not indicate if the measurement is east or west of the prime meridian. The map makers assume that you have a general idea of which hemisphere of the earth you are in. If for some reason you were unsure, you could simply deduct that

How many positions in the world could have the same latitude and longitude coordinate if we left off the directions north, south, east, or west?

you were in the western hemisphere, as the longitude numbers increase as you head west on the map.

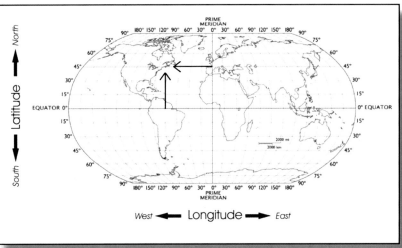

Using Latitude and Longitude Together

Latitude or longitude each by itself gives us a *line of position*, meaning that your position is somewhere on a specific line that is equidistant from either the equator or the prime meridian.

A line of position is similar to a street or road. Imagine you have an emergency and need help. You try to identify your location by saying that you are on Interstate 95. This could mean that you are somewhere on the road that runs between Houlton, Maine and Miami, Florida. Obviously, you would want to also give a second line of position that would coincide with your location along that interstate, such as a road that ran east-to-west and intersected I95, such as Interstate 90. If we give our location as the intersection of I95 and I90, we have now precisely pinpointed our location as the position where two lines of position intersect, I95 and I90 in Boston, Massachusetts.

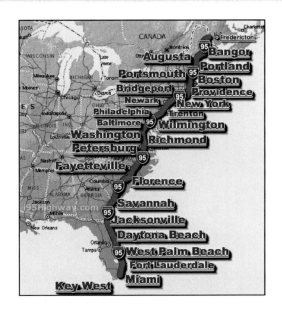

This is exactly how using latitude and longitude as intersecting lines of position can be used to uniquely identify any location on the earth.

When referencing your position using latitude and longitude, remember that latitude is always referenced first, followed by longitude. You can remember this by realizing that their order is alphabetical; latitude comes before longitude in the dictionary.

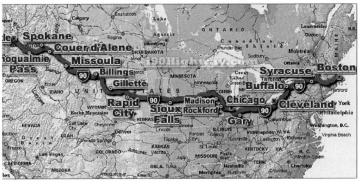

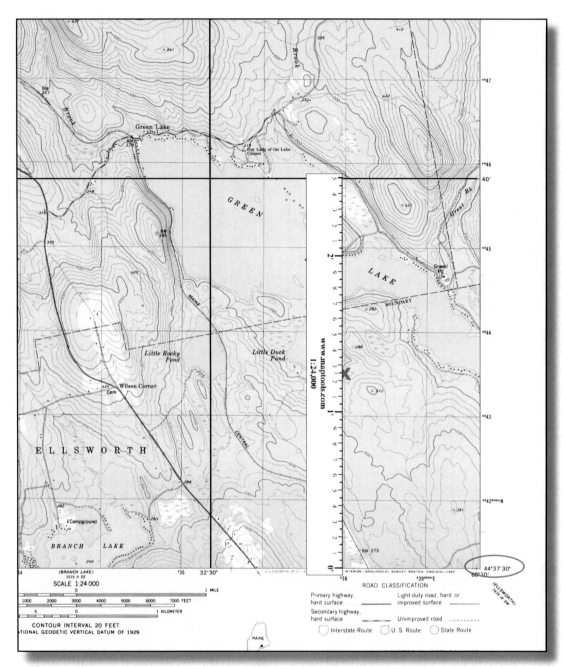

For example, if you wanted to refer to your position using latitude and longitude, you would write *42°30' N, 68°35' W.* If we look again at our 7.5 minute series topographic map, we'll notice that latitude and longitude markings in the margins are only provided every 2.5 minutes, or 2 minutes and 30 seconds. So, if we want to refer to a position that lies in between these markings, we will need a latitude longitude ruler. These can be purchased from map stores or can be found in Appendix B of this text.

To determine the latitude of the location of the red "X" on the map, simply place the ruler as shown and measure the degrees of latitude north of the bottom edge of the map. The red "X" is 1.25 minutes north of 44°37'30"N. (In order to add these together, we'll need to convert minutes and seconds to decimal minutes):

$$44°37.5' + 1.25' = 44°38.75' N$$

50

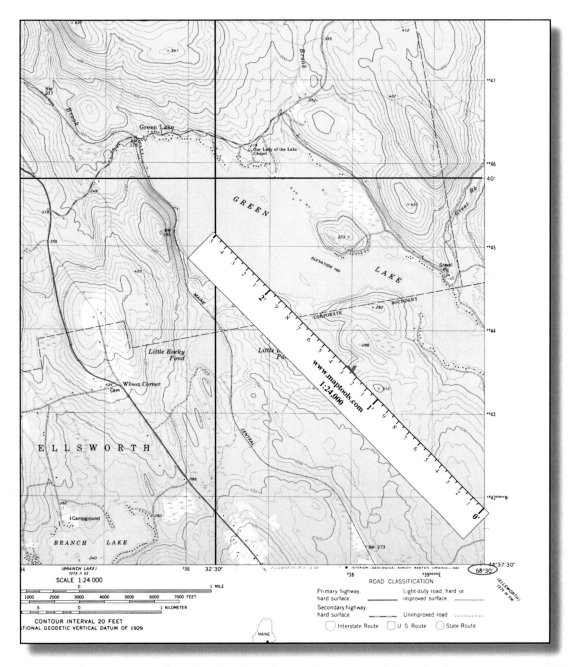

In order to accurately calculate longitude, we can use the same minute ruler, but will need to angle it so that it fits within the 2.5 minute tick marks on the map. Because the distance between longitude lines change as we travel north or south on the globe, the amount we have to angle the ruler to fit within the guidelines will vary depending upon where we are on the earth.

When using this method, be sure that both ends of the ruler intersect the edges of the longitude lines, while ensuring the measuring edge of the ruler intersects the red "X" on the map.

Here we can see that the red "X" lies 1.25 minutes west of 68°30' W. Notice that the ruler is measuring distance *west* of 68°30' because longitude in the western hemisphere is measured in a westerly direction from the prime meridian. Hence, we will add 1.25 minutes to 68°30' W to calculate our longitude:

$$68°30' + 1.25' = 69°31.25' W$$

UTM Coordinate System

Another common coordinate system used by recreationalists today is the Universal Transverse Mercator system, or UTM system. This system is gaining in popularity particularly due to its ease of use and accuracy.

The UTM system is similar to latitude and longitude in that it is a grid-based coordinate system. However, it tends to be more intuitive to users due to the fact that it uses distance in meters from an origin, rather than degrees, minutes, and seconds.

In the UTM system, the entire earth is separated into 60 zones. Each zone is 6 degrees of longitude wide, and approximately 600 kilometers wide at the equator. Each zone is numbered starting at 180° longitude heading eastward and continuing around the globe. Each football-shaped zone is then broken into north and south regions: one north of the equator and one south of the equator.

The UTM coordinate system uses two measurements to pinpoint one's location. The ***easting*** is the distance in meters east from the start of the grid in either hemisphere. The ***northing*** is the distance in meters north of the equator in the northern hemisphere and the distance in meters north of the bottom of the grid in the southern hemisphere.

The coordinate itself is written with three parts: the zone number, the easting in meters, and the northing in meters. The UTM coordinate of the red "**X**" in the illustration to the right would be written as:

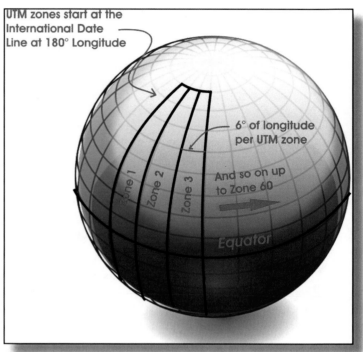

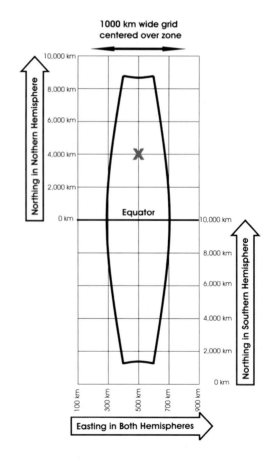

19	*0500000 E*	*4000000 N*
zone	easting	northing

The three different components of the UTM system can be found in different locations on your map. First, the UTM zone number can be found in the credit legend in the lower left hand border of the map.

Most 7.5 minute series USGS topo maps will have the UTM grid superimposed across the entire map, appearing as fine black-line grid squares. Others may only include the easting and northing scales along the margins.

The easting scale can be found in the top and bottom margins of the map. Notice that the eastings and northings may appear in different formats, sometimes only revealing the first few digits of the measurement from the start of the UTM grid. Usually, the first one or two numbers are also printed smaller than the other, more important numbers. Finally, notice that the first zero is commonly left off from the easting as well.

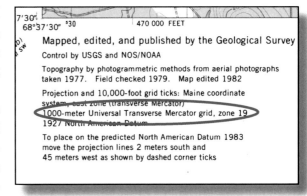

The UTM zone number is found in the credit legend in the bottom left corner of the margin

^{5}38 would be understood as 0538000 E

^{5}39^{000m}E would be understood as 0539000 E

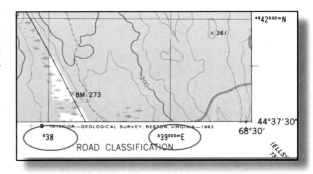

The easting values can be found along the bottom and top margins of the map

The northing scale is indicated on the right and left margins of the map, as they are measuring distance north of the equator in this zone. Similarly to the easting notations, the northings may appear in a variety of different formats, sometimes requiring looking at parts of the scale in order to deduct the complete coordinate.

If we have a good understanding of the UTM system, we could communicate the location of the red "X" on the map to the right as:

19   0538000 E   4942000 N

Interpretation of this coordinate would tell us that we are currently 530,000 meters (or 530 km) east of the western edge of the grid in zone 19, and 4,942,000 meters (or 4,942 km)

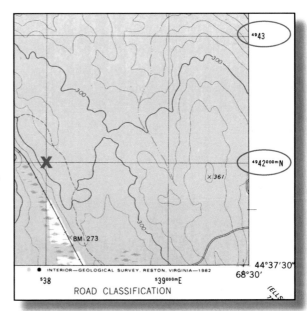

The northings can be read along the right and left margins of the map

north of the equator.

Hopefully, this all seems very simple and straight-forward. However, you may be wondering how to calculate the UTM coordinate of a location that lies somewhere off the gridlines, such as the red "X" on the map to the right.

In order to calculate this coordinate, we can either estimate the values, or we can utilize a UTM coordinate tool, which will give us accuracy to within 10 meters.

First, let's estimate our location. Follow the UTM gridlines that form the "box" around the "X". Notice that the height and width of the box are each 1000 meters (or 1 km). Therefore, the UTM gridlines that appear on the 7.5 series USGS topo maps form a 1 square kilometer grid.

The location of the red "X" is a little less than half of the way east of the 0538000 reading. A little less than half of 1000 meters is around 400 meters. Therefore, the estimated easting of the red "X" is 0538400.

To estimate the northing of the red "X", simply estimate the distance in meters north of the 4942000 reading. Since it is about 2/3rds of the way north in the 1 km square grid, we'll estimate that it is about 700 meters north of the bottom of the grid square. Therefore, we can estimate the northing of the red "X" to be about 4942700.

Our complete estimated UTM coordinate is:

19 0538400 E 4942700 N

How accurate is our estimate? Consider that even if we were off by 50 meters in any direction in our estimation, we would still be accurate to within a 100-meter square area, or roughly the size of a football stadium. Considering that the world is a very large place, it is remarkable that we are able to easily and quickly estimate our location on the planet to within a football stadium using the UTM coordinate system.

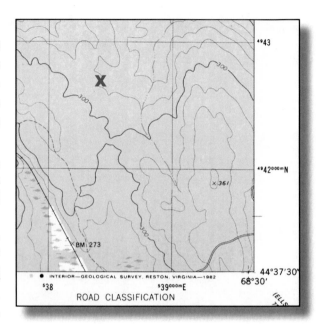

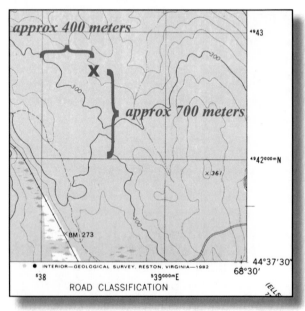

It is possible to estimate the UTM coordinate without using any tools and be accurate within about 100 meters

However, if we want to reference our exact location, rather than an estimation, we will need to use a UTM coordinate tool. These are available from various map supply stores and web sites, or can be found in Appendix B and then photocopied on to a clear acetate sheet. When printing from a computer, be sure to retain the proper size and scale for 1:24,000, 7.5 minute series maps.

When we overlay the grid tool onto the appropriate 1 km square, we can see how the grid tool divides the square into smaller 100-meter squares. If we look closely, we can get a more accurate reading of our location - likely with 10 meters of accuracy. The UTM coordinates of the location of the red "X" can now be read as:

Commercial UTM grid tools are available to purchase, or you can make your own using the template provided in Appendix B

19 0538470 E 4942670 N

This coordinate reading is likely within 10 meters of accuracy, which is about the size of large room in a house or an average classroom. This is usually accurate enough for recreational purposes; if you can communicate your location to another person within 10 meters in the wilderness, you are very likely to be located.

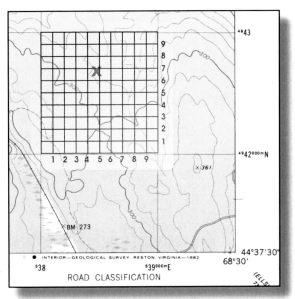

Line the UTM grid plotter tool up with the UTM 1 km square gridlines

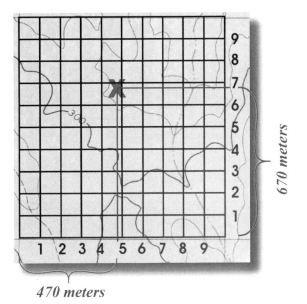

470 meters

Then estimate the distance of your location from the edge of the tool. This will be the last three digits of your easting and northing

What would the UTM coordinate of your location be if you moved 1 km west and 2 km north?

Latitude and Longitude Coordinate Exercises

Using the Green Lake USGS Quadrangle N4437.5-W6830/7.5 find the feature for the following coordinates:

	Coordinate	*Feature*
1.	44°39.52'N 68°36.33'W	_____
2.	44°41.88'N 68°30.93'W	_____
3.	44°42.35'N 68°37.27'W	_____
4.	44°44.5'N 68°33.03'W	_____
5.	44°40.95'N 68°36'W	_____
6.	44°41.89'N 68°37.35'W	_____

On the same map, find the latitude and longitude coordinates to the following features:

	Coordinate	*Feature*
7.	_____	Southernmost outlet to Hatcase Pond
8.	_____	Northernmost occupied dwelling on Hatcase Pond
9.	_____	Outlet to Little Hatcase Pond (south end of Mountainy Pond)
10.	_____	Highest point on the easternmost island on Phillips Lake
11.	_____	Southernmost inlet to Mountainy Pond
12.	_____	Highest of all the summits on Big Hill

UTM Coordinate Exercises

Use the Reversing Falls topographic map to answer the following questions:

A.   You are standing at the location 19 0648923 E, 4972706 N. Where are you?

B.   What is the elevation at UTM coordinates 19 0648461 E, 4971605 N?

C.   Is the location 19 0647400 E, 4971304N accessible by car?

D.   You are at the highest point on Dram Island. What are your UTM Coordinates?

Zone _____ Easting _____ Northing_____

E.   You are on the northern most shore of Mink Island. What are your UTM Coordinates?

Zone _____ Easting _____ Northing_____

F.   You are stranded on an island and can recognize the tip of Denbow Island at a bearing of 238 degrees Magnetic at a distance of approximately 1.7 miles. Declination is 018 degrees W. What are your UTM coordinates?

Zone _____ Easting _____ Northing_____

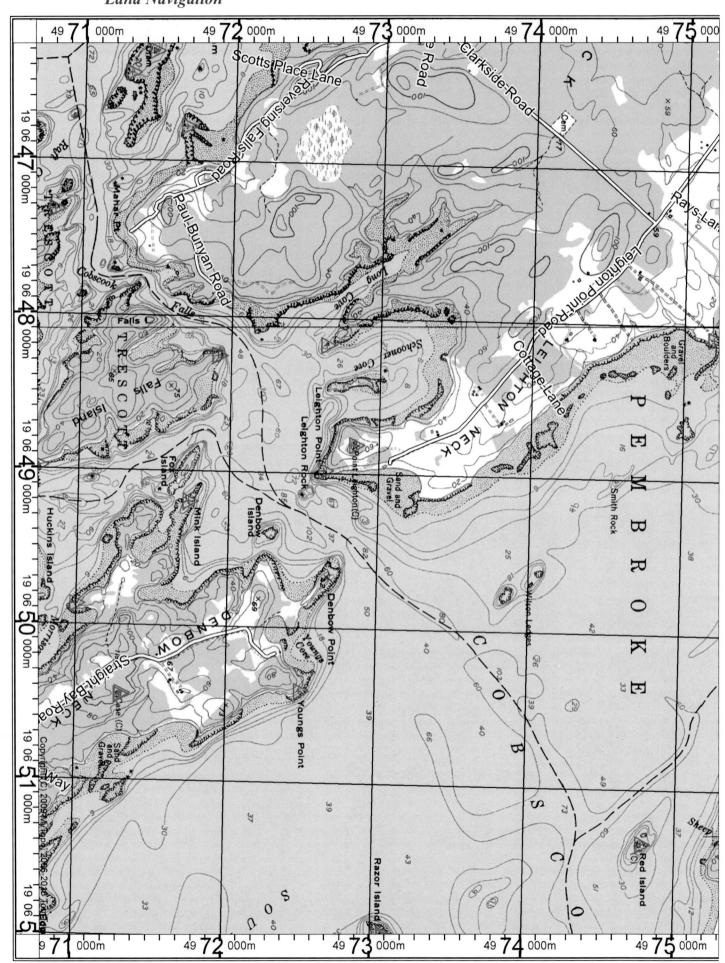

Chapter 5
Navigating with Map and Compass
Tips and Techniques for Orienteering

Chapter Objectives:
- Demonstrate how to triangulate using map and compass
- Demonstrate understanding an application of various routefinding techniques

---

Now that you have a fairly complete understanding of our navigation tools, let's discuss some situations in which you might need to use them.

Orienteering is the art and science of using your map and compass to navigate to specific checkpoints. This chapter will introduce you to several techniques that will help you become more skilled at orienteering.

Basic Routefinding

For this section, let's consider a scenario to help explain our thinking process and application of some basic rules of thumb and tips related to navigation. For this scenario, consult the Rainbow Lake East quadrangle 45069-G1-TF-024 or the map on the next page.

Let's say you are hiking along a beautiful section of the 100-Mile Wilderness on the Appalachian Trail. You get into your campsite at Hurd Brook lean-to early after a fairly easy day. You meet some other hikers who tell you they heard of a really beautiful beach at the northeastern-most corner of Hurd Pond. You still feel energized, and are considering a day hike to find the beach. You consult your map to look for the easiest route.

Tip #1: Take a bearing to your destination and write it down. Before heading out on any route you decide to take a bearing off the map from your current location to the beach area on the northern corner of Hurd Brook. You draw your bearing line on the map and measure it to be 140T. You consult your map to find that your magnetic declination is 019W. You remember that magnetic bearings will always more than true bearings (west is best) and add your declination to 140 to arrive at 159M. You dial in this bearing, box your needle on your compass and face the direction you'll be travelling. This will give you a general sense of where you're headed, and will provide a reference for you no matter what route you end up selecting.

Tip #2: Use existing trails and roads. As you look carefully at the map, you notice a dashed line (trail) leading southeast from your campsite where it eventually intersects with a double dashed line (unimproved road). Both of these features will take you very close to your destination. So at this point, your choices are to A: bushwhack through the woods following a compass course straight at the beach, or B: follow a trail and road to get almost all of the way there, and then follow a compass bearing. If you have spent any time wandering through the woods, you are probably aware of how difficult it can be travelling through dense woods, particularly in the eastern US, where forest harvesting is still very active, leaving dense young growth in the understory of the woods - nearly impenetrable terrain if you stumble into an area that has been cut in the past 15 years. So, you wisely decide to look for the trail head leading from the lean-to in a southeasterly direction.

Tip #3: The most efficient path between two points is not always a straight line. You look at the trail again on your map and notice that it meanders a little from your straight-line bearing. You begin to think that travelling straight for your destination might be a shorter distance than the trail, but after thinking more about your options, you remember how difficult it is to travel through the underbrush and

again wisely decide to look for the trail head.

However, after about twenty minutes of looking around, you are unable to find any remnant of a trail. You look again at your map to find that the last publication date was 1988 - nearly thirty years ago, and surmise that the trail has probably grown in. So, you are forced to consider some other options.

Tip #4: Use handrails. You take another look at your map and notice a stream (hurd brook) that also leads directly to Hurd Pond. As you look closer, you notice a white area (vegetation less than 6') along the brook just south of the lean-to along with a symbol that you recall represents a swamp, and realize that there is a wetland area that you would like to avoid.

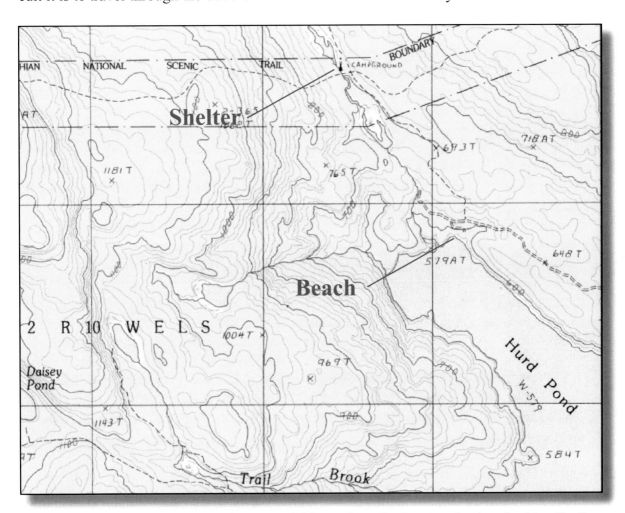

An excerpt from the Rainbow Lake East USGS quadrangle showing the Appalachian Trail campsite and the beach at Hurd Pond.

You also look closely at the contour lines and remember that they will form a "V" where they cross streams and gullies, with the "V" pointing uphill or upstream. You conclude that the brook flows in a southeasterly direction into Hurd Pond, the same direction you want to travel. You are pleased to find that your route does not include any steep terrain, as the contour lines are spaced out from each other.

So you revise your plan and decide to follow your bearing, but stay close to the stream, keeping it to your right and use it as a *handrail* as you proceed downstream toward Hurd Pond.

Tip #5: Constantly identify features along your route. As you consider your plan, you again consult your map and take note of features you expect to encounter along the way. As we mentioned before, you expect to encounter an open wetland you use your scale rule and measure .15 mile from your campsite to the open area. You convert this to feet and understand you should expect to see the open area about 800 feet southeast of your campsite. Knowing that your pace is covers 5 feet every time your right foot hits the ground, you calculate that you will expect to see the open wetland area at about 160 paces to the southeast of your campsite. You do this for the rest of the features you expect to encounter, and feel decide to head out . The last feature you expect to encounter is the double dashed line your path will intersect with and expect to come across an unimproved road at some point during your travel. You again measure and calculate that the road is .6 miles along your bearing and expect to arrive there after about 630 paces.

Looking at the area to the west across the brook, which will be on your right as you head on your bearing, you recognize that the terrain will slope upward and away from the brook. To the east, which will be on your left, the terrain should be fairly level, with some areas gently sloping up and away from the stream. As you travel along the stream, you are constantly checking in with the map, making sure that your surroundings are consistent with where you should be on the map.

Tip #6: Identify a "safety bearing". You look at the map and realize that you will be travelling in a southeasterly direction. You also recognize that the stream is to your west, and decide that if you get lost while looking for the beach, you could always walk west from your location and will encounter water of some sort: either the brook or Hurd Pond itself. Therefore, you decide to use 270M as your safety bearing, realizing you could always head in that direction until you hit water, and then re-orient yourself.

Tip #7: Use "farsighted" landmarks. Right before you head out, you consult your compass and make sure it's still set at 159M, box the needle, and sight across the direction of travel arrow. You take note that you are standing next to a large boulder, about the size of a truck, and put this fact away in your brain for a moment. You look for a notable landmark in the distance, such as the top of a tall treetop, a hilltop or summit, or a some other object that you will be able to recognize along your path. Farther objects are preferable to closer ones, as your actual route will stay closer to your bearing line. You see a large white birch tree a few hundred feet away that lies directly on your bearing, so you put away your compass and begin walking toward it, counting your paces. By using this method, you'll avoid trying to walk across uneven terrain while staring at your compass - an accident waiting to happen.

Tip #8: Use "back bearings" to ensure that you're on your desired bearing. When you arrive at the white birch tree you sighted in, you take a moment to turn around and see where you've come from. You see the boulder where you started from, and hold up your compass and sight it in. Looking at the bezel, you notice that the opposite (magnetic south) end of your magnetic needle is now boxed, signalling that the boulder is exactly 180 degrees from your intended route. This informs you that you are directly on your intended bearing, and can now turn back around and sight in your next landmark.

Tip #9: Walk around obstacles if necessary, but have a plan to get back on your bearing and maintain measuring your distance. As you bushwhack along your route, you encounter a large wet area that didn't appear on your map. You realize that what you're looking at is a recently-flooded area due to the work of some very clever beavers who have built a dam on the brook. You wisely decide that going around the flowage is much easier than wading through it. So you sight in across the flooded area and sight in a very distinct tree on the other side. You could simply put your compass away and bushwhack

around the pond until you arrive at the tree on the other side, and then continue on your bearing. However, doing so would mean losing count of your pacing and therefore your distance from your campsite. So, you decide to follow a side bearing until you are clear of the pond. Then, you turn and follow your bearing, counting your paces again, until the white pine tree is perpendicular to your bearing (see diagram below, left). You turn again and walk toward the tree, at which point you are back on your original bearing, without disrupting counting your paces.

Tip #10: Aim off your intended target. "Aiming off " is a strategy used to intentionally head slightly to one side or another of your desired target. For example, let's say you park your vehicle along a road and follow a bearing of 068M into the woods to hunt for wild mushrooms. After you've filled your basket with prize black trumpets and morels (position "A"), you decide to head back to your vehicle. You dial in your back bearing

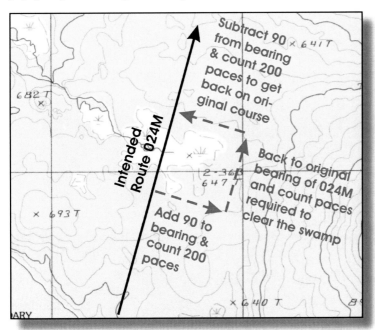

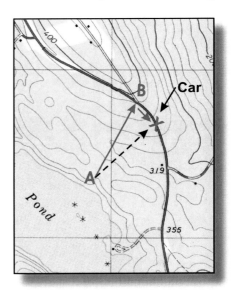

"Squaring Off" *is an effective technique for getting around objects in the field such as swamps, cliffs, rapids, etc. Note that the navigator is able to get back on the original course by carefully counting steps.*

"Aiming Off" *is a technique in which you intentionally head for one side or the other of your intended target so you will always know to which side of it that you are positioned.*

Land Navigation

(dotted black line), but realize if you follow that bearing and get set off to one side or the other while following it out, you may arrive at the road to find that you don't see your vehicle. Which direction is your vehicle - should you head left or right?

By intentionally subtracting about five or so degrees from your bearing, you'll know when you hit the road that you'll need to turn right and follow the road to find your vehicle. This technique is called "aiming off" and is very handy when planning a route to a destination that lies on a road that intersects your bearing.

Triangulation

Triangulation is a technique that will allow you pinpoint where you are if you aren't quite sure. However, it does require that you have a general idea of your location, and that you are able to identify at least two or three features on your map and in the field. The basic concept of triangulation involves taking field bearings to two or more known features in the field, transferring those bearings to a map as **lines of position (LOP's)**. Where these LOP's cross is your current location on the map.

Let's say you are fishing on Lake George and drop your prize Pfleuger reel overboard. You want to mark the location, so that you can come back and dive on the exact spot to retrieve your reel.

You pull out your compass and look for some notable features around the lake. You take a bearing to Jewell Hill of 130M, and another to the point at the northern end of the lake at 007M. You write these two bearings down so that you can plot them on a map later.

When you get home, you pull out your map and plot the two lines of position (see Chapter three for how to do this). What you immediately notice is that the two lines cross at the exact location where you took the bear-

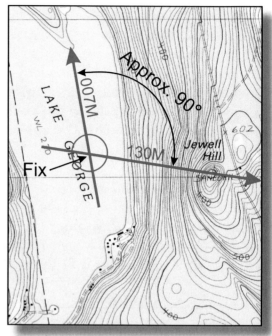

Two lines of position that are approximately 90 degrees apart intersect to identify a "fix"

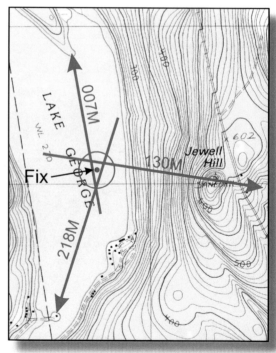

Three lines of position intersect to form a triangle. The fix is in the center of the triangle and will be more accurate than using only two LOPs.

64

ings. Where these two lines cross is the only place in the entire world where you could be 130 degrees from Jewell Hill **and** 007 degrees magnetic from the point at the northern end of the lake **at the same time**. This known position resulting from triangulation is known as a "*fix*".

When selecting features for triangulation, it is important to look for objects in the field that are about 90 degrees apart from each other. This will ensure greater accuracy, as the point at which the resulting lines of position cross will be more defined. What you want to avoid are features that are close to 0 or 180 degrees apart from each other, as the point where they cross will be less defined.

If you wanted even more accuracy, you might a bearing to a third known feature, again avoiding features that are close to 0 or 180 degrees apart from another. As you plot the third LOP, you'll notice that they will form a triangle. In order to average out any potential error in your field measurements and plotting procedure, your *fix* will be a point in the geometric center of the resulting triangle.

You can now return to that same location later on by moving your boat until all two (or three) bearings come back into alignment. Alternatively, you could read the UTM or Latitude/Longitude coordinates of your fix from the map and enter them into a GPS and use electronic navigation to help pinpoint the location of your prized reel.

Orienteering Exercise 1

The map below identifies six checkpoints (A-F) to be visited starting with A and ending with F. Considering the navigation tips and procedures provided in this chapter, draw the route you would use to visit each checkpoint in order. In addition, provide a written description for each leg of your route. Be sure to provide specific landmarks and indicate bearings wherever you are not following a road, trail, or handrail.

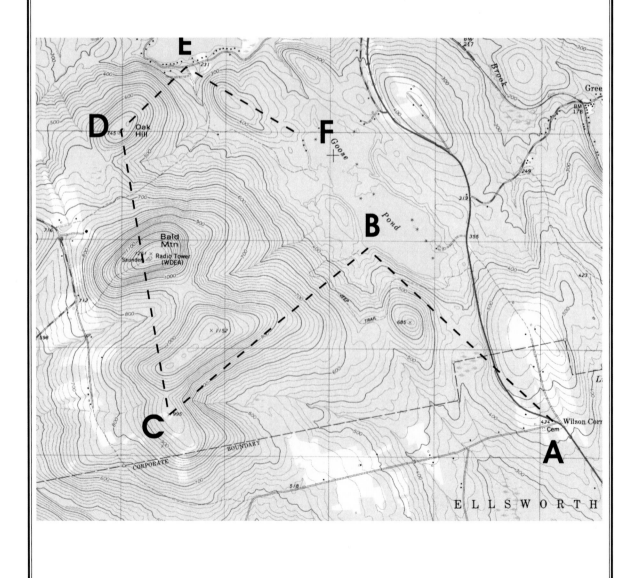

Orienteering Exercise 2

Obtain a map of your local area. Plan a route that contains checkpoints that can be walked in a day. Be sure to include some off-trail travel that will require employment of the strategies you have learned. Follow your intended route and provide a journal entry of your experience. What specific strategies did you use and what did you learn about them? What worked, what didn't? How would you plan your route differently next time? (Note: Bring a friend or two and be sure to bring a small day pack with water, food, emergency and first aid kit, and anything else you may need to be safe in the back country.)

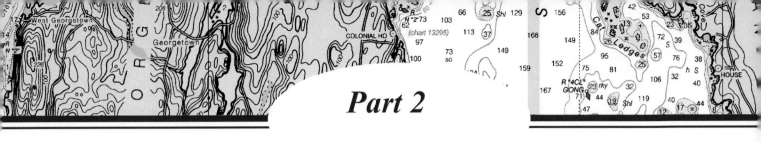

Part 2

Navigation
at
Sea

Chapter 6

The Nautical Chart

A Map of the Ocean

Chapter Objectives:
- Demonstrate how to obtain a find a nautical chart
- Demonstrate knowledge of basic chart symbols
- Demonstrate understanding of nautical chart features and their role in navigation

---

A **nautical chart** is essentially nothing more than a map of the ocean. Instead of describing land features, a nautical chart contains information that allows the trained user to navigate potential hazards such as rocks, shoals, currents, and other hazards to navigation.

Nautical charts used for navigation on the ocean are published by the **National Oceanic and Atmospheric Administration (NOAA)**, an agency of the United States Department of Commerce. Chart publication is only one of many services provided by NOAA, which has its roots dating back to 1807 when it was created to survey the coast of the US.

The process of constructing a nautical chart has evolved over the past several thousand years and today involves the use of satellite imagery, laser measurement tools, and field data collection.

Just as we discussed in chapter 4, nautical charts are constructed based upon a **datum**, a collection of measurements from a variety of sources. Today, all nautical charts in North America are constructed using a set of measurements called the **North American Datum of 1983 (NAD83)**. The NAD83 is part of a world-wide datum called World Geodetic Survey of 1984 (WGS84) and is therefore accurate with any GPS or coordinate system

based on WGS84. For all intents and purposes in North America, WGS84 and NAD83 are interchangeable.

Where to Find NOAA Charts

Up until 2013, NOAA printed nautical charts and distributed them to various marine stores and retailers for purchase by consumers. Today, NOAA no longer prints nautical charts. However, NOAA charts are available through a variety of means and can be referenced using online tools or a **Chart Catalogue**.

Print on Demand (POD) Paper Charts: A number of private, third-party printers have been certified through NOAA and will print and sell charts and are available primarily through the internet. A list of these printers is available at https://nautical-charts.noaa.gov/publications/print-agents.html#paper-charts.

NOAA's Nautical Charts and Publications Website contains links to download various types of charts and documents for navigation.

The advantage of print-on-demand charts is that you can be sure that they are current, as each time they are printed using information that has been updated weekly by NOAA. These charts meet the US Coast Guard requirements for carrying navigation equipment on commercial vessels.

Portable Document Format (PDF) Download: NOAA nautical charts are also available as a downloadable file in "PDF" format. Files of this type can be viewed using any number of free PDF reader programs such as Adobe Acrobat Reader available at http://adobe.com. These PDF documents are actually full-size images of the same chart one would receive printed on paper from a POD service and can be printed using a large-format printer such as a plotter capable of plotting 36" wide to acquire a chart that is full size. It is notable that mariners using paper charts to meet US Coast Guard chart carriage requirements should use charts printed by certified print-on-demand (POD) vendors.

NOAA BookletChart™: BookletCharts™ are also downloadable for free from NOAA's website as a PDF file. Each document contains a complete chart that has been represented as a series of tiles so that it may be printed on 8.5" x 11" paper, stapled or bound, and used as a booklet. Most of these BookletCharts™ are reduced to 75% of the original chart scale so users must use the scales printed in the BookletChart and not standard scales of other charts.

BookletCharts also contain excerpts from the Coast Pilot document that are pertinent to the area they cover. Like POD and PDF products, the BookletCharts are also updated weekly by NOAA and contain the most recent updates from the Notice to Mariners document.

Raster Navigational Charts (RNC®) Download: These files are actually digital images

What would be the most appropriate and useful chart format to use for navigating in a kayak?

How about in a sailboat or power vessel? Why?

of charts that are geo-referenced. This means that the images contain a digital layer of coordinate information that assigns each location on the chart a specific coordinate. This is especially useful in computer-based navigation systems such as GPS or Geographic Information System (GIS) applications such as Google Earth. Like all other NOAA downloads, these files are updated weekly to include any corrections.

Electronic Navigational Charts (ENC®) Downloads: Similar to RNC's, ENC's are electronic geo-referenced charts that are useful in computerized navigation systems. The advantage of ENC charts is that they are comprised of vector data (lines) rather than raster data (little dots or pixels). This becomes a huge advantage when zooming in to view details of a specific area. With a raster-based document, the zoomed image becomes pixilated and difficult to see, much like zooming in to a photograph reveals little dots or pixels. Because an ENC is comprised of lines instead of dots, there is no pixilation of the zoomed image. Because of this feature, ENC's have become the standard file to be utilized with most electronic chart and display information systems.

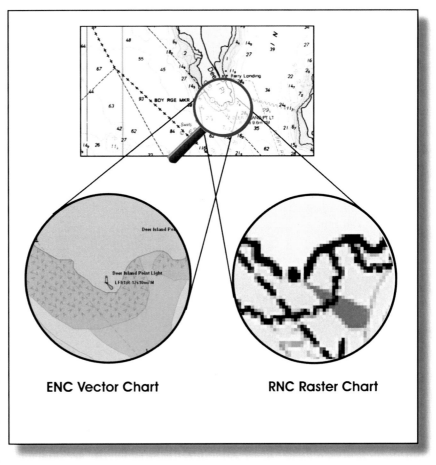

ENC Vector Chart   **RNC Raster Chart**

The pixels of a digital RNC raster chart are visible when zoomed in using a computer navigation system, as opposed to a vector ENC chart which is made up of lines.

The ability to read and interpret nautical charts, along with a good understanding of Aids to Navigation (Chapter 7) are important skills to help mariners stay in navigable waters, rather than running aground like this sailboat in the Intracoastal Waterway.

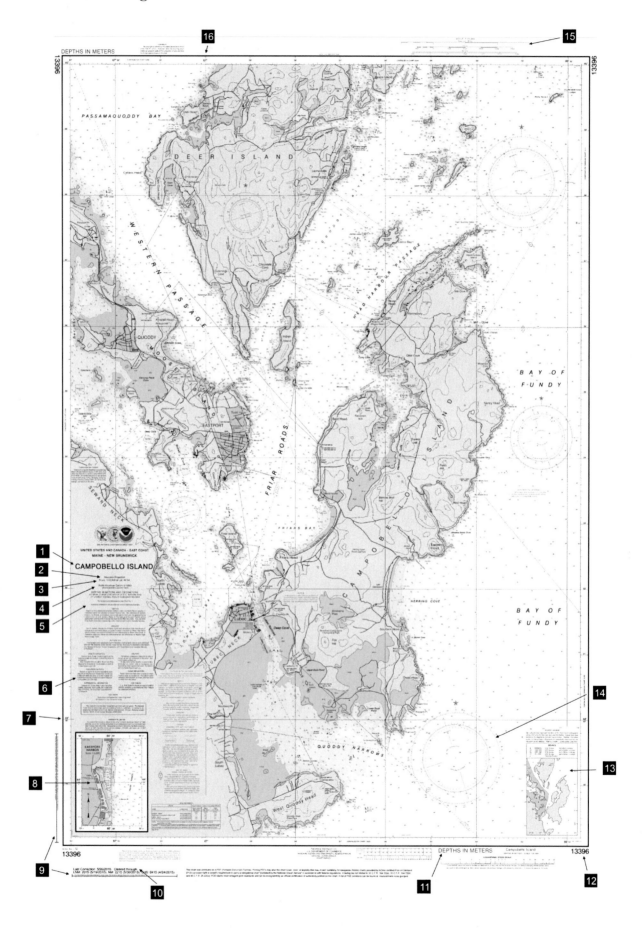

NOAA Chart Margin Information

1. Chart title - Each chart is given a name that is representative of the most prominent feature within the chart.

2. Chart projection - the projection used to create the map. This is usually Mercator Projection for coastal charts, as it offers the least distortion for navigating over short distances.

3. Chart scale - this chart is drawn 1/20,000th the size of the real world. Unlike USGS maps which are offered in series of similar scales (such as the 1:24,000, 7.5 minute series), NOAA charts are offered in various scales depending upon the size of the area it is intended to represent. Common scales are 1:20,000, 1:30,000, 1:50,000, and 1:100,000 for coastal charts.

4. Chart datum - the datum used to draw the chart. All NOAA charts covering North America use North American Datum of 1983 (NAD83), which is part of the World Geodetic Survey of 1984 (WGS84). This information is most important when using the chart with GPS or other electronic navigation systems.

5. Depth measurement information - these paragraphs explain the reference point for depth measurements on the chart.

6. Explanatory notes - various notes about the chart construction and notices about various features represented on the chart.

7. Latitude markings - latitude in degrees, minutes and decimal minutes are represented by tick marks. There are also tick marks for seconds in some places.

8. Chart inset - a smaller-scale chart of a particular feature on the chart that requires more detail, such as a harbor. This inset has a scale of 1:5,000.

9. Print scale - this feature is found on Print-On-Demand (POD) charts to help ensure that when printed, it will be the proper scale. The line represented on the chart should measure six inches in length.

10. Notice to Mariner correction information - this area contains the dates of the last correction of the chart. This will usually be within a week of the date the chart was downloaded.

11. Unit of measurement for depths - reference to the units used for water depth measurement. This can be in feet, fathoms, meters, or yards.

12. Chart number - This number represents the unique number of this chart in the national chart series. The first two numbers (13) identify the zone of the area represented by the chart. The chart number can be used to look up specific charts on the NOAA website or in the chart catalogue.

13. Source diagram - identifies the source of the data utilized to build specific areas of the chart. Navigators should be cautious in areas where surveys are old or inadequate.

14. Compass rose - used to determine bearings or azimuths.

15. Bar scale - used to measure distances on the chart, much like a bar scale is used on a topographic map.

16. Longitude markings - measurements of longitude in degrees, minutes, and decimal minutes. There are also tick marks for seconds in some places.

Chart Colors and Symbols

Just as with USGS topo maps, NOAA nautical charts are drawn using a system of colors and symbols. All of the colors and symbols, as well as any other information found on NOAA nautical charts, are defined in great detail in ***NOAA Chart No. 1***. This 132 page document is found in Appendix C in this text. It is organized according to the type of feature, and is relatively easy to use. However, a description of colors is included here for the beginner to become acquainted with charts.

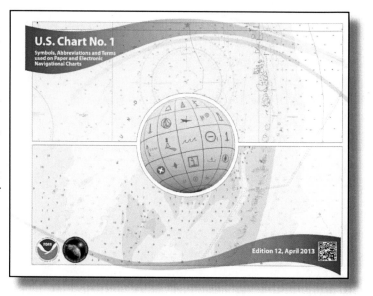

- Magenta (red) - elements significant to marine navigation such as lights, compass roses, and regulated areas.
- Blue - areas of water that may include hazards to navigation. This is usually shallow water or submerged obstructions.
- White - areas of water that are free of obstructions.
- Buff (tan) - land and other features that are always dry.
- Green - intertidal areas that are uncovered at low tide, but are covered at high tide.

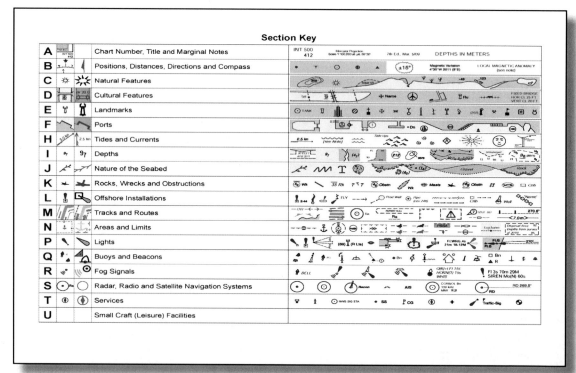

The NOAA Chart No. 1 has several sections (A through U) that define the various symbols used on nautical charts. Chart No.1 is included in Appendix C.

Notice to Mariners

The coastal waters of the US are in a constant state of change. For example, aids to navigation are installed, changed, or moved, natural shoaling occurs from strong currents or storms, channels are dredged, and new ports and berthing facilities are developed. Once a chart or map is printed, it becomes out of date. Therefore, there are two basic types of updates that are published to be used to correct nautical charts. The **Notice to Mariners (NM)** is published weekly by the National Geospatial-Intelligence Agency (NGA), and includes correction data that is intended for deep draft vessels in US waters or making a port of call from overseas. In addition, the US Coast Guard publishes **The Local Notice to Mariners (LNM)** weekly which contains correction information for all vessels, commercial and recreational, deep and shallow draft, offshore or near coastal. This information is collected from various sources, such as the US Coast Guard, commercial and recreational mariners, local port authorities, or anyone who uses waterways that notices an error in the chart. All of the NOAA charts now available through their website are automatically updated with

the weekly NM and LNM corrections. However, once your chart is printed, you will need to update your printed chart manually, or reprint it each time you want to use it. Both NM and LNM documents are available for download as PDF files from the NOAA website.

The Light List

The US Coast Guard publishes a list of every lighted **aid to navigation (ATON)** in the United States including lighted buoys and lighthouses. Similar to NOAA's Coast Pilot, information on lighted aids is published in several volumes and is organized according to regions or districts.

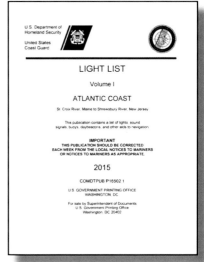

Volume 1 of the **Light List** covers the east coast from the St. Croix River, Maine to the Shrewsbury River, New Jersey. Like other navigation documents and charts, the Light List is updated weekly so that it is always current. If you use a printed document, be sure to update it frequently. Updates are included in the Local Notice to Mariners, as well as via download from the US Coast Guard Light List website.

Both the Local Notice to Mariners and the Light List are available for download from the US Coast Guard's Navigation Center website at http://www.navcen.uscg. gov

The Compass Rose

The compass rose is really nothing more than a protractor that is drawn in several positions on the nautical chart. It is intended to help the navigator measure bearings or azimuths that are drawn on the chart. Notice that there are actually two protractors in each compass rose: one inside the circle, and one outside the circle. The outside protractor is oriented with its "zero" pointing to the true north pole, or true north, and therefore measures angles relative to true north, or true bearings. The inner protractor is oriented with its "zero" pointing to magnetic north, and therefore measures magnetic bearings. The difference between magnetic and true north on land is called "declination". However, on the water and on a nautical chart, it is referred to as "*variation*". The variation in the region covered by the chart is also given in the center of the compass rose. Notice that it is given in degrees and minutes. Also notice that the amount of change in variation each year is also given. The process of measuring both true and magnetic bearings using the compass rose on a nautical chart is covered in detail in the next chapter.

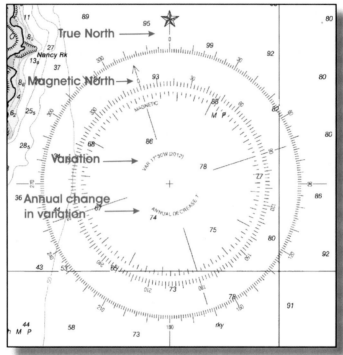

The Coast Pilot

There are several other publications that are useful for navigating at sea. In addition to Chart No. 1, and the Chart Catalogue, NOAA publishes the ***United States Coast Pilot***®. This is a series of books that include a variety of textual information for mariners about different areas around the coastal United States. Information such as harbors, anchorages, bridge clearances, currents and tidal information, and hazards to navigation is included in a collection of nine volumes, each pertaining to a certain area of the coast.

The availability of the Coast Pilot documents is similar to that of NOAA charts. You can purchase printed documents from a variety of third-party printers, or you can download a digital copy of the different volumes as PDF files from the NOAA website.

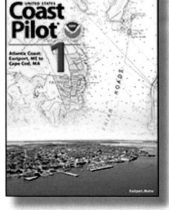

The United States Coast Pilot is available for download from the NOAA website (https://nauticalcharts.noaa.gov/publications/coast-pilot/), or can be ordered as a printed book from a number of third-party vendors.

NOAA Chart Symbols Activity

Using NOAA chart 13396 and the Chart No. 1, find the following symbols on your chart and draw them in the space provided:

1. Green can buoy number 1 that flashes a green light every 4 seconds and has a whistle.

2. Fairway buoy WQ that has a bell.

3. Red nun buoy number 6.

4. Red nun buoy named UH2 that flashes a red light

6. A lighthouse that flashes a red light every 6 seconds

7. A water tank

8. A church steeple or spire

9. A submerged rock of unknown depth

10. A submerged rock of known depth

11. A rock which is covered at high tide, but uncovered at low tide

12. The international border line between the US and Canada

13. A depth reading of 24.5 meters

Chapter 7
Aids to Navigation (ATONs)
A system for navigation at sea

Chapter Objectives:
- Demonstrate understanding and knowledge of various ATONs
- Recall specific rules of navigation that pertain to ATONs
- Identify various ATONs in the field and their respective symbols on a nautical chart
- Apply knowledge of ATONs to navigate and avoid hazards

Similar to how street signs and stoplights help motorists to locate themselves on a road, the waters of the United States are marked with a series of buoys, lights, and markers using shapes and colors to communicate how to navigate safely through an area. This system on the ocean is referred to as *Aids to Navigation (ATONs)* and is consistent with markings on NOAA nautical charts. ATONs consist primarily of two types of aids: *beacons* and *buoys* and are constantly monitored and maintained by the US Coast Guard.

Beacons are those aids that are affixed to land, such as a ledge on shore, or an island. Beacons that are lighted are called "*lights*" and beacons that are not lighted are called "*daybeacons*".

Buoys are aids that are *floating* and are somehow affixed to the sea bed via an anchor system.

The current ATON system that is used in the United States is referred to as the *International Association of Lighthouse Authorities (IALA) "B"* system. The *IALA B* system uses beacons and buoys that are either red, green, or red and white, along with lights that are red,

green, and white to mark safe navigable water.

The *IALA B* system also incorporates various sound signals such as horns, bells, whistles, and gongs that are emitted from ATONs. These sounds help mariners determine the location of the ATON when visibility is reduced (as in fog), and also help to distinguish ATONs from one another.

(Left) This green daybeacon is a beacon because even though it is in the water, it is fixed to land by means of several posts. (Right) A buoy, however is a floating aid and is affixed to the sea bottom by way of an anchor system.

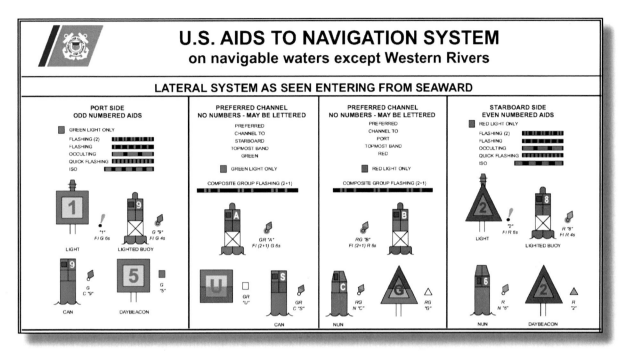

The Lateral System of IALA B

The *IALA B* system consists mainly of a **lateral** buoy system, meaning that the ATONs mark **each side** of a navigable waterway. The system uses colors, shapes, numbers, sounds, and light patterns to codify buoys and beacons that mark the waterway.

*COLOR*S- IALA B uses the colors red, green, white, and yellow to identify a navigable channel. The basic concept of this system is summarized by the phrase "**RED RIGHT RE-TURNING**". This means that when r*eturning* to port, keep the *red* ATONs to your *right* (and consequently keep the green ATONs to your left).

Looking at the diagram above, you can see that the green ATONs are on the left side of the chart, meaning keep them to your left when entering from seaward (returning to port). If you look at the far right side of the diagram, you'll see the red ATONs, meaning keep them to your right when returning to port.

In the middle of the diagram above, between the green and red ATONs, you'll find two categories of *preferred channel* markers. These buoys and beacons feature both red and green colors, and can be treated as either a red or a green buoy. This means that navigator

This preferred channel daybeacon uses red and green colors to identify the preferred channel.

Which side of the preferred channel marker above would you want to pass if you were headed in to a harbor from the open ocean?

can safely pass to either side of the marker. The color that appears on the top of the ATON is the color of the preferred channel. For example, a green over red buoy indicates that it is preferred to treat this buoy as a green buoy, and therefore keep it to your left as you are returning from seaward or returning to a harbor. However, it is also acceptable to treat it as a red buoy and leave it to your port as well.

A vertically-striped red and white ATON is called a **safe water** or **fairway** marker. This ATON usually marks the center of the channel, and is commonly found at the entrance to a channel. Safe water marks are most useful to vessels entering a channel from seaward, and gives them a target to aim for when lining up to be in the center of the channel.

A red and white safe water or "fairway" buoy marks the center or entrance of a channel

Safe water marks may be floating aids like this large buoy, or can also be a spherical buoy or even a daybeacon. They are always vertically striped red and white. Safe water buoys that are lit usually flash the Morse code pattern for the letter "A" (long, short).

Yellow buoys or beacons are considered special marks and usually denote a research buoy or data collection buoy.

Yellow triangle and square markings are also used to identify navigation aids marking the Intracoastal Waterway (ICW), an inland canal system on the eastern US that connects Florida to New York.

SHAPES - There are two basic shapes of ATONs that are found in the IALA B system: squares and triangles. The square shapes are associated with the color green and mark the left side of the channel as one is returning to port. The triangles are associated with the color red and mark the right side of the channel when returning to port.

The square and triangle shapes can sometimes be incorporated into the shape of a buoy. A red buoy that is not lighted is usually cone-shaped at the top and referred to as a "**nun buoy**" or a "**red nun**". Green buoys that are not lighted are usually flat-topped and is referred to as a "**can buoy**" or a "**green can**".

This nun buoy has a conical (triangular) top, is red in color, and has an even number on it.

NUMBERS - Notice that each ATON is marked with a number, letter, or both. Green buoys will always be marked using **odd** numbers, and red buoys and beacons will be marked with **even** numbers. The numbers that appear on ATONs will usually increase the closer they are to the harbor. In other words, the first buoy a mariner encounters when entering a channel from the open sea will be numbered with a "1" and the numbers will increase as he travels inland toward the harbor. Preferred channel markers and safe water ATONs are marked with a letter or combination of letters.

SOUNDS - Several ATONs will be fitted with some type of noise making device. Loud horns are commonly found affixed to a lighthouse and are sounded at even intervals which can be found on the chart or on the light list.

Buoys often have a bell, horn, or gong that can be heard for miles as one approaches. These sounds help the mariner to determine the general location of the ATON in the field, and also help them to distinguish one ATON from another.

LIGHTS - Many ATONs are also fitted with lights to help identify it at night or in poor visibility. Typically, red ATONs have red lights, green ATONs have green lights, and lighthouses have white lights. In addition, ATONs can flash their lights in a particular pattern, which can help distinguish each one from another. This is particularly helpful to the mariner when following a series of buoys marking a long channel at night. When each buoy flashes its own unique pattern, it can be much easier to determine which buoy one is looking at. The chart below explains the pattern systems and their symbols used on the chart.

Common Light Symbols Found on Charts

Symbol on Chart	Class of Light	Light Pattern
F	Fixed (always on)	
Fl	Flashing	
Fl (2)	Group Flashing (groups of 2 or more flashes)	
FL (2+1)	Composite Group Flashing (groups of patterns of flashes)	
Iso	Isophase (both light and dark are equal)	
Oc	Occulting (light is longer than dark)	
Q	Quick Flashing (flashing quickly - approx 50-60 times per minute)	

Other Common Chart Symbols Associated with ATONs

Symbol on Chart	Meaning	Symbol on Chart	Meaning
B	Black	N	Nun Buoy
Bn	Beacon	Pri	Private
C	Can Buoy	R	Red
G	Green	S	Square Dayboard
J	Juntion (S or T Dayboard)	s	seconds
M	Safe Water	W	White
MO	Morse Code	Y	Yellow

Note: See Chart No. 1 for a complete listing of symbols used on NOAA charts

Daybeacons

Daybeacons are unlighted markers that are mounted on a pile, tower, or other means of affixing to land or the bottom. Daybeacons are not lighted, but are consistent with other ATON characteristics with

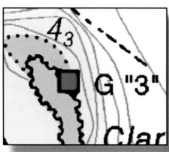

Daybeacons appear as a green square or a red triangle on the chart

regard to shape, color, etc. They are labelled either by number, letter, or combination of the two.

Range Dayboards

A *range* is a general navigation term that refers to the alignment of two or more objects in the field to yield a *line of position (LOP).* (See chapter 9 for explanation of this piloting technique).

Range dayboards are markers that allow the mariner to use a range for determining position. Range dayboards appear in the field as vertically-striped rectangular markers.

Range Dayboard in the Sandy Hook Channel in New Jersey

Intracoastal Waterway Marks

The intracoastal waterway is an inland waterway along the eastern US coast that extends from Florida to New York. This canal system utilizes its own unique navigational marking system that includes yellow squares and triangles. These yellow shapes often appear on other ATONs where the ICW intersects other navigation channels

This green daybeacon also includes an ICW yellow square marking

connecting the open ocean to inland ports and harbors. The shape system is consistent with IALA B convention in that the yellow triangle shape marks the right side of the channel and the squares identify the left side of the channel, when travelling south (clockwise) along the eastern coast.

Lighthouses

Although all lighthouses in the US are now fully automated and no longer manned, the iconic lighthouse of the past is still used

Head Harbor Light on Campobello Island, New Brunswick, Canada

Draw what you would expect the green daybeacon #3 described on the chart at the top left of this page to look like in the field.

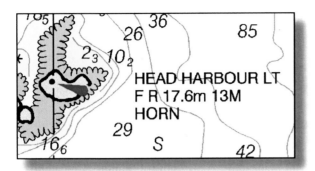

Symbols on the chart describe Head Harbor Light as having a fixed red light that is 17.6 meters above high tide, is visible for 13 nautical miles, and has a horn

today for navigational purposes. Usually located near the entrance to harbors, lighthouses provide a visual and often audible landmark for mariners to use for navigation. Lighthouses are represented on the chart using a light symbol, and include information about the frequency, intensity, and height of the light as well as whether or not the lighthouse also has a horn or other audible signal.

The Cardinal Buoy System

In addition to using a lateral system of buoys that mark the sides of a navigable waterway, IALA B also employs a cardinal buoy system. As indicated by its name, the cardinal system uses four buoys (N, S, E, W) that mark the cardinal boundaries of a hazard. Each buoy is designated by a system of colored bands and topmarks, both of which are indicated on the chart.

The cardinal system is not used often in US waters, but can often be seen marking hazards to navigation in Canadian waters.

Western River System

The Mississippi River and its tributaries utilize a slight variation of the IALA-B system, most notably being the reference to the direction of current in the rivers. Similar to the "red right returning" rule use elsewhere in the US, red ATONs mark the right side of the channel when navigating upstream, or against the current. Likewise, the green ATONs mark the left side of the channel when heading downstream or with the current.

Aside from this subtle difference, the Western River System is very similar to other rules, symbols, and characteristics of the IALA-B system used throughout the United States and the rest of North America.

(See the ATON guide in Appendix D for a more complete record of the Western River System.)

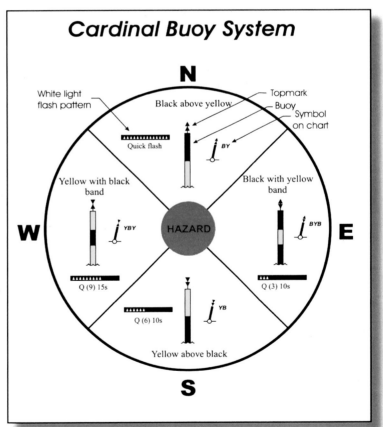

The cardinal buoy system uses a system of four buoys to mark the north, south, east, and west boundaries of a hazard to navigation

Putting it all together...

Each of these individual buoys and beacons combine to create a system of navigational "road signs" to aid the navigator. The diagram below displays what one might typically expect to see when navigating a channel using the IALA B system.

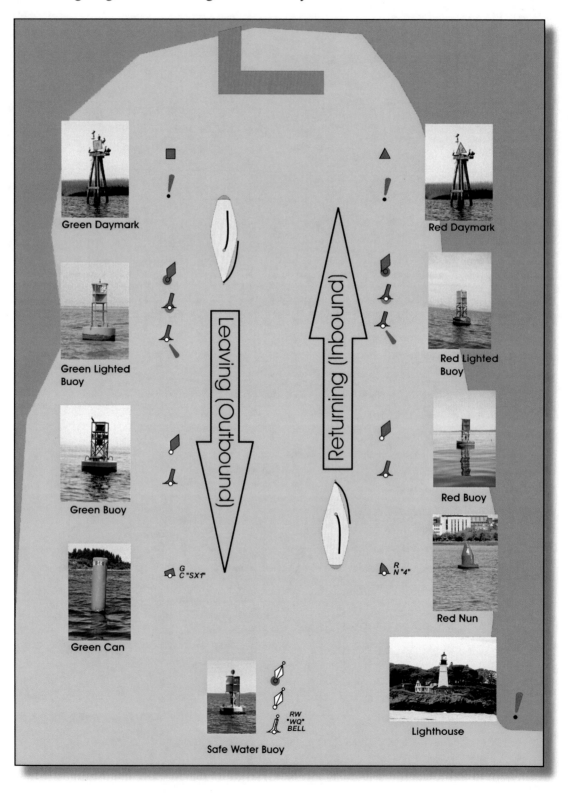

ATONs ID Activity

Using Chart 13394 and Chart No. 1 in Appendix C, find and circle each of the ATONs below on your chart.

1. Red nun with "UH4" printed on it

2. The number 3 daybeacon at Clark Ledge

3. Red nun number "4"

4. Green can number "5"

5. A lighted green buoy with a bell

6. A green buoy with a whistle

7. A lighthouse

8. A safe water buoy

9. A North cardinal buoy

10. A West cardinal buoy

11. A private yellow buoy

12. A buoy that flashes the Morse code for the letter "A"

Identify the type of ATON and define its associated symbols using Chart No. 1

13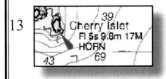

14

15

16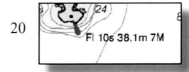

17

18

19

20

ATON Identification

Using the visual buoyage guide below and Chart No. 1, draw a chart that includes the ATON symbols that you would expect to see on a chart representing this area. Be sure to include all symbols and notations as listed in Chart No. 1.

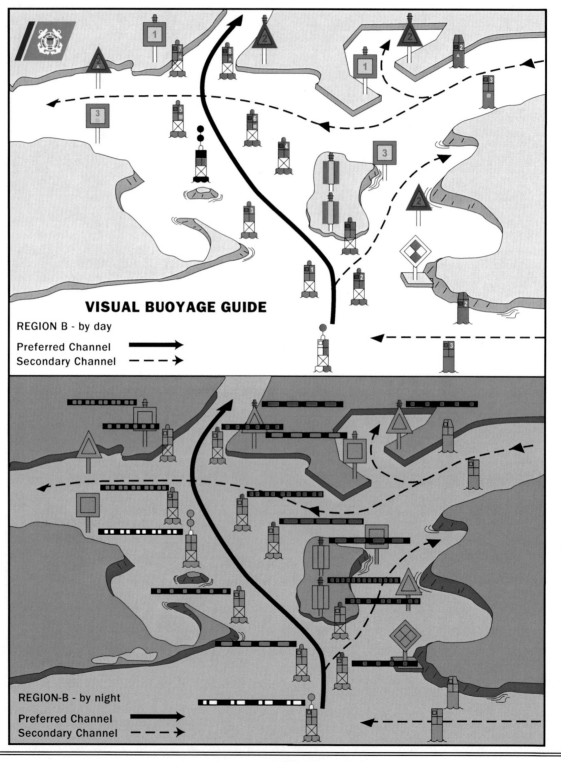

Chapter 8
Plotting and Dead Reckoning
The foundation of nautical navigation

> ***Chapter Objectives:***
> * Demonstrate an understanding of the basic tools used for plotting
> * Demonstrate ability to measure distance using a divider
> * Demonstrate the ability to plot latitude and longitude coordinates on a chart
> * Demonstrate a working knowledge of dead reckoning methods including plotting, labeling, measuring, and determining DR positions; speed, time, distance formulas and problem solving

Navigating on the ocean is an ancient art dating back several thousand years. The methods described in this chapter have been adapted from those tested over time to be applicable to small craft, namely small powerboats, sailboats, and kayaks. These methods can collectively be referred to as "***dead reckoning***," an abbreviated form of the term "deductive reckoning," which refers to the scientific and mathematical estimation of one's position particularly when the navigator is planning a course or is unable to use landmarks or ATONs for navigation.

Throughout this chapter, you will learn various components of the dead reckoning process and the building-block skills related to these methods. Toward the end of the chapter, each of these components will be put together into a systematic method of determining one's position and course at sea.

It's worth noting that many of these techniques can be adapted to be used in navigation on land.

Plotting Tools

Drawing your position or course, whether known or estimated while planning, on a chart is referred to as "***plotting***". There are a few tools that you will want to use with your chart that will allow you plot accurately.

A ***parallel rule*** or other device capable of transferring bearings to a chart is necessary to accurately plot your location or intended route. These come in various sizes and styles, however consider what you will really need. If you are kayaking, you may want a smaller

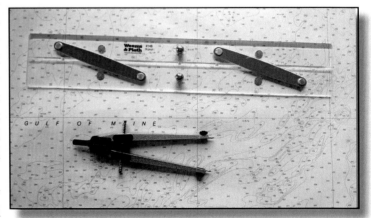

In addition to a pencil and eraser, a good quality parallel rule (top) and a pair of dividers (bottom) are essential tools for plotting

88

device that fits easily in your chart bag.

A good quality set of **dividers** will allow you to accurately measure distances on your chart. On all boats, but especially in a kayak, take care to protect the sharp points on the ends of the divider. Carrying them in a hard plastic case is a good way to avoid them puncturing your gear or your skin.

A sharp pencil is also a necessary tool for plotting. Either a standard pencil with means to sharpen it, or a mechanical pencil with spare graphite leads are a must. Using an ink pen on a chart is not recommended. A large eraser is very helpful, especially when first learning how to plot.

Measuring Distance

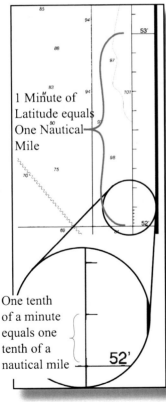

1 Minute of Latitude equals One Nautical Mile

One tenth of a minute equals one tenth of a nautical mile

52'

Distance on the water is measured in **nautical miles.** One nautical mile is equal to one minute of latitude (or 1/60 of a degree), which equates to about 6076 feet or 1.15 statute miles.

On the chart, we can measure distance in nautical miles using our dividers and the latitude scale on the left or right borders of the chart. If we look closely at the latitude scale in the margin of the chart, we'll see that each minute of latitude is broken into tenths of a minute, thus tenths of a nautical mile.

If we want to measure the distance of

Step 1: Place each point of the dividers on the beginning and end of the straight-line distance you want to measure.

Step 2: Without changing the distance between the legs of the dividers, lift the dividers off the chart and place them on the latitude scale on the side of the chart closest to what you are measuring. Place one point of the divider on a minute mark and allow the other to touch the scale wherever it falls preserving the distance measured.

Step 3: Read the distance in nautical miles between the two points of the dividers. Interpolate between tenths of a minute to read hundredths of a mile. This distance measures 1.37 nautical miles.

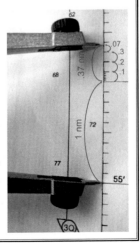

each leg of the course we laid out in the previous exercise, we would simply place each end of the dividers on the beginning and ending of each leg, then transfer the dividers to the latitude scale at the side of the chart closest to our course.

Plotting Latitude and Longitude

The Latitude and Longitude coordinate system is the primary position reporting system utilized on the ocean. In Chapter 4, we learned about this system and how to use a lat/long scale tool to measure and plot latitude and longitude on a 1:24,000 scale, 7.5 minute series UGSG map. Because nautical charts are printed at various scales, we would need to carry a separate tool for each scale of chart published, making it simply not practical to use a lat/long tool on a chart.

Instead, we will use a parallel rule to measure location using the latitude and longitude scales found in the margins of the chart.

If we are trying to determine the coordinates of a location of any specific point on the chart, whether it is an ATON, a good fishing spot, or a point of land, the process is the same. This process is also the same if we are trying to find the coordinates of our known location, or a "*fix*". This process is described in detail to the right. The various methods used to *acquire* a fix are described in detail in Chapter 9.

If we are trying to plot a location for which we already know the latitude and longitude coordi-

---

3-Step Process for Finding your Latitude and Longitude on a Chart

Step 1: Place your parallel rule on a *latitude* line that is closest to your fix. "Walk" the rule so that one edge aligns with your fix and follow the edge of the rule to where it intersects with the latitude scale in the margin of the chart. Read the latitude of your fix.

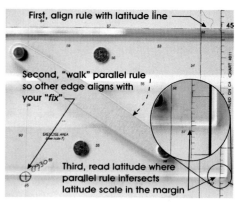

Step 2: Similar to step 1, place your parallel rule on a *longitude* line that is closest to your fix. "Walk" the rule so that one edge aligns with your fix and follow the edge of the rule to where it intersects with the longitude scale in the top or bottom margin of the chart. Read the longitude of your fix.

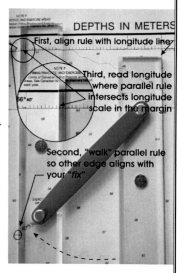

Step 3: Record the latitude and longitude in that order, being sure to include descriptors N or S (for latitude) and E or W (for longitude). If

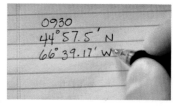

this coordinate represents a fix, it is always a good idea to record the time of the fix along with the coordinate.

3-Step Process for Plotting a Known Latitude and Longitude on a Chart

Step 1: Find and mark the latitude of the position you want to plot on the latitude scale on the side of the chart. Similarly, find and mark the longitude of your position on the longitude scale across the top or bottom margin of your chart.

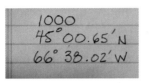

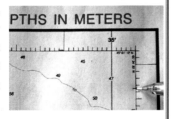

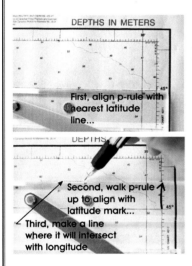

Step 2: Position your parallel rule on the latitude line nearest to your latitude. "Walk" the rule so that one edge lines up with your latitude. Draw a line across the chart where it will be likely to intersect with your longitude.

Step 3: Position your parallel rule on the longitude line nearest your longitude. "Walk" the rule so that one edge lines up with your longitude. Draw a line across the chart where it will intersect your latitude. Where these two lines cross is your latitude/longitude fix.

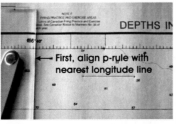

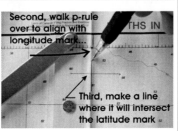

nates, we will essentially reverse the steps used above. Because we already know the coordinates, we start with finding each coordinate on the appropriate margin of the chart and then transfer that coordinate across or down the chart to where the two coordinates intersect. This intersection represents the location of the coordinate plotted.

Interpreting Degrees, Minutes, and Seconds on the Chart

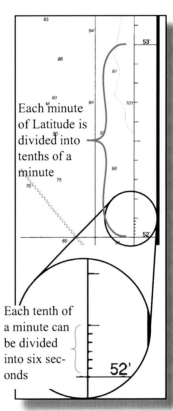

If we look closely at the latitude scale in the margin of the chart, we'll see that each minute of latitude is broken into tenths of a minute. In select places on the latitude scale, we will see that each tenth is broken into six more subunits. Since 6 X 10 = 60, each one represents one sixtieth of a minute, or one second of latitude. These markings allow us to measure latitude and longitude coordinates that are described in either decimal minutes, or degrees, minutes, seconds format.

To record the coordinates

using degrees, minutes, and decimal minutes (sometimes represented as *DD°MM.MM'*) like 66°39.17' in the process outlined to the right, simply use the tenth of a minute markings for tenths. If the measurement falls between two "tenth" markings, estimate the hundredths measurement by visually dividing each tenth into ten subunits and estimate how many hundredths this is. This process is exactly the same as if you were measuring distance in decimal nautical miles. The longitude coordinate of the location represented by the red tick mark in the example to the right is 17 hundredths of a minute (.17') west of 66°39', or 66°39.17'.

If, however, you wanted to measure latitude or longitude using degrees, minutes, and seconds (sometimes represented as *DD°MM'SS"*) like 66°39'10", we'll need to divide each tenth of a minute into six subunits to represent seconds.

Each tenth of a minute we will count as six seconds. For locations that do not fall directly on a tenth mark, we can transfer the distance of into the next tenth using dividers. In the example to the right, the red tick mark lies one tenth (six seconds) plus

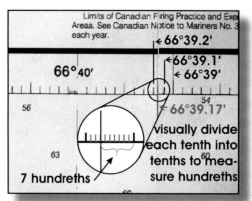

Measuring Longitude in Degrees, Minutes, and Decimal Minutes (DD°MM.MM')

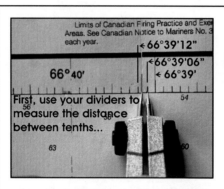

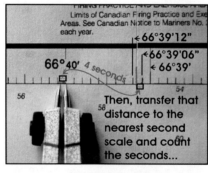

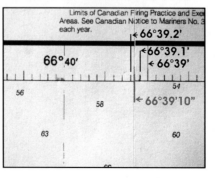

Measuring Longitude in Degrees, Minutes, and Seconds (DD°MM'SS')

four more seconds (measured by the dividers) for a total of 10 seconds west of 66°39'. Therefore, the longitude coordinate of this position is 66°39'10".

Plotting a Course

Plotting a course involves drawing the intended course on the chart using plotting tools. The process begins with studying the chart carefully to determine a reasonable and safe route, being careful to interpret all ATONs to ensure safe passage that is appropriate for the vessel. For example, a large tanker may want to stay in the deep channel, whereas a sea kayaker or small power or sailboat will want to avoid the heavier traffic in the channel and plan a route through shallower, quieter water.

For this example, let's use Chart No. 13394 and plan a route from the city pier in Eastport out to Head Harbor Light. Simply draw a series of straight course lines starting from the Eastport Breakwater/ Pier past Cherry Islet Light and out Head Harbor Passage. Write the direction of each leg of the course on top of the course line, and the distance of each

CLARIFYING NAVIGATION TERMS

There are a few terms that are often used incorrectly by even the most seasoned navigator. *Heading, bearing,* and *course* are all similar terms, but actually mean very different things.

A *course* is an accurate, intended path that you wish travel. It is represented on a chart as a *vector*, or a line that represents both a direction and a distance.

Your *heading* is the direction your boat is pointing. If you drew a line through the center of your boat from stern to bow and extended it out in front of you, this would be your heading.

A *bearing* is a direction that is defined by a measured angle from either true or magnetic north to another object.

It is certainly possible that you could be heading at 220 degrees magnetic on a course that is 220 degrees magnetic, toward an object in the distance that is bearing 220 degrees magnetic.

However, it is not uncommon that you would need to be heading at 220 degrees magnetic to stay on a course of 200 degrees magnetic, while taking a bearing to an object of 150 degrees magnetic.

leg of the course under the course line. The box on page 94 provides a 3-step process for plotting a course.

Dead Reckoning

As discussed in the beginning of this chapter, *dead reckoning (DR)* is used to predict your position when you are planning your route or when you are unable to determine your position using other methods described in Chapter 9. The DR plot is considered a universal skill and is appropriate for use whether paddling a sea kayak, sailing a 30-foot sailboat, or piloting a 600-foot tanker. Ideally, it should be completed before heading out on the water to give the navigator a clear navigational plan.

The backbone of the DR plot is a course line (see p.94 step 1), which can be considered the "road" on which you'd like to travel. After drawing this line or series of lines, you'll add more information to your DR plot that will help you determine where you will be and when you'll be there. This information can be represented by symbols and specific formatting of time, direction, speed, and distance. Think of a DR plot as being its own language. If we all use this same language, then we can easily interpret each other's DR plots.

After drawing our course line and labelling it with the course direction and distance, the next step is to calculate how long it will take us to travel each leg of the course.

Name a couple of reasons why your heading could be different from your course.

3-Step Process for Plotting a Course on a Nautical Chart

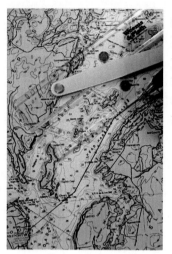

Step 1: Using your parallel rule as a straightedge, draw a course line (or series of lines) that represents your desired course. If you need to change direction, begin your new course line where the last one ended. (Note that your course lines may not be exactly as drawn in this example, as there are multiple ways to travel out Head Harbor Passage.)

— Align one edge of parallel rule with course line...

then, while holding down that side of the parallel rule, rotate the other side...

Step 2. Measure the direction of each course line. Do this by first aligning one edge of the parallel rule along the course line. Then, "walk" the parallel rule across the chart toward the nearest compass rose. To do this, press down firmly on one

to intersect the <u>center</u> of the compass rose and the inner <u>(magnetic)</u> bearing circle

side of the parallel rule, and gently move the other side toward the rose. If necessary, alternate holding and moving each side of the parallel rule until you reach the rose. Continue walking until one edge of the parallel rule intersects the center of the compass rose. Read the bearing where the parallel rule intersects the inner (magnetic) circle. This is the direction in degrees magnetic of the course line. This course measures 074 degrees magnetic. (Note that the direction of the course line might not be exactly 074 M.)

Step 3: Label each leg of the course with its direction and distance. Place the course bearing on top of the course line and make sure to include the "*M*" for magnetic after the number to distinguish it from a true bearing. Measure the length of each leg of the course and write that distance under the course line. Repeat this process for each leg of the course. (Again, note that the distance of each leg of the course you draw may not be exactly the same as in this example.)

Let's say you've planned your route and drawn your course lines from the Eastport breakwater heading out Head Harbor Passage (as described in the 3-step process on p. 94) and begin travelling that route. If the fog rolled in, how would you know where you were? Or, how would you know when to change your heading so you could stay on course?

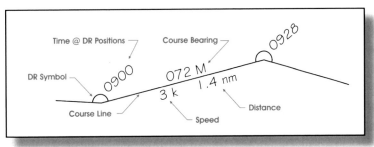

DR plots are communicated through a specific "language" of symbols and formatting

The answer is "speed and time". Since we already know the distance of each leg of the route, if we carefully monitor speed and time, we will know when to change course. This is because speed, distance, and time are all related. This relationship can be represented using a mathematical formula:

$$\text{Speed} = \text{Distance} \div \text{Time}$$

This relationship can also be represented as a fraction:

$$\text{Speed} = \frac{\text{Distance}}{\text{Time}}$$

The easiest way to remember this is to think about what "speed" is measuring. If you look at the speedometer in you car, you can find that you are travelling at 60 miles per hour. Your speed is equal to 60 miles per (divided by) one hour. So...

$$S_{(mph)} = D_{(miles)} \div T_{(hours)}$$

or

$$S_{(mph)} = \frac{D_{(miles)}}{T_{(hours)}}$$

Understanding this relationship allows us to calculate any one of the three factors if we know the other two. For example, if we know the distance of the leg and we know our speed, we can calculate how long it will take us to travel that leg. Looking at the first leg of the course leaving the breakwater, we can see that we'll need to travel 1.4 nautical miles before we need to change our heading. If we sail 3 nautical miles per hour (or knots) we can calculate how long it will take us to travel along that particular leg, and hence when we will need to change our heading:

$$S_{(mph)} = D_{(miles)} \div T_{(hours)}$$

$$3_{(knots)} = 1.4_{(miles)} \div T_{(hours)}$$

Let's simplify our formula and solve for T ...

$$3 = 1.4 / T$$
$$3T = 1.4$$
$$T = 1.4 / 3$$
$$T = .467 \text{ hours}$$

Great! We now know that if we travel along our course from the Eastport breakwater at 3 knots for .467 hours, we should at our first heading change. The problem is, however, that we don't keep time in decimal hours; .467 hours isn't a time format that we can set on our watch. We'll need to convert decimal hours to minutes.

We know that one hour equals 60 minutes. We can use a ratio to calculate how many minutes are in .467 hours:

$$\frac{1 \text{ (hr)}}{60 \text{ (min)}} = \frac{.467 \text{ (hr)}}{M \text{ (min)}}$$

You may recall from basic algebra that in order to solve this equation for "M" (how many minutes are in .467 hours), we'll need to cross-multiply:

$$\frac{1 \text{ (hr)}}{60 \text{ (min)}} = \frac{.467 \text{ (hr)}}{M \text{ (min)}}$$

$$1 \times M = 60 \times .467$$
$$M = 28.02 \text{ minutes}$$

This means that if we travel along our course heading at 3 knots for slightly more than 28 minutes we will need to change our heading. Because we know that there are 60 seconds in a minute, we could use the same equation to calculate how many seconds are in .02 minutes. However, we can usually round to the nearest minute when calculating DR positions, as calculating seconds exceeds the real-world accuracy of using DR.

Now that we have this information, we can add it to our course plot, thereby converting it to a "DR" plot. First, simply add the speed under the course line next to the distance. Then, add a "DR" symbol to each point where the course changes. A "DR" symbol looks like a half-circle whose center is at the turning point of each leg. Each "DR" symbol should include a time you are predicted to be there. If you leave the Eastport Breakwater at 0900 (use military time), and travel at 072 degrees magnetic at 3 knots, you'll

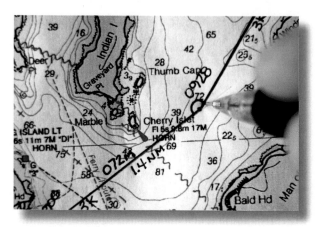

DR symbols drawn on a chart. Note how important it is to be very neat and organized when drawing DR plots, as charts can get crowded.

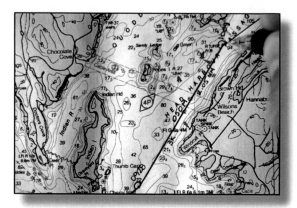

Each leg of the DR plot is labelled in a similar fashion.

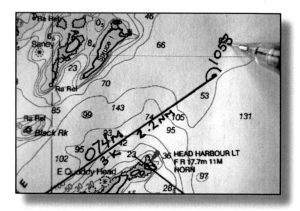

The end of the course is labelled, identifying the time at which you can expect to arrive

need to change your heading at 0928 to 050 degrees magnetic. To determine when you'll need to change course again, simply use the Speed = Distance / Time formula again:

$$S = D/T$$
$$3 = 2.05/T$$
$$3T = 2.05$$
$$T = 2.05/3$$
$$T = .683 \text{ hours}$$

Then, convert decimal hours to minutes...

$$\frac{1 \text{ (hr)}}{60 \text{ (min)}} = \frac{.683 \text{ (hr)}}{M \text{ (min)}}$$

$$1 M = 60 \times .683$$
$$M = 40.98 \text{ minutes}$$

Let's round up to 41 minutes. This means that if we travel at 050 degrees magnetic at 3 knots for 41 minutes, we'll need to change our heading at 1009. If we repeat this process for every leg of the route, we will arrive at our destination north of Head Harbor Light at 1053.

DR Plot Tutorial on YouTube at https://www.youtube.com/watch?v=8_uBYkI-iLfs

---

3-Step Process for a DR Plot

Step 1: Draw course line (track). Measure and label course headings, distances, and speed for each leg of the course (see 3-step process on p. 94).

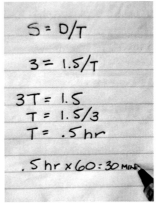

Step 2: Using the speed and distance of each leg, calculate the time it will take to travel each leg of the course in hours and minutes.

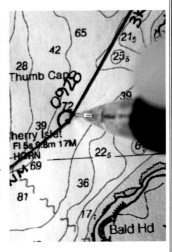

Step 3: Using the times calculated in step 2, calculate the time for each course change. Place a DR symbol and anticipated times at regular time intervals and at course changes.

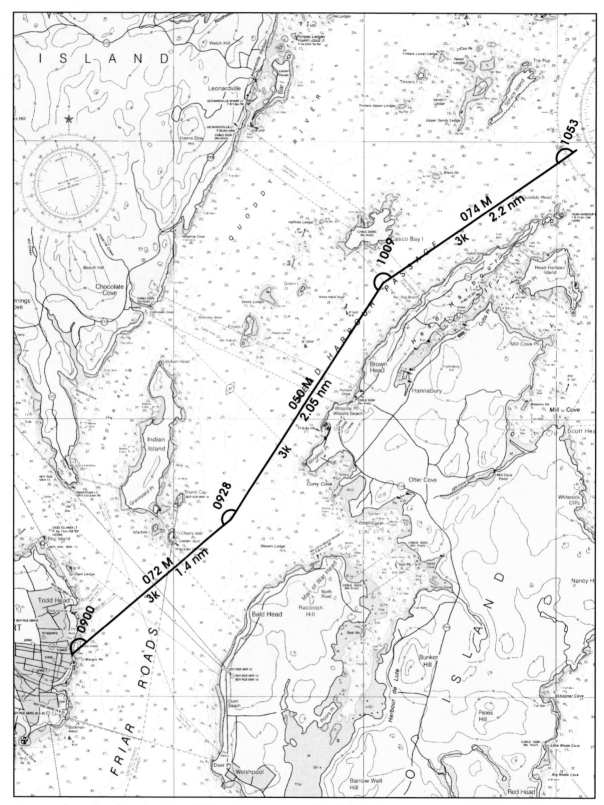

A complete dead reckoning (DR) plot contains all of the information needed to predict where you might be given time, direction, speed, and distance. It is important to note that the DR plot represents the theoretical predicted location of your vessel and does not account for errors in steering or the effects of wind, current, or waves.

Latitude and Longitude Plotting Exercises

Plot the Following Locations on Nautical Chart No. 13394 and write in the name of the geographic feature at that location.

Geographic Feature	Latitude	Longitude
_____	44°56.21' N	66°44.01' W
_____	44°55.12' N	66°59.35' W
_____	44°52'58" N	67°07'49" W
_____	44°53'49" N	67°04'30" W

Find the coordinates to the following geographic features on Chart No. 13394:

Geographic Feature	Latitude	Longitude
Cherry Islet Light	_____	_____
Head Harbour Light	_____	_____
Swallowtail Light on Grand Manan	_____	_____
The "WQ" safe water buoy Near West Quoddy Head	_____	_____

Course Plotting Exercises

Plot the following courses on Chart No. 13394:

1. Starting at 44°54.37' N 66°59' W plot the following course:

048° T for 1 NM
033° T for 1.5 NM
046° T for 2.4 NM
110° T for .75 NM

End Location _____ (lat) _____ (long)

2. Starting at the Eastport Breakwater, plot the following course:

123° M for .5 NM
230° M for 1 NM
300° M for 1 NM
318° M for 1.3 NM
312° M for .5 NM

End Location _____ (lat) _____ (long)

3. Starting at 44°48'02"N 66°47'11" W, plot the following course:

025T for 13.4 NM
272T for 8.2 NM
216T for 3.3 NM
175T for 3.2 NM
148T for 7.5 NM

4. Plot a course from the light at Long Eddy Point at the northernmost tip of Grand Manan through the Quoddy Narrows to Lubec. List the bearings and distances below:

_____ for _____ NM
_____ for _____ NM
_____ for _____ NM
_____ for _____ NM
_____ for _____ NM
_____ for _____ NM
_____ for _____ NM

DR Course Plotting Homework

Plot the following courses on Chart No. 13394:

1. Starting at 44°54.37' N 66°59' W plot the following DR course for starting at 0900 and turning at 4 knots:

055° M for .5 NM
338° M for 3.25 NM
017° M for 2.15 NM
134° M for 3800 Ft

End Location _____ (lat) _____ (long)

Geographic Name of End Location _____

Time of arrival_____

2. Starting at 44°51'42"N, 066°58'56"W, plot the following DR course if you start at 1230 and paddle at 3 knots:

026° M for 1 NM
332° M for 1 NM
228° M for 1 NM
137° M for 1.23 NM

End Location _____ (lat) _____ (long)

ATON at End Location _____

Time of arrival_____

3. Starting at the "WQ" safe water buoy near West Quoddy Head at 1000 and sailing at 6 knots, plot a DR course to the following landmarks :

Swallowtail Light on Grand Manan, then to…
Southern Wolf Island Light, then to…
Head Harbor Light on Campobello, then to…
The Eastport Breakwater
Time of arrival_____

Chapter 9
Basic Piloting
An introduction to some basic techniques

Chapter Objectives
- Demonstrate understanding of basic components of piloting
- Demonstrate how to plot a line of position (LOP)
- Demonstrate how to plot a running fix
- Demonstrate how to plot a fix from triangulation
- Demonstrate how to correct and uncorrect compass bearings

Piloting is considered to be both an art and a science, and is defined as the use of landmarks, ATONs, and other observations in the field to navigate through a waterway. Sometimes piloting is simply a matter of recognizing ATONs and other land features in the field and, by referencing these objects on the chart, figuring out where you are. Other times, piloting requires the use of bearings, ranges, and other tricks that help you to make your way safely along a waterway. The concept of piloting includes dozens of techniques, formulas, and strategies to help navigate when visual clues are present. This chapter will introduce a few of the more common and basic strategies and techniques that will utilize observations in the field combined with a nautical chart to help the navigator pilot a vessel safely through an area.

We have already discussed Aids to Navigation (ATONs) and their role in identifying navigable waterways, along with techniques for planning a course through safe waters. The *science* of piloting includes several techniques that we will discuss in this chapter. The *art* of piloting involves knowing when to use which technique given a particular situation, and even combining two or more tech-

niques when appropriate. Becoming a "piloting artist" requires lots of practice in the field.

Lines of Position (LOPs)

Remember from Chapter 5 that a *line of position (LOP)* is a line drawn on the map (or chart in this case) that represents a direction between you and a known object. It repre-

A sighting compass can help provide accurate bearings in the field that can be transferred to the chart as LOP's. This bearing reads 325 degrees magnetic.

sents a line on the chart on which you must be located.

To acquire an LOP, you must be able to identify a *fixed* object in the field that you can also identify on your chart. It is important that this object is fixed (such as a beacon or point of land) and not something that changes position (such as a floating ATON buoy) so that the LOP is as accurate as possible.

In the field, simply take a bearing to a known object in the field using your baseplate compass (see Chapter 4), or a sighting compass (p. 102, bottom, right). In the example to the right, let's say you can see Head Harbor Light, a lighthouse on Campobello, and it lies 325 degrees magnetic to your current position.

To plot this LOP, use your parallel rule to transfer the magnetic bearing from the center (magnetic) circle of the compass rose on the chart to the known object. Note that because the center circle of the compass rose is aligned with magnetic north, there is no need to convert your magnetic bearing to a true bearing as we did with plotting bearings on topographic maps.

This LOP plotted on the chart represents a line on which you must be located. In other words, if your bearing to the object was 325 magnetic, you have reduced all of the possible locations you could be in the world to a line that represents that bearing to the object.

3-Step Process for Plotting an LOP on a Nautical Chart

Step 1: Align the parallel rule with the compass rose nearest to the object sighted. Be sure to align the rule so that one edge intersects the center of the compass rose and the bearing measurement on the *magnetic* (inner) circle of the rose (in this case, 325 degrees magnetic).

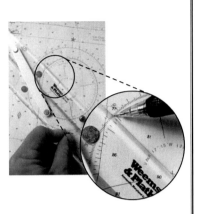

Press down and hold this side...

While sliding this side toward object sighted in...

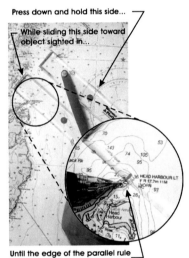

Until the edge of the parallel rule intersects the object sighted in

Step 2: "Walk" the parallel rule across the chart. To do this, press down firmly on one side of the parallel rule, and gently move the other side toward the object sighted on the chart. Continue walking until one edge of the parallel rule intersects the object sighted.

Step 3: Draw a line on the chart along the edge of the parallel rule from the object sighted in the direction toward what would be center of the compass rose if it were still under the parallel rule. Write the bearing on top of the LOP.

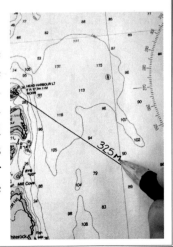

Triangulation

Lines of position are helpful in that they provide a one-dimensional line on which we are located. However, a single LOP is only one half of the information required to obtain a *fix* which is a *known point (rather than a line) that represents your location.* In Chapter 5 we discussed the process of *triangulation* which uses two or more LOP's to obtain a fix.

This process is similar when on the ocean, with the exception being that our position is rarely stationary while floating on water. As a result, we will want to take bearings to two objects *at the same time* if we want our fix to be accurate. If we plot the LOPs to those two known positions on the chart, where they cross will be our *fix*. This point represents the only place in the entire world that we can have the measured bearing to each of the two known points at the same time.

When using two or more LOP's to triangulate, remember from Chapter 5 that the two objects used should be as close to 90 degrees apart as possible.

When using three or more LOPs to determine position, they should theoretically all cross at a single point, yielding a fix. However, in practice, the three LOPs will likely form a small triangle due to small errors in taking bearings and in

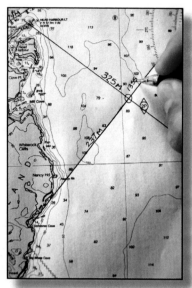

Triangulation involves plotting two (or more) LOP's taken at the same time that are approximately 90 degrees apart from each other and provides a "fix". Note that the fix includes a circle around the intersection and the time written at an angle above the fix.

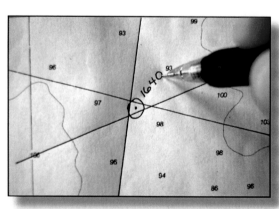

This fix is derived by placing a dot in the center of a triangle formed by three LOPs. This averages the error and results in a more accurate fix.

plotting. When this occurs, the errors in the fix are averaged out by placing a dot in the center of the triangle which represents your location.

Running Fix

A *running fix* is a valuable technique to utilize when you only have one object with which to measure an LOP. The running fix is not as accurate as a fix calculated using triangulation or GPS, as it is actually a combination of an LOP and DR. As such, the accuracy of a running fix is highly dependent upon accurate measurement of distance covered and speed.

To plot a running fix, start with a DR plot and measure and plot an LOP to a known object. After travelling a measured distance (either measured by log, or calculated from time and speed), measure and plot a second LOP to either a new object or the same as the original one. Finally, "advance" the original LOP the distance along the DR track that was travelled. Where the advanced LOP and the second LOP cross is your running fix. This should be labelled with "R FIX" and the time so that it can be distinguished from a real fix.

3-Step Process for Plotting a Running Fix

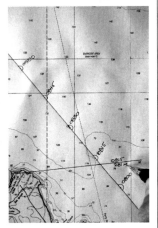

Step 1: Begin with a DR Plot. Take a bearing to and draw an LOP to the first known object.

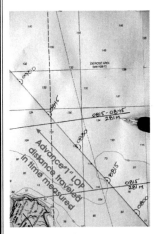

Step 2: Travel a significant distance along your course. Advance your LOP the distance and direction you have travelled.

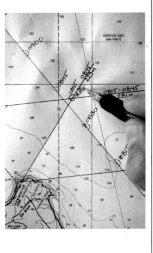

Step 3: Take a second bearing to the same or another known object. Draw this LOP on the chart. Where the second LOP and the advanced first LOP intersect is the running fix. Label this point with an "R" and the time to note it as a running fix.

Ranges

In Chapter 6 we discussed briefly how *range dayboards* provide two points of reference which, when aligned with each other provide an LOP. LOP's from ranges are sometimes already marked on the chart (below, bottom), but may also be drawn in by the navigator. Although there are specific ATONs that are intended to be used for ranges, consider that any two fixed objects when they are aligned can be used to provide an LOP.

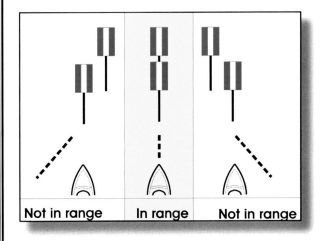

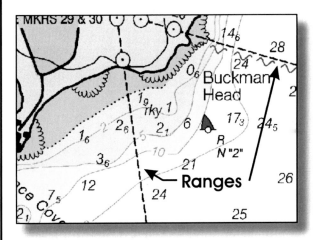

When two objects are aligned with each other, they can provide an LOP that can be transferred to the chart. Actual range dayboards (left) or towers (right) can provide an LOP that can be used for piloting.

The Marine Compass

On land, we are likely to use a baseplate type compass for taking or following bearings. Although this technique can be used on the water, most mariners opt to use a compass mounted on their boat. In a kayak, this is likely to be a ***deck compass*** that is either per- manently mounted into the deck, or

A kayaking deck compass. Note that the reading is taken from the front of the card and is therefore a direct compass.

strapped to the top deck using a bungee or other attachment device. Similarly, most powerboats or sailboats use a fixed compass mounted either on a pedestal or in a bulkhead within plain view of the helm, and are usually gimballed to self-level and ensure accuracy in case the vessel heels or pitches.

Marine compasses have some differ- ences from baseplate compasses. The most

An indirect compass with its lubber line on the opposite side of the card from the user.

obvious differ- ence is that in- stead of a mag- netic needle, a marine compass utilizes a mag- netic card that rotates inside a fluid-filled dome. The card is numbered with 360 degree markings, al- lowing the user to read the bearing from the card where it aligns with a "lubber line".

There are two distinct types of marine compasses: direct and indirect. A ***direct*** com- pass allows the user to read the bearing at the lubber line on the front (user side) of the card. An ***indirect*** compass is read at the back side (opposite the user) of the card.

Deviation

Any time we use a magnetic compass, we need to be aware of any local magnetic dis- turbances such as ferrous metals, or an elec- tromagnetic field caused by electric motors or power lines, for example.

This awareness becomes especially important when using a compass on a boat. When using a deck compass on a kayak, we need to be careful when loading our boats to keep radios, electronics, and any gear that may contain iron stowed away from the deck com- pass so as to not compromise its accuracy.

On a sailboat or powerboat, we need to account for any local magnetic disturbanc- es that may be caused by the engine, radios, radar, or other electronic devices that are also permanently mounted to the boat. The mag- netic field created by these devices interferes with the earth's magnetic field and causes er- rors in the accuracy of our compass readings. This error is referred to as ***deviation*** and must be accounted for when using a marine com- pass for navigation.

Deviation on large vessels is usually corrected by the use of small magnets mount- ed under the compass. A professional ***com- pass adjuster*** is usually hired to make sure that deviation is correctly measured and ac-

What direction (clockwise/counter-clockwise) do the bearing numbers increase on the card of a direct compass? How about an indirect compass? What do you think are the advantages/disadvantages of each?

counted for.

For smaller vessels, the deviation can be calculated using a variety of methods in the field, such as following a known range on a chart. If the range on the chart measures 180 degrees magnetic, and your compass measures 190 degrees magnetic, your compass has an error, or a ***deviation*** of 10 degrees west *at that heading.* It is important to know that deviation changes with the heading of the vessel. For example, the same compass may also have a deviation of 004 degrees west at a heading of 270 degrees magnetic.

Because of this, deviation is usually accounted for using ***deviation card***, a chart that denotes common compass headings and the deviation that exists at each heading.

In order to account for deviation, the user must consult the card and either add or subtract the deviation to the magnetic bearing. A magnetic bearing that has been corrected for deviation is called a "***compass bearing***". Compass bearings are denoted using the letter "C" after the bearing number, just as the letter "T" and "M" are used for true and magnetic bearings.

The process for converting true bear-

True	*200T*
Variation	*018 W*
Magnetic	*218 M*
Deviation	*004 W*
Compass	*222 C*
Add	
West	

Compass	*222 C*
Deviation	*004 W*
Magnetic	*218 M*
Variation	*018 W*
True	*200 T*
Add	
East	

Process for converting True to Compass (top) and Compass to True (bottom) bearings.

ings to compass bearings can be remembered using the phrase "*TeleVision Makes Dull Children, Add Wilderness,*" with the first letter of each word referring to each step of the process. This reminds us that, starting with a True bearing, we will Add West variation (which means we'll subtract East variation) and arrive at our Magnetic bearing. From there, we Add West Deviation (again subtracting East deviation) to arrive at our Compass bearing.

The same process can be run in reverse and remembered by using the phrase "*Can Dead Men Vote Twice At Elections?*". Starting with a Compass bearing, we will Add East Deviation (or subtract West deviation) to arrive at a Magnetic Bearing. From there, we Add East Variation (or subtract West variation) to arrive at our True bearing.

Sample deviation card for a compass on a US Navy ship. Image from http://www.globalsecurity. org/military/library/policy/army/ fm/55-501/chap6.htm

Triangulation Exercises

Plot the following 2- or 3-LOP fixes on Chart No. 13394 by using triangulation:

1.

		End Location
Long Eddy Point Light	167M	_____(lat)
Southern Wolf Island Light	093M	_____(long)

2.

		End Location
Southern Wolf Island Light	075M	_____(lat)
Head Harbor Light	333M	_____(long)

3.

		End Location
Long Eddy Point Light	087M	_____(lat)
West Quoddy Head Light	346M	_____(long)

4.

		End Location
Northern tip of Eastern Wolf Island	346M	_____(lat)
Southern Wolf Island Light	320M	_____(long)
Swallowtail Light	241M	

5.

		End Location
Southern Wolf Island Light	145M	_____(lat)
Radar shows you are 5.2 nm from Southern Wolf Island Lt.		_____(long)

6.

		End Location
Swallowtail Light	211M	_____(lat)
Southern Wolf Island Light and Head Harbor Light are lined up as a range		_____(long)

Running Fix Exercises

Plot the following running fixes using Chart No. 13394

1.   You are at 44°46.72'N 66°51.45'W heading at 049M at 4 knots at 0900 when you lose your electronics on board. 30 minutes later, you see the lighthouse on Long Eddy Point at 120M. After another 30 minutes, you can see the same lighthouse at 168M. What are the coordinates of your location?

2.   You are sailing at 4 knots heading 336M somewhere off the eastern side of Grand Manan Island. At 0800 you plot a fix at 44°46.72'N 66°43.47'W. At 0820, the fog rolls in and you can only see Long Eddy Point Light at 266M. At 0845 you take another bearing to Eddy Point Light of 223M. What are your coordinates of your location?

3.   At 0900, you are position 45°00.45' N 66°37.1'W steaming at 5 knots on a heading of 228M. At 0930, you see the norther end of Eastern Wolf Island at 341M. 30 minutes later, you can see Southern Wolf Island Light at 276M. What are the coordinates of your location?

Bearing Correction Exercises

"Uncorrect" the following bearings using the compass card on p. 107:

T	045T	036T	180T	245T	110T	325T
V						
M						
D						
C						

Correct the following bearings using the compass card on p. 107:

C	225C	129C	036C	096C	228C	333C
D						
M						
V						
T						

Chapter 10
Navigating Tide and Current
Navigating on a moving waterway

Chapter Objectives:
- Demonstrate understanding of what causes the tides
- Define the relationship between tide and current
- Demonstrate ability to read a tide chart and current table
- Demonstrate the ability to compensate for set and drift

Up until now, all of the navigation techniques discussed in this text have assumed that the navigator is traveling on a stationary surface. However, the water in the ocean is constantly in motion. The primary force behind the movement of water in the ocean is due to both the gravitational pull of the sun and moon, and the centrifugal force of the Earth's rotation. We'll discuss these forces and their resultant effects upon the oceans, as well as some basic strategies to account for this motion when navigating.

Tide

The vertical rise and fall of water in the ocean is referred to as **tide**. The height of the change between high and low water levels, called the **tidal range**, can vary drastically from place to place based upon a number of factors.

As the earth revolves around the sun and the moon revolves around the earth, the sun and moon exert gravitational pull on the earth. As a result, water is pulled toward each the sun and moon in at varying directions and levels of force. Because the relative position of the sun an moon constantly changes, so do the forces they exert on the earth. As a result, we experience variation in the height of the tides from day to day. If we look at the tide chart for Eastport, Maine during the month

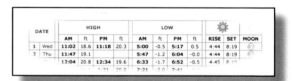

of July, 2015, we'll notice that there are two high tides each day and two low tides each day. Notice that the time between each high and low is approximately six hours. Actually, the average time between low and high tide is 6 hours and 12-1/2 minutes. This is because the moon returns to the same relative position

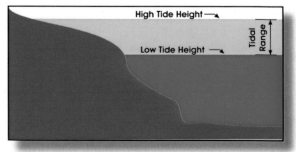

The difference between high tide and low tide is the tidal range.

112

in the sky every 24 hours and 50 minutes, which divided by four (two high and two low cycles) is 6 hours 12-1/2 minutes.

One of the high and low tides each day is caused by the gravitational force of the sun and moon. If we look at the alignment of the sun and moon throughout the 30-day cycle it takes for the moon to revolve all the way around the earth, we will see that the relationship of the moon changes not only to the earth, but to the sun as well.

For the purpose of trying to understand

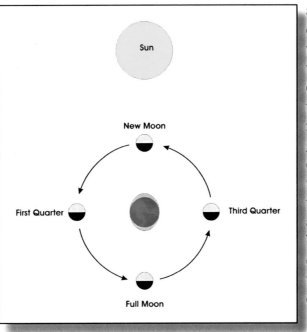

and focus just on the effects of forces on water, let's assume that the earth is covered entirely by water; pretend there is no land. The moon's gravitational force on the earth pulls the oceans' water toward it, creating a *tidal bulge* (see below). This bulge exists on the side of the earth that is closest to the moon.

The sun also exerts a gravitational force on the earth. Although less than that of the moon, the sun's gravitational force is combined with the moon's force, sometimes

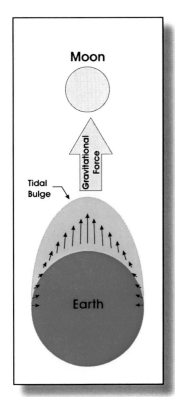
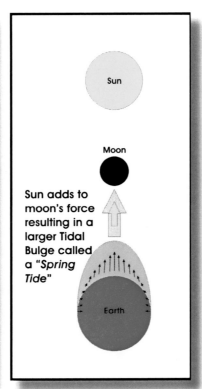
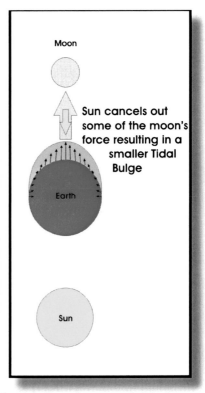

The gravitational force of the moon pulls water away from the earth to form a tidal bulge (left). The gravitational force of the sun combines with that of the moon to either increase the force and tidal bulge resulting in a "Spring Tide" (center) or cancel out some of the moon's force to decrease the force and tidal bulge (left).

adding, and at other times subtracting to that of the moon.

The diagrams on the previous page show how the relative positions of the moon and sun effect the amount of force exerted on the earth, and thus the water in the earth's oceans.

As the earth rotates, we experience one "pass" through this tidal bulge each 24 hours, resulting in one high, and one low each day. However, as we can see from the tide chart, we experience two highs and lows each day. What causes the other high and low?

As the earth rotates, it is pulled slightly off its rotational axis by the moon's gravitational force. The resulting axis around which both the moon and earth counter-rotate is referred to as the "barycenter". Rotating around the barycenter results in a slight "wobbling" effect of the earth. The centrifugal force created by the wobbling induces a whipping action which causes another tidal bulge on earth's surface opposite of the moon.

This can be demonstrated by two peo-

The moon's pull on the earth causes the rotational axis of the earth to shift to become the "Barycenter" around which both the earth and moon rotate together

This shifting of the rotational axis causes the earth to "wobble" which then "whips" the water away from the barycenter causing a tidal bulge on the opposite side of the moon.

The gravitational force of the moon forces the earth to "wobble" as it rotates around its "barycenter" creating a second tidal bulge

ple of drastically different masses lock hands and spin. As the lighter person spins around the heavier person, they are pulled slightly off their rotational axis. If the heavier person has a ponytail, it will begin to fly outward due to centrifugal force. The ponytail is analogous to the tidal bulge on the earth created by centrifugal force.

This tidal bulge from centrifugal force is also subject to additive and subtractive gravitational forces from the sun. For example, when the sun is opposite the moon (full moon) the force it exerts on the surface of the earth adds to the force pulling water due to centrifugal force.

The sun's gravitational force adds to the centripetal force resulting in a larger tidal bulge called a *"Spring Tide"*

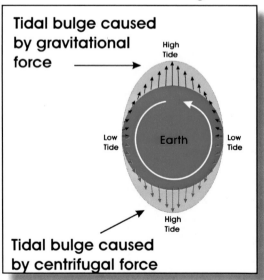

Tidal bulge caused by gravitational force

Tidal bulge caused by centrifugal force

The rotation of the earth through both tidal bulges every 24 hours yields two high and two lows each day. This cycle is referred to as "semidiurnal".

This second tidal bulge exists on the opposite side of the earth from the tidal bulge resulting from gravitational forces from the sun and moon.

If we consider that we are standing on the surface of the earth as it rotates once around every 24 hours, we will pass through both tidal bulges resulting in two highs and two lows each day. This cycle is called a "*semidiurnal*" tide cycle.

When we combine this knowledge with our understanding of the earth, moon, and sun's relative positions throughout the lunar cycle, we can begin to understand the various changes in tide heights that appear on the tide chart for Eastport, Maine.

Eastport Tides - Jul/2015

44°54'N 66°59'W

DATE		HIGH				LOW				RISE	SET	MOON
		AM	ft	PM	ft	AM	ft	PM	ft			
1	Wed	11:02	18.6	11:18	20.3	5:00	-0.5	5:17	0.5	4:44	8:19	
2	Thu	11:47	19.1			5:47	-1.2	6:04	-0.0	4:44	8:19	
3	Fri	12:04	20.8	12:34	19.6	6:33	-1.7	6:52	-0.5	4:45	8:19	
4	Sat	12:51	21.1	1:21	20.0	7:21	-2.0	7:41	-0.7	4:45	8:18	
5	Sun	1:39	21.1	2:10	20.2	8:09	-2.1	8:31	-0.9	4:46	8:18	
6	Mon	2:30	20.9	3:01	20.3	8:59	-1.9	9:23	-0.8	4:47	8:18	
7	Tue	3:23	20.5	3:55	20.3	9:51	-1.6	10:19	-0.7	4:48	8:17	
8	Wed	4:19	20.0	4:51	20.1	10:45	-1.1	11:16	-0.4	4:48	8:17	
9	Thu	5:18	19.4	5:49	20.0	11:42	-0.5			4:49	8:16	
10	Fri	6:19	18.9	6:49	19.9	12:16	-0.3	12:41	-0.0	4:50	8:16	
11	Sat	7:21	18.5	7:48	19.9	1:18	-0.2	1:42	0.3	4:51	8:15	
12	Sun	8:22	18.4	8:46	20.0	2:19	-0.3	2:41	0.4	4:52	8:15	
13	Mon	9:20	18.5	9:41	20.1	3:18	-0.6	3:38	0.4	4:52	8:14	
14	Tue	10:14	18.7	10:33	20.2	4:12	-0.8	4:31	0.3	4:53	8:13	
15	Wed	11:04	18.8	11:21	20.1	5:03	-0.9	5:20	0.2	4:54	8:13	
16	Thu	11:50	18.8			5:49	-0.9	6:06	0.3	4:55	8:12	
17	Fri	12:06	20.0	12:33	18.8	6:33	-0.8	6:50	0.5	4:56	8:11	
18	Sat	12:49	19.7	1:15	18.7	7:15	-0.5	7:32	0.7	4:57	8:10	
19	Sun	1:31	19.3	1:57	18.5	7:55	-0.1	8:13	1.0	4:58	8:09	
20	Mon	2:13	18.8	2:38	18.3	8:36	0.3	8:55	1.3	4:59	8:09	
21	Tue	2:56	18.3	3:21	18.1	9:17	0.8	9:38	1.6	5:00	8:08	
22	Wed	3:40	17.8	4:05	17.8	9:59	1.3	10:24	1.9	5:01	8:07	
23	Thu	4:26	17.3	4:52	17.6	10:44	1.7	11:12	2.1	5:02	8:06	
24	Fri	5:16	16.8	5:41	17.5	11:33	2.1			5:03	8:05	
25	Sat	6:08	16.5	6:33	17.6	12:03	2.2	12:24	2.4	5:04	8:04	
26	Sun	7:02	16.5	7:27	17.9	12:57	2.0	1:18	2.4	5:05	8:02	
27	Mon	7:57	16.8	8:20	18.4	1:53	1.6	2:13	2.1	5:07	8:01	
28	Tue	8:51	17.3	9:12	19.1	2:48	1.0	3:07	1.5	5:08	8:00	
29	Wed	9:43	18.1	10:03	19.9	3:41	0.1	4:00	0.8	5:09	7:59	
30	Thu	10:33	18.9	10:52	20.7	4:32	-0.8	4:51	-0.1	5:10	7:58	
31	Fri	11:22	19.8	11:41	21.3	5:21	-1.7	5:41	-0.9	5:11	7:57	

Local Time   © US Harbors   Tidal Data Source: Eastport (8410140)

Notice that highs are highest and lows are lowest near the full and new moons, and highs are lowest and lows are highest just after the first and third quarter moons. If we relate this back to our diagram of the relationship between the relative locations of the sun, moon, and earth, we can see how the accumulative forces of the sun and moon combine with the centrifugal forces from the whipping action to create the varied tidal pattern represented by the chart.

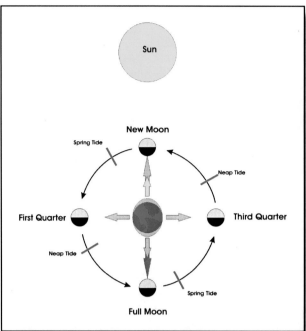

Also adding to the variation of tidal heights is the relative distance of the sun and moon from the earth. The closer the earth is to each the sun and moon, the stronger the gravitational forces are present resulting in variable tidal ranges for a given point in time.

Looking at the tide chart, we will notice that the spring and neap tides occur a couple of days after the full and new moons. This lag time is due to a number of factors including friction from the ocean floor, as well as the specific shape of the tidal basin in which the tidal heights are predicted.

Finally, while the forces that cause water to rise and fall are a result of gravitational forces from the sun and moon and the centrifugal force of the Earth and moon,

the amount of tidal range is largely due to the shape of the basin in which the water is moving. In Florida, for example where the coastline is long and straight, forces pull the water through an open, unobstructed ocean from one point to another. In the Bay of Fundy, however, where the coastline forms a giant bay, the water is pulled up into a funnel-shaped bay and has nowhere to go, so it simply builds up and rises to heights of over 38 feet in Burntcoat Head at the northern end of the Bay of Fundy.

Tidal information for specific places in the US is available from NOAA's tides and currents website. In addition, several third-party websites such as usharbors.com provide the same data in various, easy-to-read formats and are available for download for free from their websites.

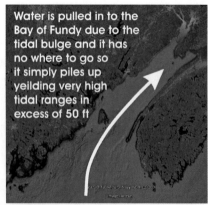

Water is pulled in to the Bay of Fundy due to the tidal bulge and it has no where to go so it simply piles up yeilding very high tidal ranges in excess of 50 ft

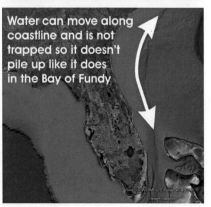

Water can move along coastline and is not trapped so it doesn't pile up like it does in the Bay of Fundy

NOAA's tide prediction website provides helpful tidal information for positions in the US.
http://tidesandcurrents.noaa.gov

Tidal Datums

If you reference any tide chart or graph, you will find tidal heights given in feet or meters. These heights are measured from a tidal datum, or baseline. Because the low tide height varies significantly from one low to another, it is difficult to pick one particular point to measure from.

In the US, NOAA provides tidal heights based on the tidal datum of "***mean lower low water***" or **MLLW**. This baseline is the average of all of the lowest lows of each tidal day. In addition, depths on NOAA nautical charts are provided using the same datum. This means that a depth reading of 10 feet is the depth of that area at the average of all the lowest low tide recordings of each day. If you are navigating through that area at high tide, you can simply add the height of the tide from the tide chart to the depth printed on the chart to calculate the depth at that point in time.

Heights of overhead obstacles and hazards to navigation, such as power lines and bridges are printed on the chart as being measured from the **MHW** datum, or **Mean High Water** datum. This datum is the average of all the high water heights observed over a given amount of time.

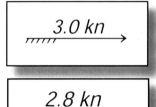

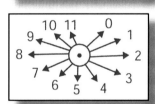

Current data can be found on the charts and referenced using Chart No. 1.

Tidal Current

We have defined tides as the vertical movement of water due to the gravitational and centrifugal forces resulting from the sun and moon.

Tidal current is the horizontal movement of water that is due to the same tidal forces. If we think of water as it is getting pulled across the ocean as moving in a gentle-sloped and gradual wave, we can imagine that it will create a horizontal force as it rises. It is these horizontal tidal currents that we will need to consider when navigating.

In general, areas that are open with few obstructions do not create the opportunity for significant currents to develop. Similar to large tidal ranges, areas that provide constriction of flow generally result in higher tidal currents. You could expect that the Bay of Fundy would (and does!) produce significant currents capable of being hazardous to navigation.

Tidal currents that are present when the tide is rising are called "***flood***" currents. Currents present when the tide is falling are called "***ebb***" currents. It is also not uncommon for people to refer to a rising tide as a ***flood tide,*** and a falling tide as an ***ebb tide***.

Besides tides, other forces produce ocean currents throughout the world. Although their sources vary, current has the same effect on navigation; moving water is moving water, regardless of the source. It is worth mentioning that the significant difference of tidal currents to other ocean currents is that they change direction and speed drastically over short periods of time, whereas most other ocean currents are predictably constant in direction and speed.

We can find current data in a few places. Current diagrams, vector arrows, and various current symbols are printed on the chart. A complete listing of current symbols and their meanings is provided in NOAA

http://tidesand-currents.noaa.gov/noaacurrents/Regions

Chart No. 1 (see Appendix C).

Tidal current data is also available online using NOAA's current prediction website which provides current direction and speed for various times throughout the tide cycle for thousands of locations throughout the US.

The US Coast Pilot and various non-government cruising guides also contain some tidal current information along with advice on what to expect and tips on what areas to avoid.

Rule of Twelfths

The rule of twelfths is a rule of thumb that we can use to estimate the height of the tide at any given time in the tide cycle. It also helps us to understand that the rate of change in the height of the tide over time is not linear. Instead, it rises slowly at first, then faster toward the middle of the cycle, and then slows again at the end of the cycle until it eventually reverses and begins to lower.

To illustrate the rule of twelfths, lets consider that a body of water has a tidal range of 12 feet. We know that in a semidiurnal tide cycle, the period of time it takes for the tide to rise from low to high is approximately 6 hours. However, the tide does not rise at an even rate of 2 feet per hour. Instead, the rule of twelfths states that it will rise 1/12 of the

total height (or 1 foot) the first hour, 2/12's (or 2 feet) the second hour, 3/12's (3 feet) the third hour, 3/12's again the 4th hour, 2/12's the fifth hour, and then 1/12 the last hour.

Using the rule of twelfths helps us see how half of the water (6/12ths) rises (or falls) in the middle two hours of the tide cycle.

This rule should be considered a general rule of thumb for semidiurnal tide cycles, but navigators should still consult tide tables for more specific tide rates for a given area.

50/90 Rule

While the rule of twelfths applies to tide, the 50/90 rule applies to tidal current. If we look at a graph of the change in tidal current over a six hour semi-diurnal tide cycle, we can cal-

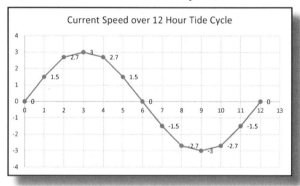

This graph of current speeds over a 12 hour semi-diurnal tide cycle illustrates the 50/90 rule

culate how fast the current will be at a given time in the tide cycle.

Notice in the graph above that the speed of the current one hour into the tide cycle is 1.5 knots, or 50% of the maximum speed of 3 knots. Next, notice that the speed of the current 2 hours into the cycle is 2.7 knots, or 90 % of the maximum current speed of 3 knots, which is

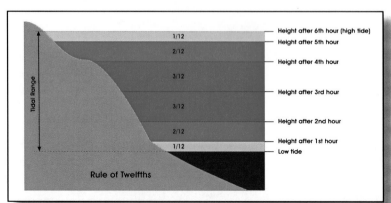

The Rule of Twelfths helps to illustrate the way in which water rises and falls due to the tide in semidiurnal tide cycles.

reached 3 hours into the tide cycle.

These observations lead us to understand the 50/90 rule, which states that 50% of the maximum tidal current speed is reached at the end of the first hour, and 90% is reached at the end of the second hour. We can apply this rule in reverse to explain that the speed of the current at the end of the 4th hour will be 90% of the maximum current speed, and at the end of the 5th hour the speed of the current will be 50% of the maximum speed.

Just as with the rule of twelfths, the 50/90 rule is a rule of thumb that helps give an understanding and estimation of tidal currents. However, many factors influence tidal currents, which can make them more complex, requiring the prudent navigator to consult tide tables for a specific area.

Navigating in Current

Ocean currents can be caused by tide, wind, temperature and salinity variations, and other forces. Regardless of their source, currents can pose a significant hazard to navigation and must be accounted for when boating through a waterway with current. Fortunately, we have developed a few strategies that can compensate for the effects of current on a vessel, whether it be a kayak, sailboat, or powerboat.

Let's consider that you are at the red and white safe water bell buoy "WQ" just northeast of West Quoddy Head on chart 13394 at 0900. You want to travel eastward at 5 knots to end up just north of Northern Head, the northernmost point on Grand Manan Island. So, you begin your DR plot, drawing your course line of 117 degrees magnetic (below, right).

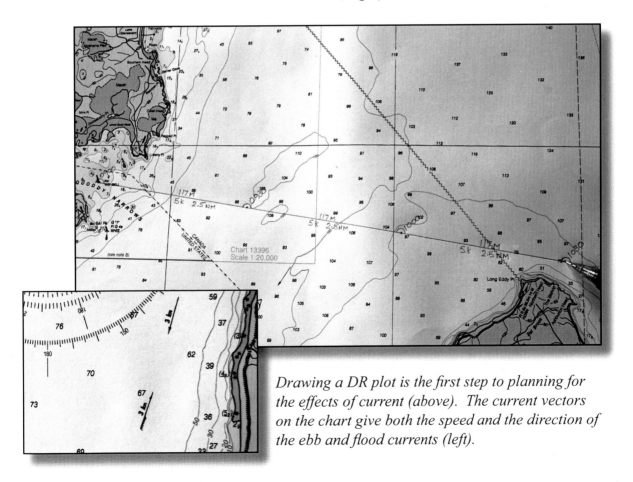

Drawing a DR plot is the first step to planning for the effects of current (above). The current vectors on the chart give both the speed and the direction of the ebb and flood currents (left).

119

You look at the chart and notice the current arrows in the Grand Manan Channel and find that the peak flood and ebb current flows at 3 knots (p.119, left). Consider that these tidal current vectors give an average speed and direction of the current. More accurate tidal current information can be found in the Tidal Current Tables downloadable from NOAA's website at http://tidesandcurrents.noaa.gov.

You look at the tide chart and notice that since low tide was at 0530, you will be travelling during a time of peak current flow. You also realize that if you head out from the WQ buoy at 0900 with a heading of 117 magnetic expecting to stay on your course line of 117, you will be also be getting *set*, or moved in the direction of the current. After traveling for 1 hour at 5 knots, you will have travelled 5 nm at a heading of 117 magnetic, but during that time you will also have been travelling at 3 knots in the direction the current is pushing you. This means that your new location would be 5 nm at a heading of 117 magnetic and 3 nm at a heading of 036 magnetic (the direction of the flood current) from where you started. This means that your actual *course over ground* (COG) would be 087 degrees magnetic - off from your desired course of 117 by 30 degrees!

It is clear to see in this example the importance of accounting for the direction of the current, called the *set*, and the speed of the current, called *drift*, when planning out and following a course plan.

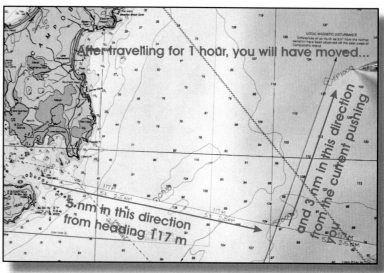

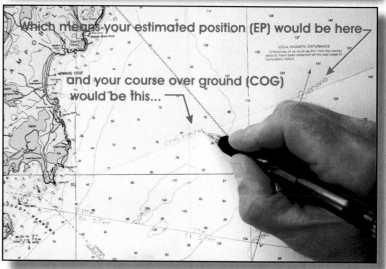

Speed Over Ground (SOG)

Now that we are familiar with the concepts of set and drift, we will need to think about and perhaps redefine what the word "speed" means.

When the water we are travelling in is moving, the speed of our vessel through the water will be different than the speed of our vessel in relation to land, or "over ground". Consider running at 5 miles per hour on a treadmill that is moving against you at 5 miles per hour. Even though your body is moving relative to the treadmill, it is not moving at all relative to everything else in the world.

Likewise, if you were on a boat moving 5 knots against a current that was moving 5 knots against you, your speed through the water would be 5 knots, but your *speed over ground (or SOG)* would be zero. If you turned your vessel around and travelled 5 knots through the water and the water was also moving at 5 knots in the same direction, your SOG would be 10 knots.

Course Over Ground (COG)

Similar to SOG, *course over ground* (COG) is the path that our vessel will take relative to land, rather than relative to the water around us. In the example in the photos on the previous page, even though our course through the water (heading) was at 117 degrees magnetic, the course over ground (COG) was actually 087 magnetic.

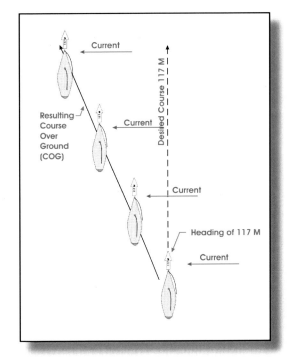

The effects of current on a vessel can drastically change its course over ground (COG) even when the vessel's heading remains constant

Compensating for Set and Drift

Figuring how set and drift will effect our vessel and, more importantly, how to counteract these forces can be calculated using our plotting tools and some basic knowledge of vectors. Vectors are lines that show both direction and distance. The angle of the line shows direction, and the length of the line represents distance on our chart.

In the example on the previous page, we have used vectors to calculate our estimated position if we were to steer a heading of 117 M with a set of 018 T and a drift of 3 knots for 1

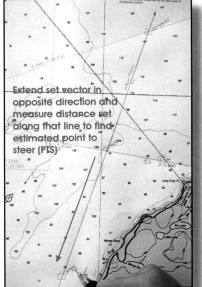

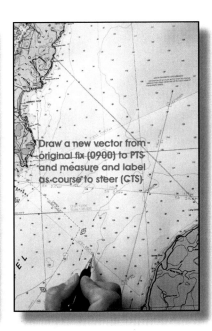

To calculate how to compensate for set and drift, first extend the drift vector the opposite direction from the set and measure the distance set along this line to calculate your PTS (left). Next, draw a new vector through from your original fix at 0900 through the PTS. Measure and label this as your CTS (right)

3-Step Process for Calculating Set and Drift

Step 1: Complete a DR plot for the desired route on the chart. (Note: Although the set and drift plot can be done anywhere on the chart, it will make more sense if you complete it using the DR plot of the route you intend to take.)

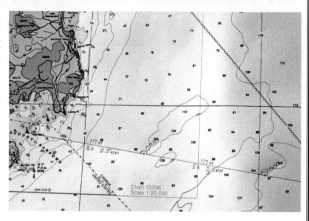

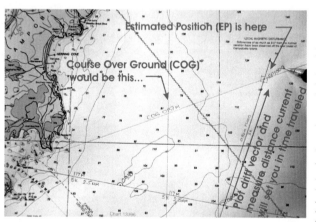

Step 2: Select a DR point on the course line and draw a line representing the direction you will be set through this point. Find the drift of the current and calculate how much the current will have set you in the time you have traveled to get to this point. Using your dividers, measure and plot this distance along your drift vector, and label this as your Estimated Position (EP) at that time if you steer your original heading. Draw a line from your original starting point through your EP. Label this line as your Course Over Ground (COG), as this would be your COG if you steered your original heading.

Step 3: Extend the set line in the opposite direction of the direction of the current. Using your dividers, measure and plot the same distance you would be set. Mark this point as your point to steer for (PTS). Draw a line from your original starting point through the PTS. Measure and label this line as your Course To Steer (CTS). This will be your heading if you want to stay on your original course line.

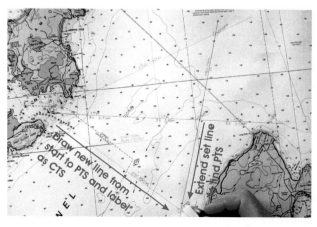

hour. If the current is setting us at 018 T, it makes sense that we will need to steer into the current the same amount it is setting us if we want to stay on our course of 117 M. But how far into the current should we steer?

This can be calculated before we head out by extending our set vector the opposite direction and measuring the same distance we'd be set in 1 hour the opposite way. This will give us a point to steer for (PTS) - see below left.

Next, we need to draw a new vector that originates from our original fix at 0900 and extends through the new PTS. Measure and label this new bearing as our course to steer (CTS). This line represents the new heading we will steer (150 M) that will keep us on our desired course track of 117 M, effectively compensating for the effect of set and drift on our vessel.

Set and Drift Exercises – Chart 13394

1. At 1000 you are at Head Harbor Light on the northern tip of Campobello Island and want to head eastward at 5 knots to Southern Wolf Island Light in the Wolves. Your set is 030T and your drift is 2 knots. What is your course to steer (CTS)?

2. At 0900 you are in position 44°53.9' N 66°38.3' W and are steaming at 10 knots. You are trying to get to Swallowtail Light on North Head on Grand Manan. Your set is 340T and your drift is 3.5 knots. What is your CTS?

3. You want to leave at 1300 from the northernmost point of Grand Manan and travel to Head Harbor Light at 5 knots at peak flood. Using the current arrows on your chart and a drift of 3.8 knots, what is your CTS?

4. You want to head from Southern Wolf Island Light to Swallowtail Light on Grand Manan at a cruising speed of 8 knots. With a set of 020T and a drift of 3 knots, what is your CTS? What is your Speed Made Good (SMG)?

5. At 1100 you are in position 44°53.82'N, 66°35.82'W heading at 294M sailing at 6 kts. At 1130, you take bearings of 308M to South Wolf Island Light, 238M to the light at Northern Head at the northernmost tip of Grand Manan, and 219M to Swallowtail Light. Using this info, answer the following questions:
a. Plot and label your fix
b. What is your set and drift?
c. What is your Course Made Good (CMG)?
d. What is your Speed Made Good (SMG)?
e. What would be your new Course to Steer (CTS) and speed required to arrive at your next DR point at 1200 on your original DR track?

Part 3

Appendices

Appendix A

USGS Topographic Map Symbols

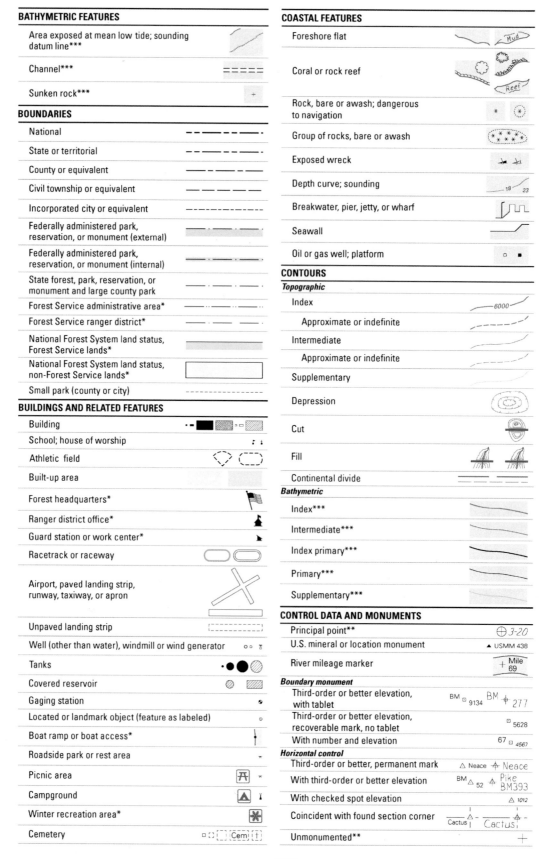

BATHYMETRIC FEATURES

Area exposed at mean low tide; sounding datum line***	
Channel***	
Sunken rock***	

BOUNDARIES

National	
State or territorial	
County or equivalent	
Civil township or equivalent	
Incorporated city or equivalent	
Federally administered park, reservation, or monument (external)	
Federally administered park, reservation, or monument (internal)	
State forest, park, reservation, or monument and large county park	
Forest Service administrative area*	
Forest Service ranger district*	
National Forest System land status, Forest Service lands*	
National Forest System land status, non-Forest Service lands*	
Small park (county or city)	

BUILDINGS AND RELATED FEATURES

Building	
School; house of worship	
Athletic field	
Built-up area	
Forest headquarters*	
Ranger district office*	
Guard station or work center*	
Racetrack or raceway	
Airport, paved landing strip, runway, taxiway, or apron	
Unpaved landing strip	
Well (other than water), windmill or wind generator	
Tanks	
Covered reservoir	
Gaging station	
Located or landmark object (feature as labeled)	
Boat ramp or boat access*	
Roadside park or rest area	
Picnic area	
Campground	
Winter recreation area*	
Cemetery	

COASTAL FEATURES

Foreshore flat	
Coral or rock reef	
Rock, bare or awash; dangerous to navigation	
Group of rocks, bare or awash	
Exposed wreck	
Depth curve; sounding	
Breakwater, pier, jetty, or wharf	
Seawall	
Oil or gas well; platform	

CONTOURS

Topographic

Index	
Approximate or indefinite	
Intermediate	
Approximate or indefinite	
Supplementary	
Depression	
Cut	
Fill	
Continental divide	

Bathymetric

Index***	
Intermediate***	
Index primary***	
Primary***	
Supplementary***	

CONTROL DATA AND MONUMENTS

Principal point**	
U.S. mineral or location monument	
River mileage marker	

Boundary monument

Third-order or better elevation, with tablet	
Third-order or better elevation, recoverable mark, no tablet	
With number and elevation	

Horizontal control

Third-order or better, permanent mark	
With third-order or better elevation	
With checked spot elevation	
Coincident with found section corner	
Unmonumented**	

128

CONTROL DATA AND MONUMENTS – *continued*

Vertical control

Third-order or better elevation, with tablet	BM $\times$ 5280
Third-order or better elevation, recoverable mark, no tablet	$\times$ 528
Bench mark coincident with found section corner	BM + 5280
Spot elevation	$\times$ 7523

GLACIERS AND PERMANENT SNOWFIELDS

Contours and limits	
Formlines	
Glacial advance	
Glacial retreat	

LAND SURVEYS

Public land survey system

Range or Township line	
Location approximate	
Location doubtful	
Protracted	
Protracted (AK 1:63,360-scale)	
Range or Township labels	R1E T2N R3W T4S
Section line	
Location approximate	
Location doubtful	
Protracted	
Protracted (AK 1:63,360-scale)	
Section numbers	1 - 36 1 - 36
Found section corner	
Found closing corner	
Witness corner	WC
Meander corner	MC
Weak corner*	

Other land surveys

Range or Township line	
Section line	
Land grant, mining claim, donation land claim, or tract	
Land grant, homestead, mineral, or other special survey monument	
Fence or field lines	

MARINE SHORELINES

Shoreline	
Apparent (edge of vegetation)***	
Indefinite or unsurveyed	

MINES AND CAVES

Quarry or open pit mine	$\times$
Gravel, sand, clay, or borrow pit	$\times$
Mine tunnel or cave entrance	
Mine shaft	
Prospect	X
Tailings	Tailings
Mine dump	
Former disposal site or mine	

PROJECTION AND GRIDS

Neatline	39°15' 90°37'30"
Graticule tick	55'
Graticule intersection	
Datum shift tick	

State plane coordinate systems

Primary zone tick	640 000 FEET
Secondary zone tick	247 500 METERS
Tertiary zone tick	260 000 FEET
Quaternary zone tick	98 500 METERS
Quintary zone tick	320 000 FEET

Universal transverse metcator grid

UTM grid (full grid)	273
UTM grid ticks*	269

RAILROADS AND RELATED FEATURES

Standard guage railroad, single track	
Standard guage railroad, multiple track	
Narrow guage railroad, single track	
Narrow guage railroad, multiple track	
Railroad siding	
Railroad in highway	
Railroad in road	
Railroad in light duty road*	
Railroad underpass; overpass	
Railroad bridge; drawbridge	
Railroad tunnel	
Railroad yard	
Railroad turntable; roundhouse	

RIVERS, LAKES, AND CANALS

Perennial stream	
Perennial river	
Intermittent stream	
Intermittent river	
Disappearing stream	
Falls, small	
Falls, large	
Rapids, small	
Rapids, large	
Masonry dam	
Dam with lock	
Dam carrying road	

RIVERS, LAKES, AND CANALS – *continued*

Perennial lake/pond	
Intermittent lake/pond	
Dry lake/pond	
Narrow wash	
Wide wash	
Canal, flume, or aqueduct with lock	
Elevated aqueduct, flume, or conduit	
Aqueduct tunnel	
Water well, geyser, fumarole, or mud pot	
Spring or seep	

ROADS AND RELATED FEATURES

Please note: Roads on Provisional-edition maps are not classified as primary, secondary, or light duty. These roads are all classified as improved roads and are symbolized the same as light duty roads.

Primary highway	
Secondary highway	
Light duty road Light duty road, paved* Light duty road, gravel* Light duty road, dirt* Light duty road, unspecified*	
Unimproved road Unimproved road*	
4WD road 4WD road*	
Trail	
Highway or road with median strip	
Highway or road under construction	
Highway or road underpass; overpass	
Highway or road bridge; drawbridge	
Highway or road tunnel	
Road block, berm, or barrier*	
Gate on road*	
Trailhead*	

SUBMERGED AREAS AND BOGS

Marsh or swamp	
Submerged marsh or swamp	
Wooded marsh or swamp	
Submerged wooded marsh or swamp	
Land subject to inundation	*Max Pool 431*

SURFACE FEATURES

Levee	*Levee*
Sand or mud	*Sand*
Disturbed surface	
Gravel beach or glacial moraine	*Gravel*
Tailings pond	*Tailings Pond*

TRANSMISSION LINES AND PIPELINES

Power transmission line; pole; tower	
Telephone line	*Telephone*
Aboveground pipeline	
Underground pipeline	*Pipeline*

VEGETATION

Woodland	
Shrubland	
Orchard	
Vineyard	
Mangrove	*Mangrove*

USGS Topo
Symbols PDF

Map Tools for 1:24,000 Scale

Photocopy these tools at 100% on to a piece of acetate or clear acrylic
and use with your 1:24000 USGS Topographic maps.

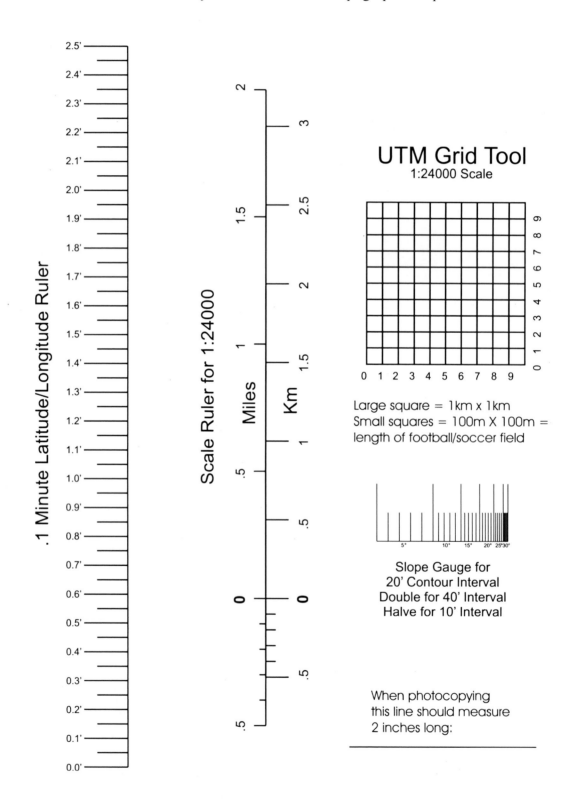

UTM Grid Tool
1:24000 Scale

Large square = 1km x 1km
Small squares = 100m X 100m =
length of football/soccer field

Slope Gauge for
20' Contour Interval
Double for 40' Interval
Halve for 10' Interval

When photocopying
this line should measure
2 inches long:

.1 Minute Latitude/Longitude Ruler

Scale Ruler for 1:24000

U.S. Chart No. 1

Symbols, Abbreviations and Terms used on Paper and Electronic Navigational Charts

 12th Edition, April 15, 2013
Corrected through NM Nov. 16, 2013
Corrected through LNM Nov. 12, 2013

Prepared Jointly by

Department of Commerce
National Oceanic and Atmospheric Administration

Department of Defense
National Geospatial-Intelligence Agency

ECDIS

New in Edition 12: ECDIS Symbols and Other ECDIS Information

Symbology for displaying Electronic Navigational Charts (ENCs) on an Electronic Chart Display and Information System (ECDIS) has been added to U.S. Chart No. 1. See the Preface and Introduction sections for more details.

In addition to the ECDIS symbols shown in the traditional lettered sections of U.S. Chart No. 1, there are now several special pages devoted exclusively to providing important details about ECDIS. These pages are distinguished by the ECDIS icon, as shown in the top left corner of this page. The ECDIS pages are also listed in the table of contents in italic type.

One major difference in the use of paper charts and ENCs is the ability of ECDIS to display the same feature differently depending on user settings and other conditions, such as a ship's draft. An important example is that ECDIS displays wrecks, rocks and other obstructions with their traditional "paper-chart" symbols if they are at or deeper than the depth of the safety contour set for the ship. Dangers that are shoaler are portrayed with the unique ECDIS "isolated danger" symbol shown at left. (See the ECDIS Portrayal of Depths page for more information about the ECDIS safety contour.)

Another advantage that ECDIS provides over paper charts is enabling users to obtain more information about a feature through a "cursor pick." Some feature attribute values that can be obtained by cursor pick are noted throughout U.S. Chart No. 1. This is especially true if a particular value, such as height, vertical clearance or the like is included in the INT symbol description. The cursor pick icon, shown at left, is used to indicate when a reference to a cursor pick is made.

There are many other attribute values that users may obtain through a cursor pick that are not specifically noted. These include, but are not limited to, the purpose, seasonality, periodicity, status, color, height, type of structure and the visual or radar conspicuousness of features; shape, color or color pattern of buoys; characteristics of lights; category of obstructions and wrecks; radar wave length, radio frequency, communication channel and call signs; the presence of AIS transmitted signals; information regarding pilotage services and many more.

No man is an island and no single reference document stands on its own. U.S. Chart No. 1 is a handy guide for ECDIS users, but it is no substitute for mandated ECDIS training.

The ECDIS user and developer communities are invited to help improve the presentation of ECDIS symbology and information in U.S. Chart No. 1. We want to know what you think works well, which parts are a little rocky, and what additional information you would like to have included in the next edition of U.S. Chart No. 1.

Please send any recommendations or corrections to:

USChart1@noaa.gov

or

National Ocean Service, NOAA (N/CS2)
Attention: U.S. Chart No. 1
1315 East West Highway
Silver Spring, MD 20912-3282

2

SYMBOLS, ABBREVIATIONS AND TERMS

Contents

Document Sections and *ECDIS Pages*

Symbol Sections

GENERAL

A   Chart Number, Title, Marginal Notes
B   Positions, Distances, Directions, Compass

TOPOGRAPHY

C   Natural Features
D   Cultural Features
E   Landmarks
F   Ports
G   (Not currently used)

HYDROGRAPHY

H   Tides, Currents
I   Depths
J   Nature of the Seabed
K   Rocks, Wrecks, Obstructions, Aquaculture
L   Offshore Installations
M   Tracks, Routes
N   Areas, Limits
O   (Not currently used)

NAVIGATION AIDS AND SERVICES

P   Lights
Q   Buoys, Beacons
R   Fog Signals
S   Radar, Radio, Satellite Navigation Systems
T   Services
U   Small Craft (Leisure) Facilities

4

This Page Intentionally Left Blank

PREFACE

Presentation of Two Symbology Sets

This edition of U.S. Chart No. 1 has a new name and a new look. Its title is now *Symbols, Abbreviations and Terms used on Paper and Electronic Navigational Charts*. For the first time, U.S. Chart No. 1 presents both of the major symbology sets used for marine navigation.

As in previous editions, the symbols used on paper nautical charts produced by the National Oceanic and Atmospheric Administration (NOAA) and the National Geospatial-Intelligence Agency (NGA) and digital raster representations of those charts, such as NOAA Raster Nautical Charts (NOAA RNCs®), are presented in lettered sections organized in categories, such as Landmarks, Depths, and Lights. New in this edition is the inclusion of the corresponding symbols used to portray Electronic Navigational Chart (ENC) data on Electronic Chart Display and Information Systems (ECDIS) as specified by the International Hydrographic Organization (IHO).

Other Non-ECDIS Digital Displays May Portray Data Differently

Navigation systems certified to meet the exacting performance standards established by the International Maritime Organization (IMO) are said to be ECDIS "type approved." The symbology used to display ENCs or other non-ENC nautical navigational data on *non-ECDIS systems*, such as geographic information systems, recreational GPS and other chart display systems can differ significantly from the symbology specified for ECDIS type approved systems. U.S. Chart No. 1 *only shows the symbology used on ECDIS*.

INTRODUCTION

New Column Headers

The orientation of this edition of U.S. Chart No. 1 has been rotated 90° into a landscape format to allow two additional columns to be added to the right side of the page. These columns hold the ECDIS symbols corresponding to the paper chart symbols shown on the left side.

"INT 1" symbols, as specified in the *Regulations of the IHO for International (INT) Charts and Chart Specifications of the IHO*, appear in the second column from the left, after the symbol number. Any variations from INT 1 symbology that are used on charts produced by NOAA or NGA are shown in the NOAA, NGA and the "Other NGA" columns (columns 4a, 4b, and 5 respectively).

ECDIS symbols and their descriptions are shown in columns 6 and 7 respectively. The ECDIS description usually provides the generic symbol name given in the *IHO Specifications for Chart Content and Display Aspects of ECDIS*, although sometimes other clarifying terms are also provided in column 7. The ECDIS symbols shown use the day color palette (see page 9).

When columns 4a and 4b are combined, this indicates that NOAA and NGA both use the same non-INT 1 symbol for that particular feature. When any of columns 4a, 4b, or 5 are blank, then the INT 1 symbol has been adopted for use by the organization for which that column applies.

The schematic layout following this introduction shows a typical symbol table page. It provides details about the table headers and the types of information presented in each of the columns.

Sample Chart Layouts

Section A presents two schematics showing typical layouts of the major elements of NOAA and NGA charts.

INFORMATION ON SELECTED CHART FEATURES

Soundings

The sounding datum reference is stated in the chart title. Soundings on NOAA and NGA charts may be shown in fathoms, feet, fathoms and feet, fathoms and fractions, or meters and decimeters. In all cases the unit of depth used is shown in the chart title and outside the border of the chart in bold type (see item b in Section A). For ECDIS, the sounding datum is part of the ENC metadata, which can be retrieved through a cursor inquiry.

Heights

Heights of lights, landmarks, structures, etc. refer to the shoreline plane of reference. The unit of height is shown in the chart title. When the elevations of islets or bare rocks are offset into the adjacent water, they are shown in parentheses. For ECDIS, the unit of height is meters.

Drying Heights

For rocks and banks that cover and uncover, elevations are underlined and are referenced to the sounding datum as stated in the chart title (or in the ENC metadata). When the heights of rocks that cover and uncover are offset into the adjacent water, they are shown in parentheses.

Light Range (Visibility)

A light's range or visibility is given in nautical miles, except on the Great Lakes and adjacent waterways, where light ranges are given in statute miles. For lights having more than one color, NOAA charts give only the shortest range of all the colors. On NGA charts, multiple ranges may be shown using the following convention. For lights with two colors, the first number indicates the range of the first color and the second number indicates the range of the second color. For example, Fl WG 12/8M means the range of the white light is 12 nautical miles and the range of green light is 8 nautical miles. For lights with three colors, only the longest and shortest ranges are given and the middle range is indicated by a dash. For example, Fl WRG 12-8M means that the range of the white light is 12 nautical miles, the range of green light is 8 nautical miles and the range of the red light is between 8 to 12 nautical miles. The dash can appear in any of the three positions.

Aids to Navigation Positioning

The fixed and floating aids to navigation depicted on charts have varying degrees of reliability. Floating aids are moored to sinkers by varying lengths of chain and may shift due to sea conditions and other causes. Buoys may also be carried away, capsized or sunk. Lighted buoys may be extinguished and sound signals may not function, because of ice or other causes. Therefore, prudent mariners will not rely solely on any single aid to navigation, particularly on floating aids, but will also use bearings from fixed objects and aids to navigation on shore.

Colors

Color conveys the nature and importance of features found on nautical charts. Chart elements significant to marine navigation, such as lights, compass roses and regulated areas, are emphasized with magenta. Lateral marks on NOAA charts are shown with a red or green fill. Shades of blue depict potential hazards to navigation, typically shallow water and submerged obstructions. Areas of deeper water believed to be clear of obstructions are shown as white. Land, and other features that are always dry, are depicted with buff on NOAA charts and gray on NGA charts. Foreshore and other intertidal features are portrayed with a green tint. Other colors may be used to provide additional information, such as protected areas, which are outlined in blue or green and mineral lease blocks, which are outlined in red.

Traffic Separation Schemes

Traffic separation schemes show recommended lanes to increase safety of navigation, particularly in areas of high density shipping. These schemes are described in the International Maritime Organization (IMO) publication, *Ships Routeing*. Traffic separation schemes are generally shown on nautical charts at scales of 1:600,000 and larger. When possible, traffic separation schemes are plotted to scale and shown as depicted in Section M.

Conversion Scales

Depth conversion scales are provided on all charts to enable the user to work in meters, fathoms or feet.

Correction Date

The date of each new chart edition is shown below the lower left border of the chart. The date of the latest NGA issued U.S. Notice to Mariners applied to the chart is

Shoreline

Shoreline shown on charts represents the line of contact between the land and a selected water elevation. In areas affected by tidal fluctuation, this line of contact is usually the mean high water line. In confined coastal waters of diminished tidal influence, a mean water level may be used. The shoreline of interior waters (rivers, lakes) is usually a line representing a specified elevation above a selected datum. Shoreline is symbolized by a heavy line (symbol C 1). Apparent shoreline is used on charts to show the outer edge of marine vegetation where the limit would be expected to appear as the shoreline to the mariner or where it prevents the shoreline from being clearly defined. Apparent shoreline is symbolized by a light line (symbols C 32, C 33, C p, C q and C r).

Landmarks

A structure or a conspicuous feature on a structure may be shown by a landmark symbol with a descriptive label (see Section E). Prominent buildings that could assist the mariner may be shown by actual shape as viewed from above (see Sections D and E).

On NGA charts, landmark legends shown in capital letters indicate that a landmark is conspicuous; the landmark may also be labeled "CONSPICUOUS" or "CONSPIC." On NOAA charts, all landmarks are considered to be conspicuous, and landmark legends shown in all capital letters indicate a landmark has been positioned accurately; legends using both upper and lower case letters indicate an approximate position.

ECDIS portrays conspicuous features with black symbols and non-conspicuous features with brown symbols. Only the conspicuous version is shown in the lettered sections of U.S. Chart No. 1. See the ECDIS "Conspicuous and Non-Conspicuous Features" page in front of Section E for more information.

IALA Buoyage System

The International Association of Marine Aids to Navigation and Lighthouse Authorities (IALA) Maritime Buoyage System is followed by most of the world's maritime nations; however, systems used in some foreign waters may be different. IALA buoyage is divided into two regions: Region A and Region B. All navigable waters of the United States follow IALA Region B rules, except U.S. possessions west of the International Date Line and south of 10° north latitude, which follow IALA Region A rules.

The major difference between the two buoyage regions is the color of the lateral marks. Region A uses red to port and Region B uses red to starboard (red-right-returning). The shapes of the lateral marks are the same in both regions, can to port and cone (nun) to starboard, when entering from seaward. Cardinal and other marks, such as those for isolated dangers, safe water and special marks are also the same in both regions. Section Q and Appendix 1 illustrate the IALA buoyage system for both Regions A and B.

U.S. Lateral Marks

Most of U.S. waters are in IALA Region B. In the U.S. system, on entering a channel from seaward, buoys and beacon dayboards on the starboard side are red with even numbers and have red lights, if lit. Buoys and beacon dayboards on the port side are green with odd numbers and have green lights, if lit. Preferred channel buoys have red and green horizontal bands with the top band color indicating the preferred side of passage.

6

shown after the edition date. NOAA charts also show the date of the latest U.S. Coast Guard Local Notice to Mariners applied to the chart.

ADDITIONAL RESOURCES

Information on the use of nautical charts, aids to navigation, sounding datums and the practice of navigation in general is in *The American Practical Navigator* (Bowditch), available through the "Publications" link on the NGA Maritime Safety Information portal at msi.nga.mil/NGAPortal/MSI.portal.

Tide and current data over U.S. waters is available from the NOAA Center for Operational Oceanographic Products and Services at tidesandcurrents.noaa.gov.

Detailed information about specific lights, buoys, and beacons and general information about the U.S. Aids to Navigation System and the Uniform State Waterway Marking Systems is in the U.S. Coast Guard *Light List*, at navcen.uscg.gov/?pageName=lightLists. Information about aids to navigation in foreign waters is in the NGA *List of Lights*, available through the "Publications" link on the NGA Maritime Safety Information portal at msi.nga.mil/NGAPortal/MSI.portal.

Other important information that cannot be shown conveniently on nautical charts can be found in the NOAA *U.S. Coast Pilot*®, at www.nauticalcharts.noaa.gov/staff/chartspubs.html and NGA *Sailing Directions*, available through the "Publications" link on the NGA Maritime Safety Information portal at msi.nga.mil/NGAPortal/MSI.portal.

U.S. Nautical Chart Catalogs and Indexes

NGA catalogs are available through the "Product Catalog" link on the NGA Maritime Safety Information portal at msi.nga.mil/NGAPortal/MSI.portal. NOAA catalogs are available at www.nauticalcharts.noaa.gov/mcd/ccatalogs.htm. A list of the dates of the latest editions of NOAA charts is at www.nauticalcharts.noaa.gov/mcd/dole.htm.

CORRECTIONS AND COMMENTS

Corrections to U.S. Chart No. 1 will appear in the weekly U.S. Notice to Mariners, available through the "Notice to Mariners" link on the NGA Maritime Safety Information portal at msi.nga.mil/NGAPortal/MSI.portal.

Users may send corrections or comments to USChart1@noaa.gov or by mail to:

National Ocean Service, NOAA (N/CS2)
Attention: U.S. Chart No. 1
1315 East West Highway
Silver Spring, MD 20910-3282

Schematic Layout of U.S. Chart No. 1:

(A) **K**   Rocks, Wrecks, Obstructions (B)

(C) **Rocks**

(D) Supplementary national symbol: a

| (E) No. | Plane of Reference for Heights → H | Plane of Reference for Depths → H | | | | | |
	INT	Description	NOAA	NGA	Other NGA	ECDIS	
11		Rock which covers and uncovers, height above chart datum		Uncov 1m / Uncov 1m		✳	rock which covers and uncovers or is awash at low water
						◀	underwater hazard which covers and uncovers with drying height
					⊙	✖	isolated danger of depth less than the safety contour
(1)	(2)	(3)	(4a)	(4b)	(5)	(6)	(7)

(A) Section designation

(B) Section

(C) Sub-section

(D) Reference to "Supplementary national symbols" at the end of each section

(E) Cross-reference to terms in other sections

(1) Column 1: Numbering system following the "Chart Specification of the IHO". A letter in this column indicates a supplementary national symbol or abbreviation for which there is no international equivalent.

(2) Column 2: Representation that follows the "Chart Specifications of the IHO" (INT 1 symbol)

(3) Column 3: Description of symbol, term, or abbreviation

(4a)* Column 4a: Representation used on charts produced by the National Oceanic and Atmospheric Administration (NOAA)

(4b)* Column 4b: Representation used on charts produced by the National Geospatial-Intelligence Agency (NGA)

(5) Column 5: Representation of symbols that may appear on NGA reproductions of foreign charts

(6)** Column 6: Representation used to portray ENC data on ECDIS

(7)** Column 7: Description of ECDIS symbols

*   When columns 4a and 4b are combined then NOAA and NGA both use the same symbol. When either column 4a or 4b is blank then the respective agency uses the INT 1 symbol shown in column 2.

**   When columns 6 and 7 have several rows for the same symbol number, then ECDIS portrays this feature differently depending on the ship's draft and other conditions as defined in ECDIS by the mariner (as is the case for K 11). When columns 6 and 7 combine rows to span across several symbol numbers then ECDIS portrays all of the grouped symbol numbers the same way (see C 5–C 7).

†   Signifies that this representation is obsolete, but it may appear on older charts.

✳   Signifies that a feature attribute value, such as a height, distance or name, may be obtained through an ECDIS cursor pick report. There are many attribute values that may be obtained in this manner, but the cursor pick icon is only used to note values that are specifically referred to in the description of symbols column and that ECDIS does not display next to the symbol. Height of trees in C 14 is an example.

8

Day, Dusk and Night Color Palettes

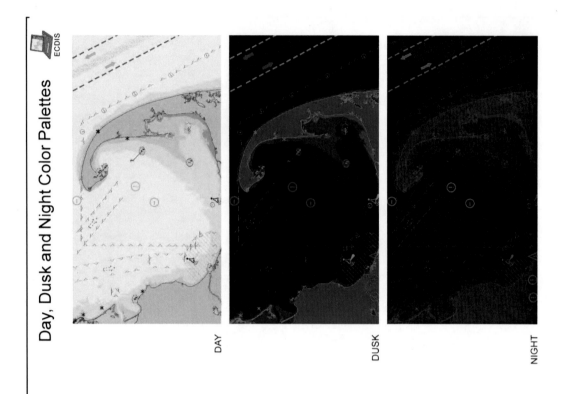

DAY

DUSK

NIGHT

ECDIS allows the mariner to change the color palette that is used to display an ENC. Three different color tables have been designed to provide the maximum clarity and contrast between features on the display under three different lighting conditions on the bridge, namely Day, Dusk and Night.

Each symbol is rendered in a different color appropriate for the lighting condition that the color table is meant for. This design provides maximum contrast for the display on a sunny day, as well as preserving night vision on a dimly lit bridge in the evening. This allows the mariner to look back and forth between the chart on the ECDIS display and out to sea through the bridge window without the mariner's eyes needing to readjust to a difference in light intensity.

- The Day Color Table, meant to be used in bright sunlight, uses a white background for deep water and looks the most like a traditional paper chart.

- The Dusk Color Table uses a black background for deep water and colors are subdued, but slightly brighter than those used in the Night Color Table.

- The Night Color Table, meant to be used in the darkest conditions, uses a black background for deep water and muted color shades for other features.

The images on the right show each of the three color palettes.

The symbols shown in the remainder of this document use the day color palette.

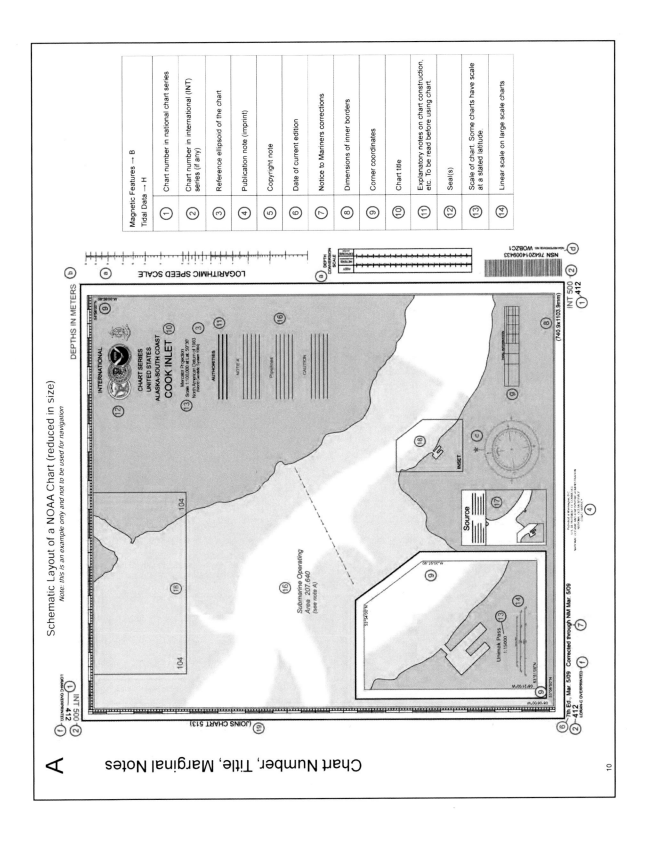

Schematic Layout of a NOAA Chart (reduced in size)
Note: this is an example only and not to be used for navigation

A   Chart Number, Title, Marginal Notes

| Magnetic Features → B | |
Tidal Data → H	
1	Chart number in national chart series
2	Chart number in international (INT) series (if any)
3	Reference ellipsoid of the chart
4	Publication note (imprint)
5	Copyright note
6	Date of current edition
7	Notice to Mariners corrections
8	Dimensions of inner borders
9	Corner coordinates
10	Chart title
11	Explanatory notes on chart construction, etc. To be read before using chart.
12	Seal(s)
13	Scale of chart. Some charts have scale at a stated latitude.
14	Linear scale on large scale charts

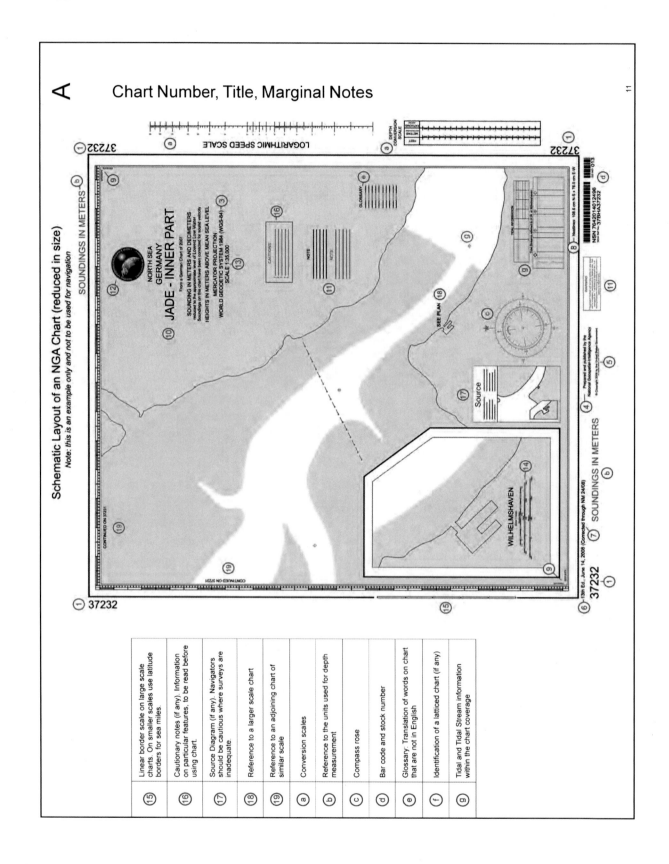

A Chart Number, Title, Marginal Notes

Schematic Layout of an NGA Chart (reduced in size)

Note: this is an example only and not to be used for navigation

⑮	Linear border scale on large scale charts. On smaller scales use latitude borders for sea miles.
⑯	Cautionary notes (if any). Information on particular features, to be read before using chart.
⑰	Source Diagram (if any). Navigators should be cautious where surveys are inadequate.
⑱	Reference to a larger scale chart
⑲	Reference to an adjoining chart of similar scale
ⓐ	Conversion scales
ⓑ	Reference to the units used for depth measurement
ⓒ	Compass rose
ⓓ	Bar code and stock number
ⓔ	Glossary: Translation of words on chart that are not in English
ⓕ	Identification of a latticed chart (if any)
ⓖ	Tidal and Tidal Stream information within the chart coverage

B Positions, Distances, Directions, Compass

No.	INT	Description	NOAA	NGA	Other NGA	ECDIS
Geographical Positions						
1	Lat	Latitude				
2	Long	Longitude				
3		International Meridian (Greenwich)				
4	°	Degree(s)				
5	'	Minute(s) of arc				
6	"	Second(s) of arc				
7	PA	Position approximate (not accurately determined or does not remain fixed)	PA	(PA)		PA — Position approximate; ⌐ — Point feature or area of low accuracy; ㉑ — Sounding of low accuracy
8	PD	Position doubtful (reported in various positions)	PD	(PD)		⌐ — Point feature or area of low accuracy; ㉑ — Sounding of low accuracy
9	N	North				
10	E	East				
11	S	South				
12	W	West				
13	NE	Northeast				
14	SE	Southeast				
15	NW	Northwest				
16	SW	Southwest				

12

Positions, Distances, Directions, Compass   B

No.	INT	Description	NOAA	NGA	Other NGA	ECDIS
Control Points						
20	△	Triangulation point				
21	⊕	Observation spot	⊕ Obs Spot			Position of an elevation or control point
22	⊙	Fixed point	⊙			○
23	⊤	Benchmark	○ BM			
24		Boundary mark	◇ Bdy Mon			
25.1	○ km 32	Distance along waterway, no visible marker	St M 32			km 7 — Canal and distance point with no mark
25.2	○ km 46	Distance along waterway with visible marker	□ Y Bn (46)			○ km 7 — Canal and distance point

Note: ECDIS uses a magenta "km" symbol to represent distance marks. However, the distances shown along waterways on NOAA-produced ENCs are displayed in statute miles.

No.	INT	Description	NOAA	NGA	Other NGA	ECDIS
Symbolized Positions (Examples)						
30	⚹	Symbols in plan: position is center of primary symbol				ECDIS follows the paper chart convention for the position of symbols, except for simplified symbols for buoys and beacons (see Q 1).
31		Symbols in profile: position is at bottom of symbol				
32	⊙ Mast	Point symbols: accurate positions		⊙ MAST		⊙ — Position of a point feature
33	○ Mast PA	Point symbol: approximate position		○ Mast		ECDIS indicates approximate position only for wrecks, obstructions, islets and shoreline features.
						Supplementary national symbols: a–m
Units						
40	km	Kilometer(s)				
41	m	Meter(s)				
42	dm	Decimeter(s)				
43	cm	Centimeter(s)				
44	mm	Millimeter(s)				
45	M	International nautical mile(s) (1852m), sea mile(s)	Mi NMi NM			
46		Cable(s) (0.1M)	cbl			

13

146

B Positions, Distances, Directions, Compass

No.	INT	Description	NOAA	NGA	Other NGA	ECDIS
47	ft	Foot/Feet				
48		Fathom(s)	fm			
49	h	Hour(s)	hr			
50	m min	Minute(s) of time				
51	s sec	Second(s) of time				
52	kn	Knot(s)				
53	t	Ton(s), Tonnage (weight)				
54	cd	Candela(s)				

Magnetic Compass

No.	INT	Description	NOAA	NGA	Other NGA	ECDIS
60		Variation	var VAR			
61		Magnetic	mag			
62		Bearing	brg			
63		True	T			
64		Decreasing				
65		Increasing				
66		Annual change				
67		Deviation	dev			
68.1	Magnetic Variation 4°30'W 2011 (8'E)	Note of magnetic variation, in position				
68.2	Magnetic Variation at 55°N 8°W 4°30'W 2011 (8'E)	Note of magnetic variation, out of position				

Supplementary national symbols: n

Varn	Magnetic variation
	Cursor pick site for magnetic variation at a point
	Cursor pick site for magnetic variation over an area

14

Appendix C

Positions, Distances, Directions, Compass   B

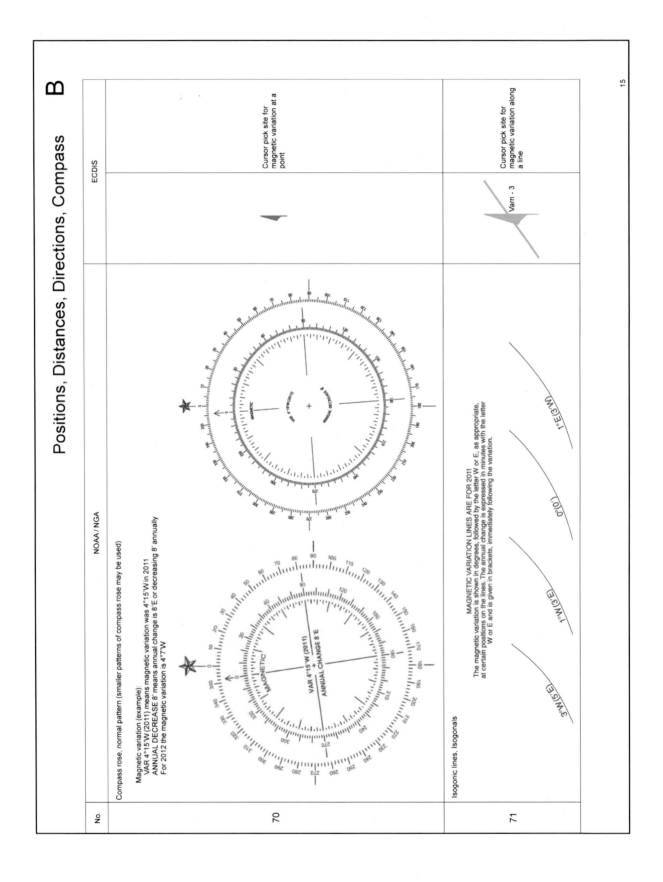

No.	NOAA / NGA	ECDIS
70	Compass rose, normal pattern (smaller patterns of compass rose may be used) Magnetic variation (example): VAR 4°15'W (2011) means magnetic variation was 4°15'W in 2011 ANNUAL DECREASE 8' means annual change is 8'E or decreasing 8' annually For 2012 the magnetic variation is 4°7'W	Cursor pick site for magnetic variation at a point
71	Isogonic lines. Isogonals	Cursor pick site for magnetic variation along a line Varn - 3

B   Positions, Distances, Directions, Compass

No.	INT	Description	NOAA	NGA	Other NGA	ECDIS
82.1	±15° Local Magnetic Anomaly (see Note)	Local magnetic anomaly: Within the enclosed area the magnetic variation may deviate from the normal by the value shown				Cursor pick site for magnetic anomaly along a line or over an area
82.2		Local magnetic anomaly: Where the area affected cannot be easily defined, a legend only is shown at the position	LOCAL MAGNETIC DISTURBANCE (see note)	LOCAL MAGNETIC ANOMALY (see note)	LOCAL MAGNETIC DISTURBANCE (see note)	Cursor pick site for magnetic anomaly at a point

Supplementary National Symbols

	Description	NOAA
a	Square meter(s)	m²
b	Cubic meter(s)	m³
c	Inch(es)	in
d	Yard(s)	yd
e	Statute mile(s)	St M St Mi
f	Microsecond(s)	μsec μs
g	Hertz	Hz
h	Kilohertz	kHz
i	Megahertz	MHz
j	Cycles/second	cps c/s
k	Kilocycle(s)	kc
l	Megacycle(s)	Mc
m	Ton(s) (U.S. short ton) (2,000lbs)	T
n	Degree(s)	deg

16

Natural Features C

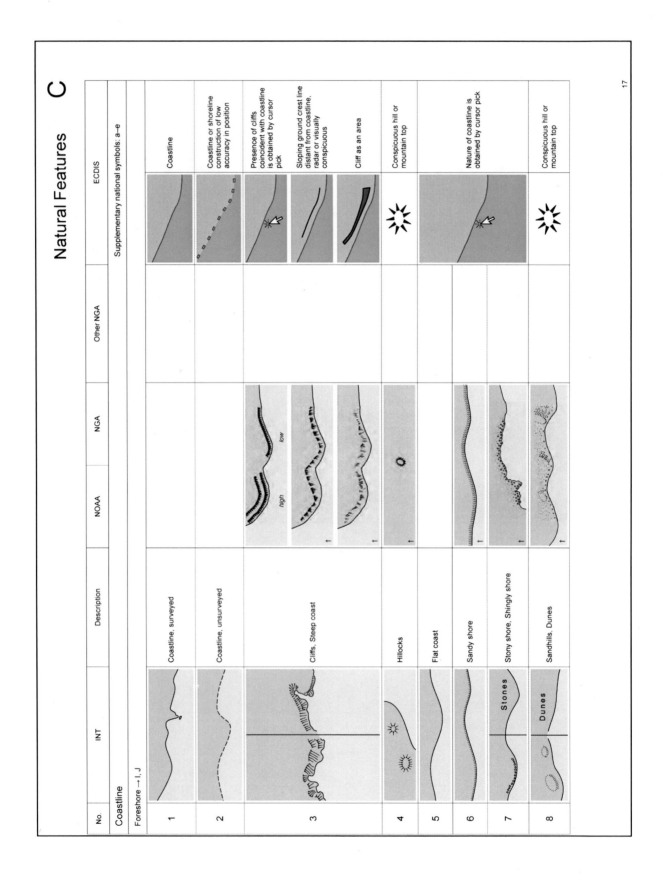

No.	INT	Description	NOAA	NGA	Other NGA	ECDIS
Coastline						Supplementary national symbols: a–e
Foreshore → I, J						
1		Coastline, surveyed				Coastline
2		Coastline, unsurveyed				Coastline or shoreline construction of low accuracy in position
3		Cliffs, Steep coast	low / high			Presence of cliffs coincident with coastline is obtained by cursor pick
						Sloping ground crest line distant from coastline, radar or visually conspicuous
						Cliff as an area
4		Hillocks				Conspicuous hill or mountain top
5		Flat coast				
6		Sandy shore				Nature of coastline is obtained by cursor pick
7	Stones	Stony shore, Shingly shore				
8	Dunes	Sandhills. Dunes				Conspicuous hill or mountain top

17

C   Natural Features

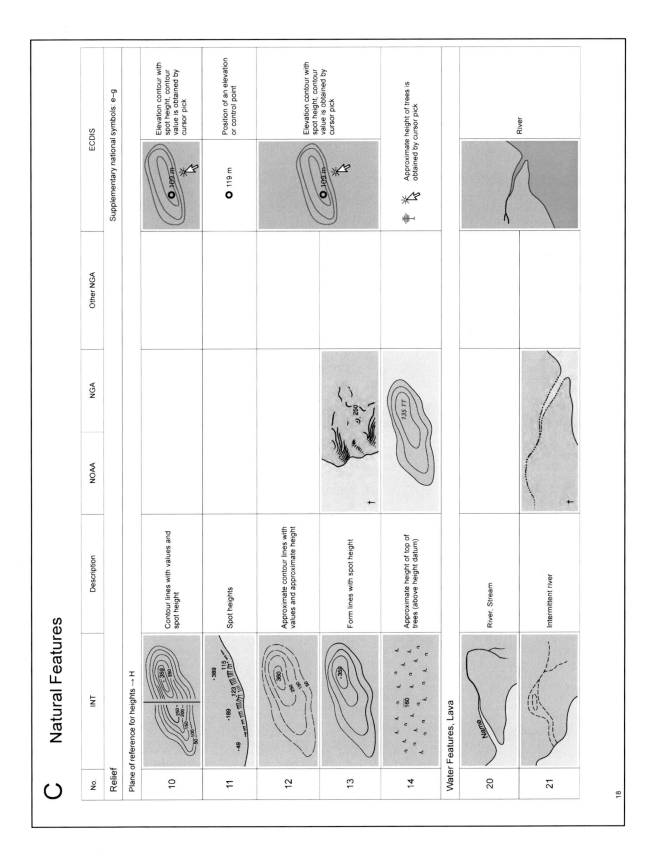

No.	INT	Description	NOAA	NGA	Other NGA	ECDIS
Relief						Supplementary national symbols: e–g
Plane of reference for heights → H						
10		Contour lines with values and spot height				Elevation contour with spot height, contour value is obtained by cursor pick
11		Spot heights				Position of an elevation or control point
12		Approximate contour lines with values and approximate height				Elevation contour with spot height, contour value is obtained by cursor pick
13		Form lines with spot height				
14		Approximate height of top of trees (above height datum)				Approximate height of trees is obtained by cursor pick
Water Features, Lava						
20		River, Stream				River
21		Intermittent river				

Appendix C

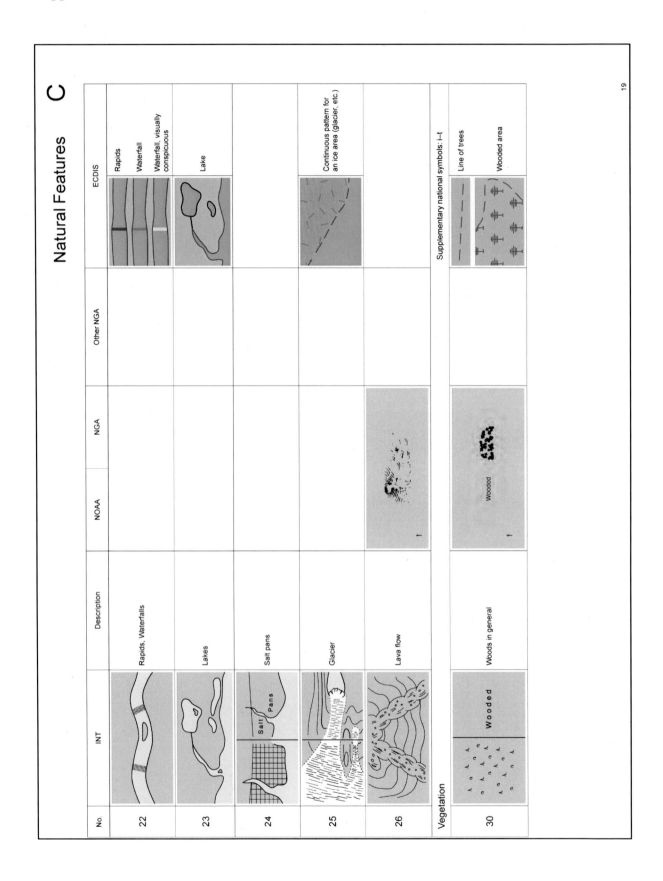

Natural Features   C

No.	INT	Description	NOAA	NGA	Other NGA	ECDIS
22		Rapids, Waterfalls				Rapids Waterfall Waterfall, visually conspicuous
23		Lakes				Lake
24	Salt Pans	Salt pans				
25		Glacier				Continuous pattern for an ice area (glacier, etc.)
26		Lava flow				

Vegetation | | | | | | Supplementary national symbols: l–t

| 30 | Wooded | Woods in general | Wooded | Wooded | | Line of trees
Wooded area |

C   Natural Features

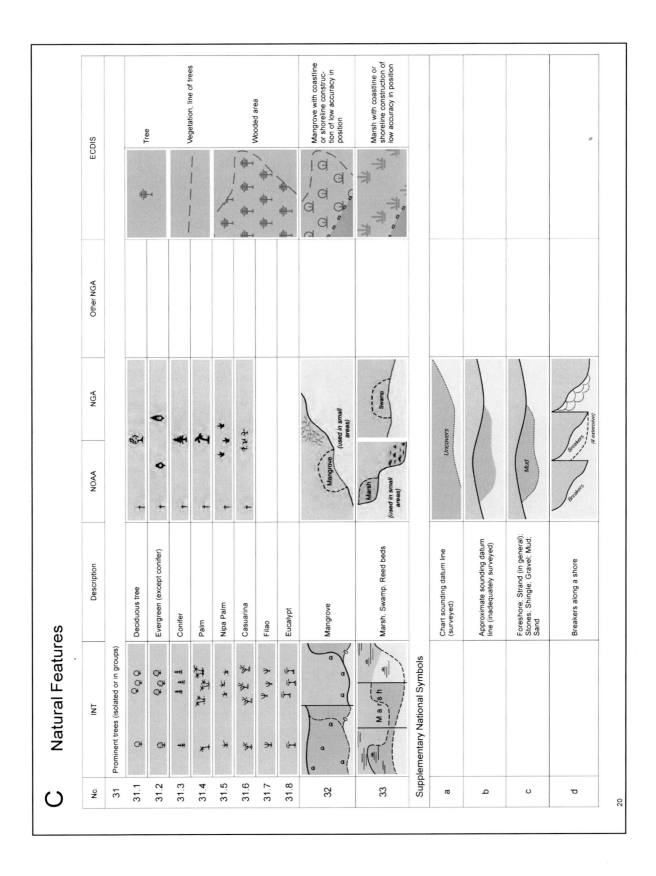

No.	INT	Description	NOAA	NGA	Other NGA	ECDIS
31	Prominent trees (isolated or in groups)					
31.1		Deciduous tree				Tree
31.2		Evergreen (except conifer)				
31.3		Conifer				Vegetation, line of trees
31.4		Palm				
31.5		Nipa Palm				Wooded area
31.6		Casuarina				
31.7		Filao				
31.8		Eucalypt				
32		Mangrove				Mangrove with coastline or shoreline construction of low accuracy in position
33		Marsh, Swamp, Reed beds				Marsh with coastline or shoreline construction of low accuracy in position

Supplementary National Symbols

a		Chart sounding datum line (surveyed)				
b		Approximate sounding datum line (inadequately surveyed)				
c		Foreshore; Strand (in general); Stones; Shingle; Gravel; Mud; Sand				
d		Breakers along a shore				

Appendix C

Natural Features   C

No.	INT	Description	NOAA	NGA	Other NGA	ECDIS
e		Rubble				
f		Hachures				
g		Shading				
i		Deciduous woodland	Wooded			
j		Coniferous woodland	Wooded			
k		Tree plantation				
l		Cultivated fields	Cultivated			
m		Grassfields	Grass			
n		Paddy (rice) fields	Rice			
o		Bushes	Bushes			
p		Apparent shoreline	*Marsh*			
q		Vegetation or topographic (Feature Area Limit-in general)				
r		Cypress	*Cypress*			
s		Grass	*Grass*			
t		Eelgrass	*Eelgrass*			

D Cultural Features

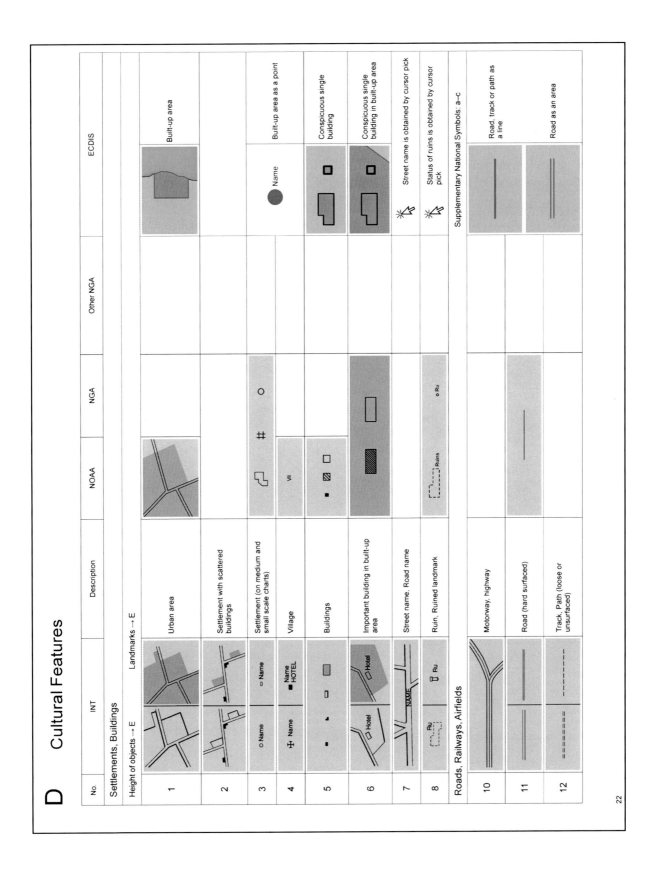

Settlements, Buildings

Height of objects → E   Landmarks → E

No	INT	Description	NOAA	NGA	Other NGA	ECDIS
1		Urban area				Built-up area
2		Settlement with scattered buildings				
3		Settlement (on medium and small scale charts)				Built-up area as a point
4		Village				
5		Buildings				Conspicuous single building
6		Important building in built-up area				Conspicuous single building in built-up area
7		Street name. Road name				Street name is obtained by cursor pick
8		Ruin, Ruined landmark				Status of ruins is obtained by cursor pick

Roads, Railways, Airfields

Supplementary National Symbols: a–c

No	INT	Description	NOAA	NGA	Other NGA	ECDIS
10		Motorway, highway				Road, track or path as a line
11		Road (hard surfaced)				Road as an area
12		Track, Path (loose or unsurfaced)				

22

Appendix C

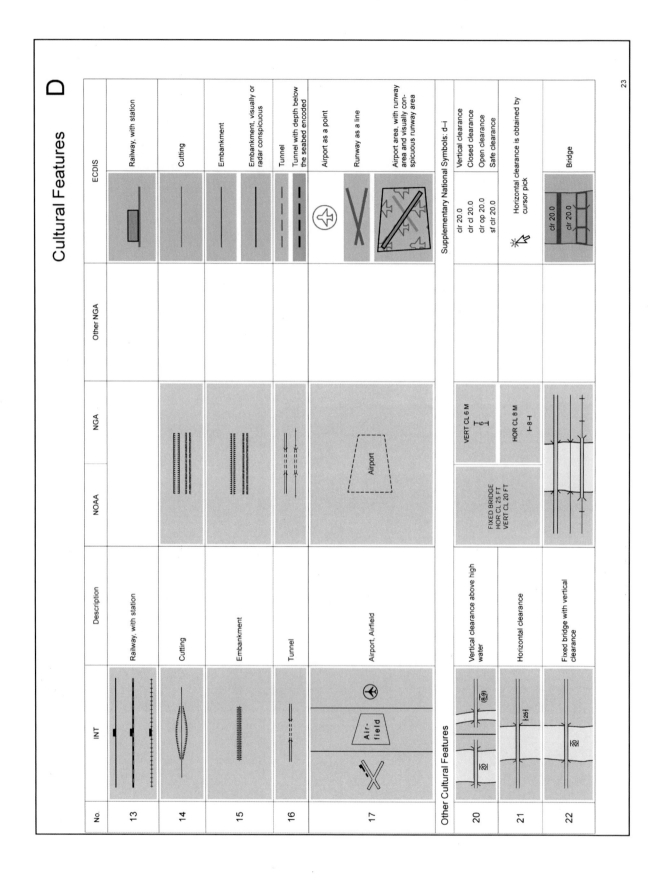

D Cultural Features

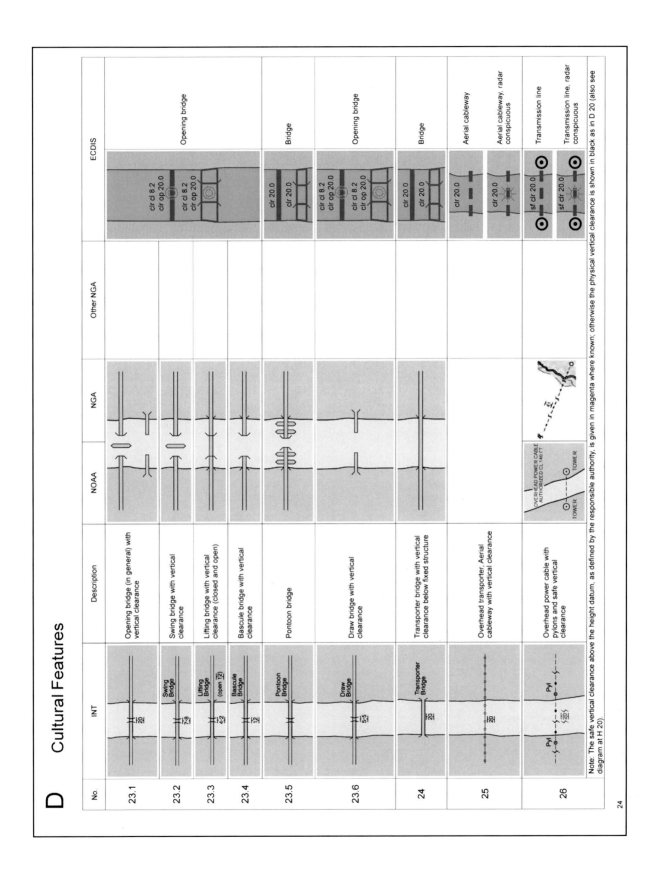

No.	INT	Description	NOAA	NGA	Other NGA	ECDIS
23.1		Opening bridge (in general) with vertical clearance				Opening bridge — clr cl 8.2 / clr op 20.0 — clr cl 8.2 / clr op 20.0
23.2	Swing Bridge	Swing bridge with vertical clearance				
23.3	Lifting Bridge (open 12)	Lifting bridge with vertical clearance (closed and open)				
23.4	Bascule Bridge	Bascule bridge with vertical clearance				
23.5	Pontoon Bridge	Pontoon bridge				Bridge — clr 20.0
23.6	Draw Bridge	Draw bridge with vertical clearance				Opening bridge — clr cl 8.2 / clr op 20.0 — clr cl 8.2 / clr op 20.0
24	Transporter Bridge	Transporter bridge with vertical clearance below fixed structure				Bridge — clr 20.0
25		Overhead transporter. Aerial cableway with vertical clearance				Aerial cableway — clr 20.0 / Aerial cableway, radar conspicuous — clr 20.0
26	Pyl	Overhead power cable with pylons and safe vertical clearance	OVERHEAD POWER CABLE AUTHORIZED CL 140 FT / TOWER / TOWER			Transmission line — sf clr 20.0 / Transmission line, radar conspicuous — sf clr 20.0

Note: The safe vertical clearance above the height datum, as defined by the responsible authority, is given in magenta where known; otherwise the physical vertical clearance is shown in black as in D 20 (also see diagram at H 20).

Cultural Features — D

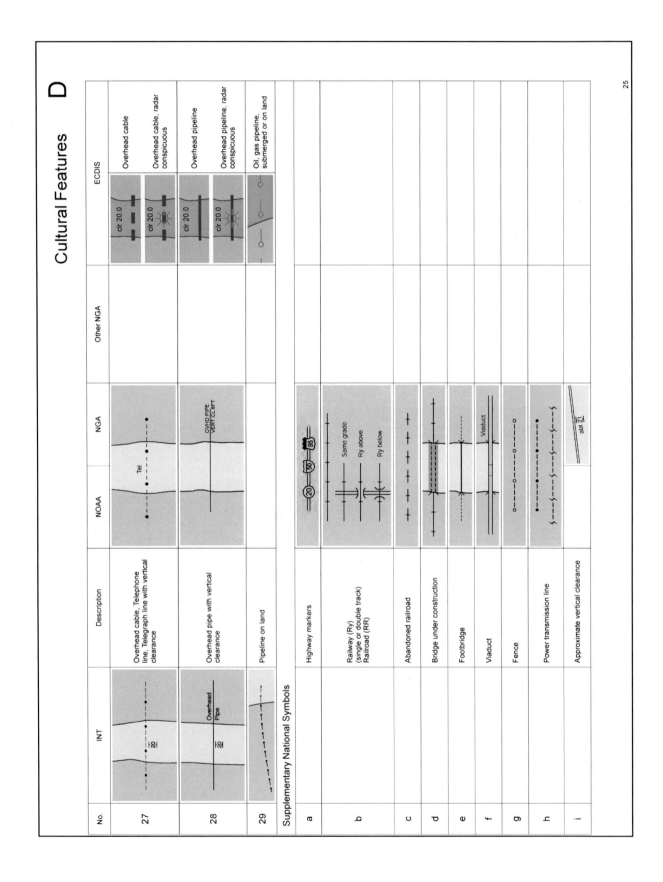

No.	INT	Description	NOAA	NGA	Other NGA	ECDIS
27		Overhead cable, Telephone line, Telegraph line with vertical clearance				Overhead cable / Overhead cable, radar conspicuous
28		Overhead pipe with vertical clearance				Overhead pipeline / Overhead pipeline, radar conspicuous
29		Pipeline on land				Oil, gas pipeline, submerged or on land

Supplementary National Symbols

No.		Description	NOAA	NGA		
a		Highway markers				
b		Railway (Ry) (single or double track) Railroad (RR)		Same grade / Ry above / Ry below		
c		Abandoned railroad				
d		Bridge under construction				
e		Footbridge				
f		Viaduct		Viaduct		
g		Fence				
h		Power transmission line				
i		Approximate vertical clearance		abt 21		

Conspicuous and Non-Conspicuous Features

ECDIS

There are 25 features for which ECDIS displays either a black symbol, if the feature is visually conspicuous, or a brown symbol if is not. Only conspicuous landmarks are depicted on NOAA paper charts and ENCs. Therefore, only the conspicuous symbol versions are shown in the symbol tables of U.S. Chart No. 1. Both versions of the symbols for these features are shown on this page.

The seven symbols shown below represent features that only have a brown symbol. There is no corresponding black, conspicuous symbol. The brown symbol is displayed regardless of the conspicuousness of the feature.

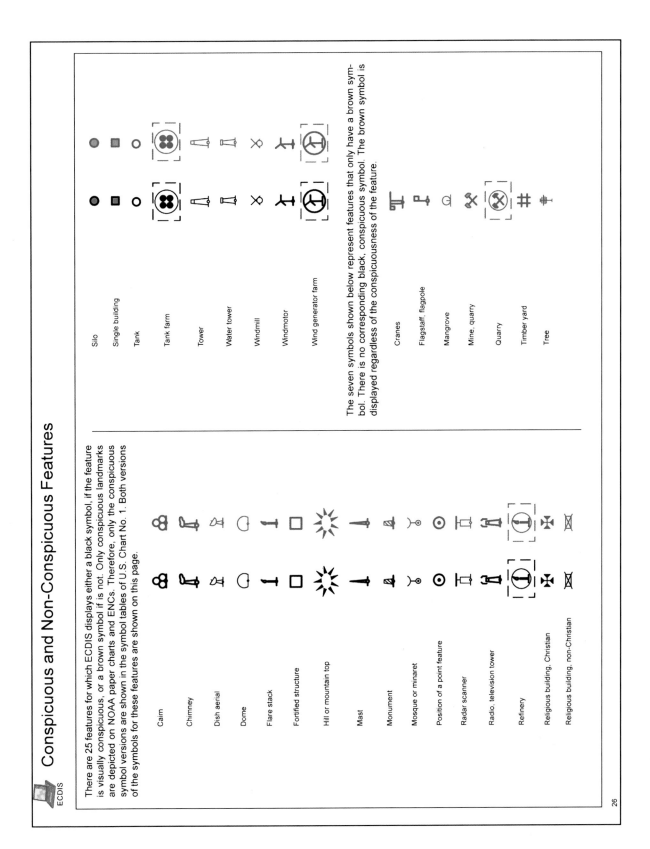

Cairn
Chimney
Dish aerial
Dome
Flare stack
Fortified structure
Hill or mountain top
Mast
Monument
Mosque or minaret
Position of a point feature
Radar scanner
Radio, television tower
Refinery
Religious building, Christian
Religious building, non-Christian

Silo
Single building
Tank
Tank farm
Tower
Water tower
Windmill
Windmotor
Wind generator farm

Cranes
Flagstaff, flagpole
Mangrove
Mine, quarry
Quarry
Timber yard
Tree

26

Landmarks   E

Plane of Reference for Height → H   Lighthouses → P   Beacons → Q

General

No.	INT	Description	NOAA	NGA	Other NGA	ECDIS
1	◆ Factory ⊙ Hotel	Examples of landmarks	⊙ TANK ○ Tr ⊙ MONUMENT			Non-conspicuous point feature; Non-conspicuous building; Non-conspicuous water tower
2	◆ FACTORY WATER TR; ○ HOTEL WATER TOWER	Examples of conspicuous landmarks (On NOAA charts, a large circle with dot and capitals indicates that position is accurate; a small circle with lowercase indicates that position is approximate.)	⊙ EMPIRE STATE BUILDING; ⊙ SPIRE; ⊙ RADAR MAST; ⊙ CHIMNEY			Conspicuous point feature; Conspicuous building; Conspicuous water tower
3.1		Pictorial sketches (in true position)				The information symbol is displayed if a supplemental image is available, which may be accessed by cursor pick
3.2		Pictorial sketches (out of position)				
4	(30)	Height of top of a structure above height datum		(30)		
5	(30)	Height of structure above ground level		(30)		Height is obtained by cursor pick

Landmarks

No.	INT	Description	NOAA	NGA	Other NGA	ECDIS
10.1	Ch ✠	Church		✠ Ch		Church as a point; Church as an area
10.2	Tr ✠ Tr	Church tower				
10.3	Sp ✠ Sp	Church spire	⊙ SPIRE ○ Spire			Church tower, spire, or dome
10.4	Cup ✠ Cup	Church cupola	⊙ CUPOLA ○ Cup			
11		Chapel		✠ Ch		Chapel

E Landmarks

No.	INT	Description	NOAA	NGA	Other NGA	ECDIS
12		Cross, Calvary				Position of a point feature
13		Temple				Religious building, non-Christian
14		Pagoda				
15		Shinto shrine, Joss house				
16		Buddhist temple or shrine				
17		Mosque, Minaret				Mosque or minaret
18	Marabout	Marabout				
19		Cemetery	Cem			Landmark area, type is obtained by cursor pick
20	Tr	Tower	TOWER / Tr	Tr		Tower
21		Water tower, Water tank on a tower	STANDPIPE / S pipe	WTR TR / Wtr Tr		Water tower
22	Chy	Chimney	CHIMNEY / Chy	CHY (208) / (202)		Chimney
23		Flare stack (on land)	FLARE	Flare		Flare stack
24	Mon	Monument (including column, pillar, obelisk, statue)	MONUMENT / Mon	Mon		Monument
25.1		Windmill	WINDMILL	Windmill		Windmill, status of ruins is obtained by cursor pick
25.2	Ru	Windmill (without sails)				
26.1		Wind turbine, Windmotor	WINDMOTOR	Windmotor		Wind motor
26.2		Wind farm	WIND FARM	Wind Farm		Wind generator farm
27	FS	Flagstaff, Flagpole	FS / FP	FS / FP		Flagstaff, flagpole

28

161

Landmarks E

No.	INT	Description	NOAA	NGA	Other NGA	ECDIS
28		Radio mast, Television mast	⊙ R MAST ⊙ TV MAST	○ R Mast ○ TV Mast		Mast
29		Radio tower, Television tower	⊙ R TR ⊙ TV TR	○ R Tr ○ TV Tr		Radio, television tower
30.1	⊙ Radar Mast Radar	Radar mast	⊙ RADAR MAST ○ Radar Mast			Mast
30.2	⊙ Radar Tr Radar	Radar tower	⊙ RADAR TR ○ Radar Tr			Radar tower
30.3	⊙ Radar Sc	Radar scanner				Radar scanner
30.4	⊙ Radome	Radome	⊙ DOME (RADAR) ○ Dome (Radar)	⊙ RADOME ○ Radome		Dome
31		Dish aerial	⊙ ANT (RADAR) ○ Ant (Radar)			Dish aerial
32	Tanks	Tanks	⊙ TANK	⊘ Silo ○ Tk		Tank
						Tank farm
33	○ Silo	Silo	⊙ SILO ⊙ ELEVATOR	⊙ Silo ○ Elevator		Silo
34.1		Fortified structure (on large scale charts)				Fortified structure
34.2		Castle, Fort, Blockhouse (on small scale charts)			⊞	Fortified structure
34.3		Battery, Small fort (on small scale charts)				
35.1	✕	Quarry (on large scale charts)				Quarry area
35.2	✕	Quarry (on small scale charts)			⚒	Quarry
36		Mine				

E Landmarks

No.	INT	Description	NOAA	NGA	Other NGA	ECDIS
37.1	(symbol)	Recreational vehicle site				
37.2	X	Camping site (including recreational vehicles)				

Supplementary National Symbols

No.	INT	Description	NOAA	NGA	Other NGA	ECDIS
a		Muslim shrine	(symbol)			
b		Tomb	(symbol)			
c		Watermill	(symbol)		✿	
d		Factory	(symbols)	Facty		
e		Well	o Well			
f		School	Sch ■	Sch ■		
g		Hospital	Hosp ■			
h		University	Univ ■	Univ ■		
i		Gable	⊙ GAB o Gab			
k		Telegraph / Telegraph office	Tel / Tel Off			
l		Magazine	Magz			
m		Government house	Govt Ho			
n		Institute	Inst			
o		Courthouse	Ct Ho			
p		Pavilion	Pav			
q		Telephone	T			
r		Limited	Ltd			
s		Apartment	Apt			
t		Capitol	Cap			
u		Company	Co			
v		Corporation	Corp			

30

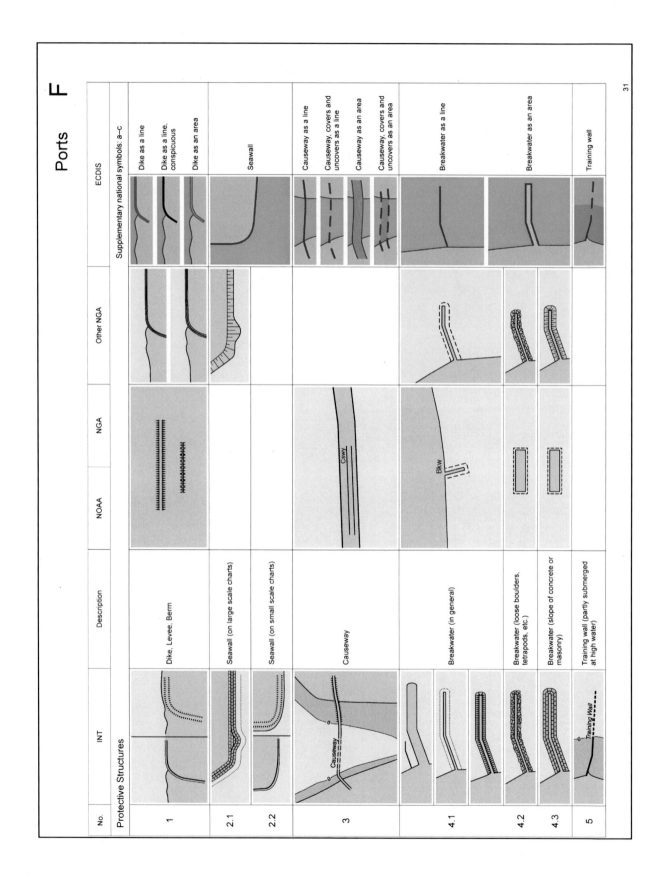

F   Ports

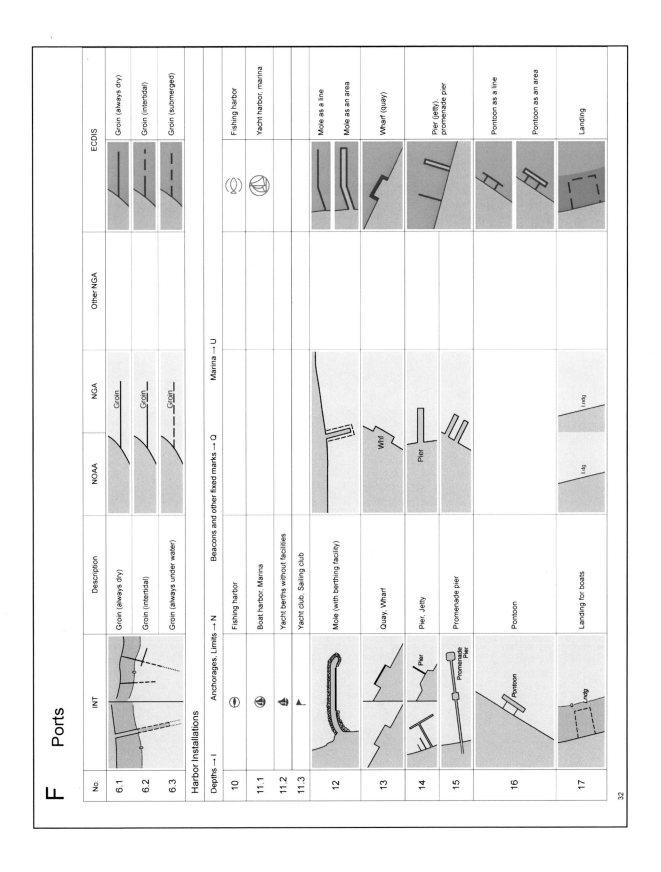

No.	INT	Description	NOAA	NGA	Other NGA	ECDIS
6.1		Groin (always dry)	Groin			Groin (always dry)
6.2		Groin (intertidal)	Groin			Groin (intertidal)
6.3		Groin (always under water)	Groin			Groin (submerged)

Harbor Installations

Depths → I   Anchorages, Limits → N   Beacons and other fixed marks → Q   Marina → U

No.	INT	Description	NOAA	NGA	Other NGA	ECDIS
10		Fishing harbor				Fishing harbor
11.1		Boat harbor, Marina				Yacht harbor, marina
11.2		Yacht berths without facilities				
11.3		Yacht club, Sailing club				
12		Mole (with berthing facility)				Mole as a line / Mole as an area
13		Quay, Wharf	Whf			Wharf (quay)
14	Pier	Pier, Jetty	Pier			Pier (jetty), promenade pier
15	Promenade Pier	Promenade pier				Pontoon as a line
16	Pontoon	Pontoon				Pontoon as an area
17	Lndg	Landing for boats	Lndg			Landing

32

Ports   F

No.	INT	Description	NOAA	NGA	Other NGA	ECDIS	
18		Steps. Landing stairs			Steps		Landing steps
19.1	Ⓐ Ⓑ Ⓐ54	Designation of berth	3 A 3			Nr 3	Berth number
19.2	∀	Visitors' berth					Yacht harbor, marina
20	□Dn □Dns	Dolphin	○ Dol ● Dol (Great Lakes) ◇ Dn ◇Dol		⚓ ○ •	■	Mooring dolphin
21	⚐	Deviation dolphin				⚐	Deviation mooring dolphin
22	·	Minor post or pile	○ Pile † Pile (Great Lakes)			•	Pile or bollard
23	Slip	Slipway. Patent slip. Ramp					Slipway, ramp
24		Gridiron. Scrubbing grid					Gridiron
25		Dry dock. Graving dock					Dry dock
26	*Floating Dock*	Floating dock					Floating dock as a line Floating dock as an area
27	7.6m	Non-tidal basin. Wet dock					Wet dock and gate
28		Tidal basin. Tidal harbor					Dock Dock, under construction or ruined

33

F   Ports

No.	INT	Description	NOAA	NGA	Other NGA	ECDIS
29.1	Floating Barrier	Floating barrier, e.g. oil barrier, security barrier				Floating hazard Boom Floating oil barrier, oil retention (high pressure pipe) Boom, floating obstruction
29.2		Oil retention barrier (high pressure pipe)			Floating Barrier	Floating oil barrier, oil retention (high pressure pipe)
30	Dock under construction (2011)	Works on land, with year date	Under construction (2011)			Ruin or works under construction
31	Area under reclamation (2011)	Works at sea. Area under reclamation, with year date	Under construction (2011)	Under constr		
32	Under construction (2011) Works in progress (2011)	Works under construction, with year date		Under constr (2011)		Year and condition of under construction or ruin is obtained by cursor pick
33.1	Ru	Ruin		Ruins		
33.2	Pier (ru)	Ruined pier, partly submerged at high water		Pier		Pier, ruined and partly submerged
34	Hulk	Hulk	Hk	Hk		Hulk

Ports F

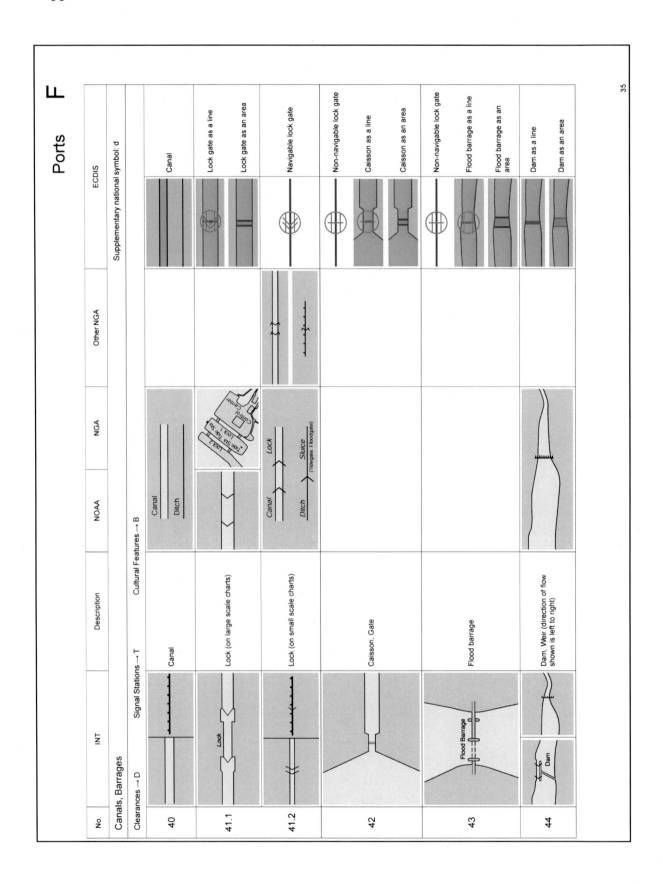

No.	INT	Description	NOAA	NGA	Other NGA	ECDIS
Canals, Barrages						Supplementary national symbol: d
Clearances → D	Signal Stations → T	Cultural Features → B				
40	Canal		Canal / Ditch			Canal
41.1	Lock (on large scale charts)			Lock Sta 2, Tide Sta, Lock Sta 1, Control Center		Lock gate as a line / Lock gate as an area
41.2	Lock (on small scale charts)		Canal / Ditch — Lock, Sluice (Tidegate. / Floodgate)		Navigable lock gate
42	Caisson, Gate					Non-navigable lock gate / Caisson as a line / Caisson as an area
43	Flood barrage					Non-navigable lock gate / Flood barrage as a line / Flood barrage as an area
44	Dam, Weir (direction of flow shown is left to right)					Dam as a line / Dam as an area

F   Ports

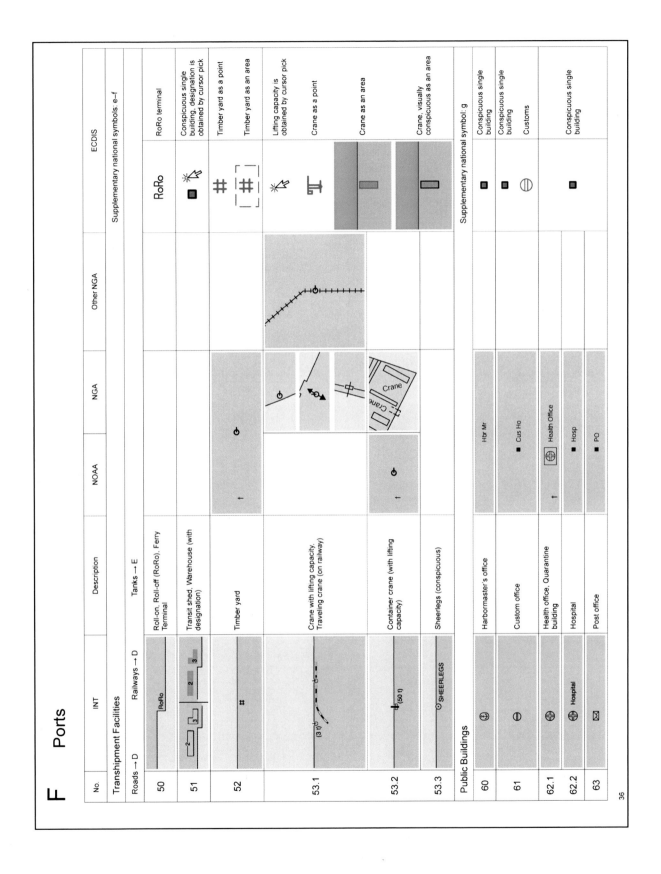

Transshipment Facilities

Roads → D   Railways → D   Tanks → E

No.	INT	Description	NOAA	NGA	Other NGA	ECDIS
						Supplementary national symbols: e–f
50	RoRo	Roll-on, Roll-off (RoRo), Ferry Terminal				RoRo RoRo terminal
51		Transit shed, Warehouse (with designation)				Conspicuous single building, designation is obtained by cursor pick
52		Timber yard				Timber yard as a point / Timber yard as an area
53.1	(3 t)	Crane with lifting capacity, Traveling crane (on railway)				Lifting capacity is obtained by cursor pick / Crane as a point
53.2	(50 t)	Container crane (with lifting capacity)		Crane		Crane as an area
53.3	SHEERLEGS	Sheerlegs (conspicuous)				Crane, visually conspicuous as an area

Public Buildings

No.	INT	Description	NOAA	NGA	Other NGA	ECDIS
						Supplementary national symbol: g
60		Harbormaster's office		Hbr Mr		Conspicuous single building
61		Custom office		Cus Ho		Conspicuous single building
62.1		Health office, Quarantine building		Health Office		Customs
62.2	Hospital	Hospital		Hosp		
63		Post office		PO		Conspicuous single building

36

Appendix C

No.	Description	INT	NOAA	NGA	Other NGA	ECDIS
Supplementary National Symbols						
a	Jetty (partly below MHW)					
b	Submerged jetty					
c	Jetty (on small scale charts)					
d	Pump-out facilities					
e	Quarantine office					
f	Mooring Canal					
g	Conveyor					

Ports   F

37

170

H   Tides, Currents

Terms Relating to Tidal Levels

INT Terms

No.	Term	Description
1	CD	Chart Datum, Datum for sounding reduction
2	LAT	Lowest Astronomical Tide
3	HAT	Highest Astronomical Tide
4	MLW	Mean Low Water
5	MHW	Mean High Water
6	MSL	Mean Sea Level
7		Height datum, Land survey datum
8	MLWS	Mean Low Water Springs
9	MHWS	Mean High Water Springs
10	MLWN	Mean Low Water Neaps
11	MHWN	Mean High Water Neaps
12	MLLW	Mean Lower Low Water
13	MHHW	Mean Higher High Water
14	MHLW	Mean Higher Low Water
15	MLHW	Mean Lower High Water
16	Sp	Spring tide
17	Np	Neap tide

Supplementary National Terms (see l–t for other terms and symbols)

No.	Term	Description
a	HW	High Water
b	HHW	Higher High Water
c	LW	Low Water
d	LWD	Low Water Datum
e	LLW	Lower Low Water
f	MTL	Mean Tide Level
g	ISLW	Indian Spring Low Water
h	HWF&C	High Water Full and Change (Vulgar establishment of the port)
i	LWF&C	Low Water Full and Change
j	CRD	Columbia River Datum
k	GCLWD	Gulf Coast Low Water Datum

Tides, Currents H

No.	

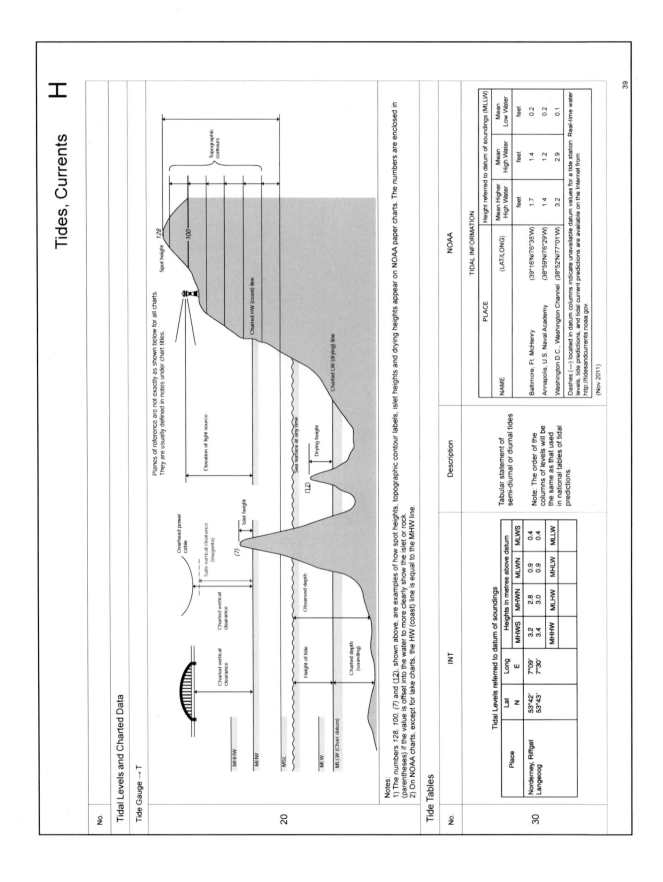

Tidal Levels and Charted Data

Tide Gauge → T

20

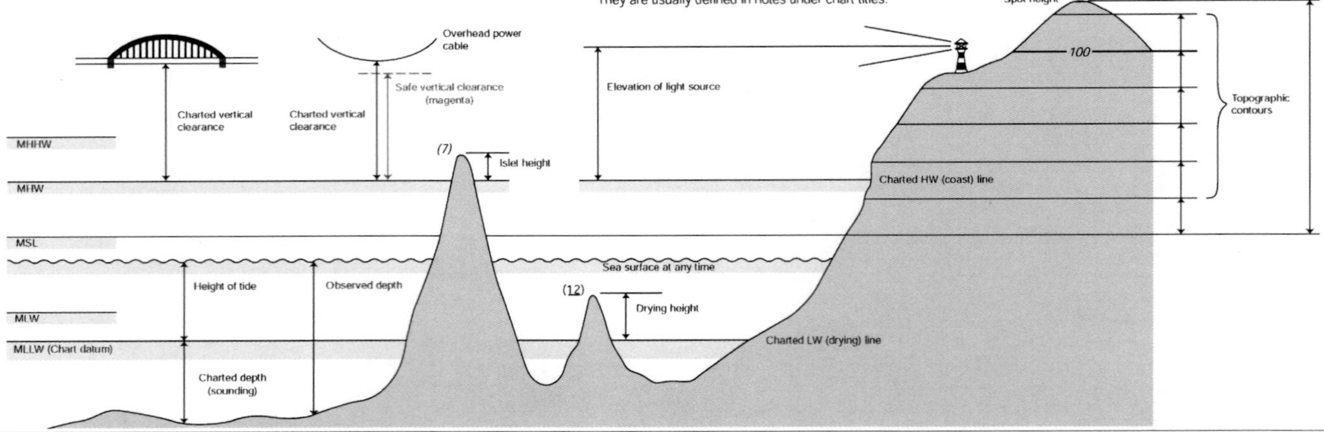
Planes of reference are not exactly as shown below for all charts.
They are usually defined in notes under chart titles.
Spot height
128
100
Overhead power cable
Safe vertical clearance (magenta)
Charted vertical clearance
Charted vertical clearance
MHHW
MHW
MSL
MLW
MLLW (Chart datum)
(7)
Islet height
Elevation of light source
Charted HW (coast) line
Topographic contours
Sea surface at any time
Height of tide
Observed depth
(12)
Drying height
Charted LW (drying) line
Charted depth (sounding)

Notes:
1) The numbers *128, 100, (7)* and (12), shown above, are examples of how spot heights, topographic contour labels, islet heights and drying heights appear on NOAA paper charts. The numbers are enclosed in (parentheses) if the value is offset into the water to more clearly show the islet or rock.
2) On NOAA charts, except for lake charts, the HW (coast) line is equal to the MHW line.

Tide Tables

No.	INT	Description	NOAA
30	(see table below)	Tabular statement of semi-diurnal or diurnal tides Note: The order of the columns of levels will be the same as that used in national tables of tidal predictions.	(see table below)

INT:

Tidal Levels referred to datum of soundings

Place	Lat N	Long E	Heights in metres above datum			
			MHWS	MHWN	MLWN	MLWS
Norderney, Riffgat Langeoog	53°42′ 53°43′	7°09′ 7°30′	3.2 3.4	2.8 3.0	0.9 0.9	0.4 0.4
			MHHW	MLHW	MHLW	MLLW

NOAA:

TIDAL INFORMATION

PLACE		Height referred to datum of soundings (MLLW)		
NAME	(LAT/LONG)	Mean Higher High Water	Mean High Water	Mean Low Water
		feet	feet	feet
Baltimore, Ft. McHenry	(39°16′N/76°35′W)	1.7	1.4	0.2
Annapolis, U.S. Naval Academy	(38°59′N/76°29′W)	1.4	1.2	0.2
Washington D.C., Washington Channel	(38°52′N/77°01′W)	3.2	2.9	0.1

Dashes (---) located in datum columns indicate unavailable datum values for a tide station. Real-time water levels, tide predictions, and tidal current predictions are available on the Internet from http://tidesandcurrents.noaa.gov.

(Nov 2011)

39

H   Tides, Currents

No.				ECDIS
31	Tidal stream table			Point or area for which a tidal stream table is available
				Boundary of an area for which there is tidal information

Tidal streams referred to . . .

	Geographical Position ◇		53°51.2'N 7°17.8'E ◇	
Hours	Directions of streams (degrees)	Rates at spring tides (knots)	Rates at neap tides (knots)	
Before High Water 6 5 4 3 2 1			-6 261 0.8 0.7 / -5 170 0.2 0.1 / -4 097 1.1 0.8 / -3 095 1.5 1.2 / -2 094 1.3 1.1 / -1 092 1.0 0.9	
High Water 0			0 081 0.7 0.6	
After High Water 1 2 3 4 5 6			+1 038 0.3 0.2 / +2 291 0.6 0.4 / +3 277 1.0 0.8 / +4 270 1.2 1.0 / +5 267 1.1 1.0 / +6 264 1.0 0.9	

Tidal Streams and Currents

Breakers → K   Tide Gauge → T

No.	INT	Description	NOAA	NGA	Other NGA	ECDIS
40	3.0 kn	Flood tide stream with rate				Flood stream, rate at spring tides 2.5 kn
						Current or tidal stream whose direction is not known
						Boundary of an area for which there is tidal information
41	2.8 kn	Ebb tide stream				Ebb stream, rate at spring tides 2.5 kn
						Current or tidal stream whose direction is not known
						Boundary of an area for which there is tidal information

Supplementary national symbols: m–t

Tides, Currents H

No.	INT	NOAA	NGA	Other NGA	ECDIS	Description
42	⇒					Current in restricted waters
43	2.5 – 4.5 kn Jan – Mar (see Note)		~~~~	~~~~ (see Note)	⬿ 2.5 kn Non-tidal current	Ocean current with rates and seasons
44		Tide rips ∿∿∿ symbol used only in small areas	∿∿	≋	∿∿ ∿∿ (point, line, and area)	Overfalls, tide rips, races
45	૯ ૯ ૯ ૯	૯ ૯ ૯ ૯ Eddies symbol used only in small areas	૯ ૯ ૯ ૯ Eddies		⟨ ∿∿∿ ⟩ Overfalls, tide rips; eddies; breakers as point, line, and area	Eddies
46	◇Ａ				◇ Point for which a tidal stream table is available	Position of tabulated tidal stream data with designation
47	▣					Offshore position for which tidal levels are tabulated

Supplementary National Symbols (Supplementary national terms relating to tidal levels are listed after H 17)

No.	INT	NOAA	NGA	Other NGA	ECDIS	Description
l		Str				Stream
m		⇢ 2 kn				Current, general, with rate
n		vel				Velocity, Rate
o		kn				Knots
p		ht				Height
q		fl				Flood
r		⬤				New moon
s		⟨☾⟩				Full moon
t		current diagram (compass rose)				Current diagram
u		Approximate location of Axis of Gulf Stream				Gulf Stream Limits

41

I Depths

General

No.	INT	Description	NOAA	NGA	Other NGA	ECDIS
1	ED	Existence doubtful				(25) Sounding of low accuracy (25) Sounding of low accuracy (212) Underwater hazard with depth greater than 20 meters (X) Isolated danger of depth less than the safety contour
2	SD	Sounding of doubtful depth				(25) Sounding of low accuracy Point feature or area of low accuracy
3.1	Rep	Reported, but not confirmed				Low accuracy line demarking area wreck or obstruction Low accuracy line demarking foul area
3.2	Rep (2011)	Reported (with year of report), but not confirmed				Obstruction, depth not stated
4	(84) (212)	Reported, but not confirmed sounding or danger (on small scale charts only)				(25) Sounding of low accuracy (5) Underwater hazard with depth of 20 meters or less (212) Underwater hazard with depth greater than 20 meters (X) Isolated danger of depth less than the safety contour Point feature or area of low accuracy

Depths   I

No.	INT	Description	NOAA	NGA	Other NGA	ECDIS
Soundings						Supplementary national symbols: a–c
	Plane of Reference for Depths → H	Plane of Reference for Heights → H				
10	12 9_7	Sounding in true position (NOAA shows fathoms and feet with vertical numbers and meters with sloping numbers)	$6\frac{1}{2}$ 6_4			9_7 Sounding shoaler than or equal to safety depth 30 Sounding deeper than safety depth
11	· (4_8) +(12) 3375	Sounding out of position	(23)	3375		
12	(4_7)	Least depth in narrow channel	(4_7)			Depths are always shown in their true position in ECDIS
13	$\overline{200}$	No bottom found at depth shown				(200) Status of no bottom found is obtained by cursor pick
14	12 9_7	Soundings which are unreliable or taken from a smaller scale source (NOAA shows unreliable soundings in fathoms and feet with sloping numbers and in meters with vertical numbers)				(12) Sounding of low accuracy
15		Drying heights and contours above chart datum	6			4 Drying height, less than or equal to safety depth
16		Natural watercourse (in intertidal area), tidal gully, tideway				Tideway

43

I Depths

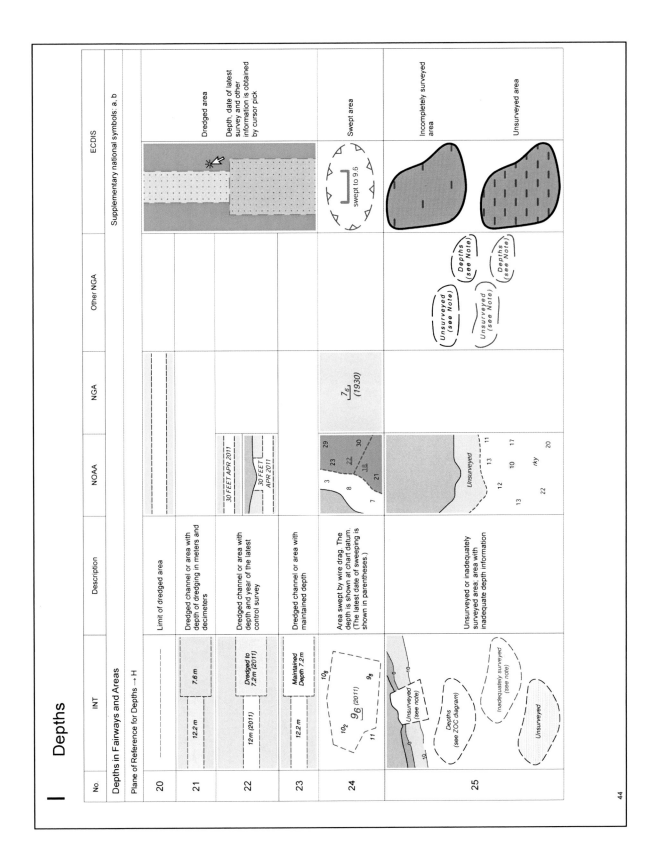

No.	INT	Description	NOAA	NGA	Other NGA	ECDIS
Depths in Fairways and Areas						
Plane of Reference for Depths → H						Supplementary national symbols: a, b
20		Limit of dredged area				Dredged area
21	7.6 m / 12.2 m	Dredged channel or area with depth of dredging in meters and decimeters				Depth, date of latest survey and other information is obtained by cursor pick
22	Dredged to 7.2m (2011) / 12m (2011)	Dredged channel or area with depth and year of the latest control survey	30 FEET APR 2011 / 30 FEET APR 2011			
23	Maintained Depth 7.2m / 12.2 m	Dredged channel or area with maintained depth				Swept area
24	10₈ / 9₆ (2011) / 10₂ / 9₈ / 11	Area swept by wire drag. The depth is shown at chart datum. (The latest date of sweeping is shown in parentheses.)	3 8 7 / 23 29 30 22 18 21	$\frac{7_6}{(1930)}$		swept to 9.6
25	Unsurveyed (see note) / Depths (see ZOC diagram) / Inadequately surveyed (see note) / Unsurveyed	Unsurveyed or inadequately surveyed area; area with inadequate depth information	Unsurveyed / 13 12 22 13 10 rky 17 20 11		Unsurveyed (see Note) / Depths (see Note) / Unsurveyed (see Note) / Depths (see Note)	Incompletely surveyed area / Unsurveyed area

44

ECDIS Portrayal of Depths

ECDIS

ECDIS depth related symbols closely resemble their paper chart counterparts; however, ECDIS provides valuable additional information to mariners that paper charts cannot.

Soundings

ECDIS enables mariners to set their own-ship "safety depth." If no depth is set, ECDIS sets the value to 30m. Soundings equal to or shoaler than the safety depth are shown in black; deeper soundings are displayed in a less conspicuous gray. Fractional values are shown with subscript numbers of the same size.

Depth Contours & Depth Areas

Depth contours in ECDIS are portrayed with a thin gray line. Each pair of adjacent depth contours is used to create depth area features. These are used by ECDIS to tint different depth levels and to initiate alarms when a ship is headed into unsafe water.

Depth Contour Labels

ECDIS depth contour labels are not centered and oriented along iso-lines as they appear on paper charts. They are displayed upright and may appear either on or next to the contour lines that they describe. The labels are black and the same size as soundings, but the labels have a light "halo" to set them apart. The graphic to the left shows depth labels and soundings both deeper and shoaler than the safety depth. Note that depths on NOAA paper charts and ENCs are usually compiled in fathoms and feet. Because ECDIS displays depths in meters, soundings and contour lines often show fractional meter values. The "own-ship safety contour" (described below) is always displayed, but mariners may choose to have all other depth contours turned off.

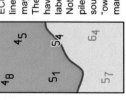

4_8 4_5

5_4

5_1 6_4

5_7

Safety Contour

ECDIS uses a "safety contour" value to show an extra thick line for the depth contour that separates "safe water" from shoaler areas. If the mariner does not set an own-ship safety contour value, ECDIS sets the value to 30m. If the ENC being displayed does not have a contour line equal to the safety contour depth value set by the mariner, then ECDIS sets the next deeper contour as the safety contour. Depending on the contour intervals used on individual ENCs, ECDIS may set different safety contours as a ship transits from one ENC to another. ECDIS will initiate an alarm if the ship's future track will cross the safety contour within a specified time set by the mariner.

Two or Four Tints for Shading Depth Areas

ECDIS tints all depth areas beyond the (green tinted) foreshore in either one of two or one of four shades of blue. This is similar to the convention used for paper charts, but the depths used to change from one tint to another are based on the safety contour and thus "customized" for each ship. If the mariner chooses two shades to be displayed, water deeper than the safety contour is shown in an off-white color, water shoaler than the safety contour is tinted blue.

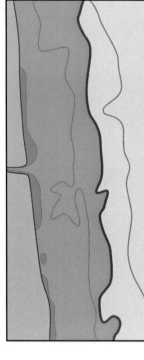

Portrayal of Depth Areas with 2 Color Settings

Some ECDIS enable mariners to define two additional depth areas for medium-deep water and medium-shallow water by setting a "deep contour" value and a "shallow contour" value. If this option is used, the safety contour is displayed between the medium deep and medium shallow contours.

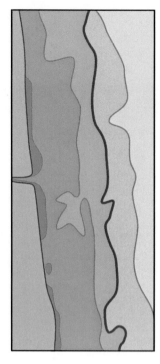

Portrayal of Depth Areas with 4 Color Setting

Some ECDIS also provide the mariner with the option of displaying a cross-hatch "shallow water" pattern over all depth areas shoaler than the safety contour.

45

I Depths

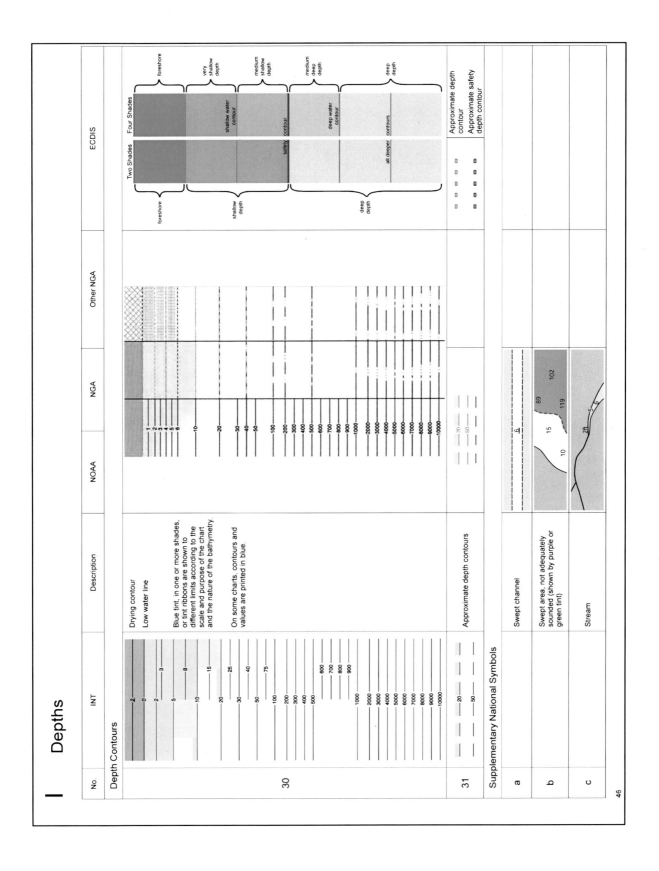

Depth Contours

No.	INT	Description	NOAA	NGA	Other NGA	ECDIS
30	2 0 2 3 5 8 10 15 20 25 30 40 50 75 100 200 300 400 500 600 700 800 900 1000 2000 3000 4000 5000 6000 7000 8000 9000 10000	Drying contour Low water line Blue tint, in one or more shades, or tint ribbons are shown to different limits according to the scale and purpose of the chart and the nature of the bathymetry. On some charts, contours and values are printed in blue.				
31	20 ——— 50 — —	Approximate depth contours				

Supplementary National Symbols

a		Swept channel				
b		Swept area, not adequately sounded (shown by purple or green tint)				
c		Stream				

46

Nature of the Seabed   J

No.	INT	Description	NOAA	NGA	Other NGA	ECDIS Supplementary national abbreviations: a–ag	
Types of Seabed							
Rocks → K							
1	S	Sand				S	Sand
2	M	Mud				M	Mud
3	Cy	Clay				Cy	Clay
4	Si	Silt				Si	Silt
5	St	Stones				St	Stones
6	G	Gravel				G	Gravel
7	P	Pebbles				P	Pebbles
8	Cb	Cobbles				Cb	Cobbles
9.1	R	Rock; Rocky	Rk; rky			R	Rock
9.2	Bo	Boulder(s)	Blds			R	Boulder
						R	Lava
10	Co	Coral, Coralline algae				Co	Coral
11	Sh	Shells (skeletal remains)				Sh	Shells
12.1	S/M	Two layers, e.g. sand over mud					
12.2	fS M Sh / fS.M.Sh	The main constituent is given first for mixtures, e.g. fine sand with mud and shells	f S M Sh				
13.1	Wd	Weed (including kelp)					Weed, kelp
13.2	(kelp symbol) Kelp, Weed			*kelp* (symbol)			Weed, kelp as an area (symbol, enclosed as area)

J Nature of the Seabed

No.	INT	Description	NOAA	NGA	Other NGA	ECDIS
14		Sandwaves	Sandwaves			Sand waves as a point Sand waves as a line Sand waves as an area
15		Spring in seabed	Spring			Spring

Types of Seabed, Intertidal Areas

		Description	NOAA	NGA	Other NGA	ECDIS
20		Area with stones and gravel		Gravel		gravel / stone — Areas of gravel and stone
21		Rocky area, which covers and uncovers		Rock		Rocky ledges or coral reef
22		Coral reef, which covers and uncovers		Coral		

Qualifying Terms

No.	INT	Description	NOAA			Supplementary national symbols: ah–bf
30	f	Fine				
31	m	Medium	only used in relation to sand			
32	c	Coarse				
33	bk	Broken				
34	sy	Sticky				
35	so	Soft				
36	sf	Stiff				
37	v	Volcanic	vol			
38	ca	Calcareous	Ca			
39	h	Hard				Rocky ledges or coral reef

48

Nature of the Seabed   J

Supplementary National Abbreviations

No.	INT	Description	NOAA	NGA	Other NGA	ECDIS
a		Ground	Grd			
b		Ooze	Oz			
c		Marl	Ml			
d		Shingle	Sn			
f		Chalk	Ck			
g		Quartz	Qz			
h		Schist	Sch			
i		Coral head	Co Hd			
j		Madrepores	Mds			
k		Volcanic ash	Vol Ash			
l		Lava	La			
m		Pumice	Pm			
n		Tufa	T			
o		Sconiae	Sc			
p		Cinders	Cn			
q		Manganese	Mn			
r		Oysters	Oys			
s		Mussels	Ms			
t		Sponge	Spg			
u		Kelp	K			
v		Grass	Grs			
w		Sea-tangle	Stg			
x		Spicules	Spi			
y		Foraminifera	Fr			
z		Globigerina	Gl			
aa		Diatoms	Di			
ab		Radiolaria	Rd			
ac		Pteropods	Pt			
ad		Polyzoa	Po			
ae		Cirripedia	Cir			
af		Fucus	Fu			

49

J   Nature of the Seabed

No.	INT	Description	NOAA	NGA	Other NGA	ECDIS
ag		Mattes	*Ma*			
ah		Small	*sml*			
ai		Large	*lrg*			
aj		Rotten	*rt*			
ak		Streaky	*str*			
al		Speckled	*spk*			
am		Gritty	*gty*			
an		Decayed	*dec*			
ao		Flinty	*fly*			
ap		Glacial	*glac*			
aq		Tenacious	*ten*			
ar		White	*wh*			
as		Black	*bl; bk*			
at		Violet	*vi*			
au		Blue	*bu*			
av		Green	*gn*			
aw		Yellow	*yl*			
ax		Orange	*or*			
ay		Red	*rd*			
az		Brown	*br*			
ba		Chocolate	*ch*			
bb		Gray	*gy*			
bc		Light	*lt*			
bd		Dark	*dk*			
be		Varied	*vard*			
bf		Uneven	*unev*			

50

Rocks, Wrecks, Obstructions, Aquaculture   K

No.	INT	Description	NOAA	NGA	Other NGA	ECDIS
General						
1	(danger line symbol)	Danger line: A danger line draws attention to a danger which would not stand out clearly enough if represented solely by its symbol (e.g. isolated rock) or delimits an area containing numerous dangers, through which it is unsafe to navigate				Obstruction, depth not stated Obstruction which covers and uncovers Underwater hazard with depth of 20 meters or less Isolated danger of depth less than the safety contour Foul area, not safe for navigation
2	$\underline{7_5}$	Swept by wire drag or diver	$\underline{21}$ Rk $\underline{35}$ Rk $\overline{4_6}$ Wk	$\underline{35}$ Rk $\overline{4_6}$ Obstn $\overline{4_6}$ Wk (1937)	$\underline{\#}$ (15₇)	4 $\underline{21}$ Swept sounding, less than or equal to safety depth Swept sounding greater than safety depth
3	$\overline{20}$	Depth unknown, but estimated to have a safe clearance to the depth shown	$\overline{4_6}$ Wk	$\overline{4_6}$ Obstn		ECDIS displays safe clearance depths in the same manner as known depths.
Rocks						
		Plane of Reference for Heights → H Plane of Reference for Depths → H				
10	(diagrams)	Rock (islet) which does not cover, height above height datum	25	(21)	▲ (4 m)	Land as a point at small scale Land as an area, with an elevation or control point (8 m)
11	(diagrams)	Rock which covers and uncovers, height above chart datum	*(2)	Uncov 1m Uncov 1m	(starburst symbols)	Rock which covers and uncovers or is awash at low water Underwater hazard which covers and uncovers with drying height Isolated danger of depth less than the safety contour
12	(diagram)	Rock awash at the level of chart datum			(*)	Rock which covers and uncovers or is awash at low water Underwater hazard which covers and uncovers Isolated danger of depth less than the safety contour

51

K Rocks, Wrecks, Obstructions, Aquaculture

No.	INT	Description	NOAA	NGA	Other NGA	ECDIS	
13		Underwater rock of unknown depth, dangerous to surface navigation					Dangerous underwater rock of uncertain depth
							Isolated danger of depth less than the safety contour
14.1		Underwater rock of known depth; inside the corresponding depth area	12 *Rk*	27 *Rk* / 21 *R*		5	Underwater hazard with a depth of 20 meters or less
						25	Underwater hazard with depth greater than 20 meters
14.2		Underwater rock of known depth; outside the corresponding depth area, dangerous to surface navigation	(5) *Rk*	(4) *Rk* / (5) *R*			Isolated danger of depth less than the safety contour
15	35 *R*	Underwater rock of known depth, not dangerous to surface navigation	35*Rk*		35 *R* +(35)	10	Underwater hazard with a depth of 20 meters or less
						25	Underwater hazard with depth greater than 20 meters
							Dangerous underwater rock of uncertain depth Obstruction, depth not stated
							Isolated danger of depth less than the safety contour
							Safe clearance shoaler than safety contour
						12₈	Safe clearance deeper than safety contour
16		Coral reef which is always covered	*Co* / *Reef line*			25₆	Safe clearance deeper than 20 meters
17	(19)(5)₉ *Br* / 18	Breakers	*Breakers* / *Br*		*West Breaker* PA		Overfalls, tide rips, eddies; breakwaters as point, line, and area

Rocks, Wrecks, Obstructions, Aquaculture　K

Wrecks and Fouls

Plane of Reference for Depths → H

No.	INT	Description	NOAA	NGA	Other NGA	ECDIS
20	Mast (1.2) Wk	Wreck, hull never covers, on large scale charts		Hk	Hk	● 1.2 m — Wreck, always dry, with height shown
21	Mast (1_2) Wk	Wreck, covers and uncovers, on large scale charts		Hk	Wk / Wk / Wk / Wk	12 — Wreck, covers and uncovers
						Distributed remains of wreck
22	6 Wk	Submerged wreck, depth known, on large scale charts			9 Wk	5 — Submerged wreck with depth of 20 meters or less
						25 — Submerged wreck with depth greater than 20 meters
						Distributed remains of wreck
23	Wk	Submerged wreck, depth unknown, on large scale charts		Hk	Wk / Wk / Wk	✖ — Submerged wreck with depth less than the safety contour or depth unknown
24	✈	Wreck showing any portion of hull or superstructure at level of chart datum			Wk / Wk / Wk / Wk	✈ — Wreck showing any portion of hull or superstructure at level of chart datum
25	Masts	Wreck of which the mast(s) only are visible at chart datum	Masts	Mast (10ft) Funnel		
26	46 Wk	Wreck, least depth known by sounding only	5 Wk		(11)	5 — Underwater hazard with depth of 20 meters or less
	25 Wk					25 — Underwater hazard with depth greater than 20 meters
						✖ — Isolated danger of depth less than the safety contour

53

186

K Rocks, Wrecks, Obstructions, Aquaculture

No.	INT	Description	NOAA	NGA	Other NGA	ECDIS
27	46 Wk · (25) Wk	Wreck, least depth known, swept by wire drag or diver	25 Wk			Swept sounding for underwater hazard less than safety depth · Swept sounding for underwater hazard greater than or equal to safety depth · Isolated danger of depth less than the safety contour
28	⊕	Dangerous wreck, depth unknown				Dangerous wreck, depth unknown · Isolated danger of depth less than the safety contour
29	‡	Sunken wreck, not dangerous to surface navigation				Non-dangerous wreck, depth unknown
30	(25) Wk	Wreck, least depth unknown, but considered to have a safe clearance to the depth shown			(4) Wk	Underwater hazard with safe clearance of 20 meters or less · Underwater hazard with safe clearance greater than 20 meters · Isolated danger of depth less than the safety contour
31.1	# (25)	Foul ground, not dangerous to surface navigation, but to be avoided by vessels anchoring, trawling, etc. (e.g. remains of wreck, cleared platform)				Foul area of seabed safe for navigation but not for anchoring · Foul ground
31.2	# · # · (#)					Distributed remains of wreck

Obstructions and Aquaculture

No.	INT	Description	NOAA	NGA	Other NGA	ECDIS
Plane of Reference for Depths → H		Kelp, Seaweed → J	Underwater Installations → L			
40	⊙ Obstn · Obstn	Obstruction, depth unknown				Obstruction, depth not stated · Isolated danger of depth less than the safety contour · Safe clearance shoaler than safety contour

Rocks, Wrecks, Obstructions, Aquaculture   K

No.	INT	Description	NOAA	NGA	Other NGA	ECDIS
41	Obstn / Obstn	Obstruction, least depth known by sounding only				5 — Underwater hazard with depth of 20 meters or less; 25 — Underwater hazard with depth greater than 20 meters; ⊗ — Isolated danger of depth less than the safety contour
						4 / 21 — Less than or equal to safety depth / Greater than safety depth (swept depth); Method of depth measurement is obtained by cursor pick
42	Obstn / Obstn	Obstruction, least depth known, swept by wire drag or diver				5 — known by diver or other means / 25; Underwater hazard with depth of 20 meters or less; Underwater hazard with depth greater than 20 meters; ⊗ Isolated danger of depth less than the safety contour
43.1	T T T / Obstn	Stumps of posts or piles, wholly submerged	Subm piles	Piles	T	Obstruction, depth not stated; Underwater hazard with depth of 20 meters or less
43.2	T	Submerged pile, stake, snag, or stump (with exact position)	Well / Deadhead / Stump; Stakes / Snags		T T	5 — Underwater hazard with depth of 20 meters or less; ⊗ Isolated danger of depth less than the safety contour
44.1		Fishing stakes	Fsh stks			Fish stakes as a point / Fish stakes as an area
44.2	Fish trap	Fish trap, Fish weir, Tunny nets	Fish trap			Fish trap, fish weir, tunny net as a point
45	Fish traps / Tunny nets	Fish trap area, Tunny nets area				Fish trap, fish weir, tunny net as an area

55

K   Rocks, Wrecks, Obstructions, Aquaculture

No.	INT	Description	NOAA	NGA	Other NGA	ECDIS
46.1		Fish haven	Obstn Fish Haven	(actual shape)		Isolated danger of depth less than the safety contour
						Safe clearance shoaler than safety contour
						Underwater hazard with depth of 20 meters or less
						Underwater hazard with depth greater than 20 meters
46.2	(2₁)	Fish haven with minimum depth	Obstn Fish Haven (auth min 42ft)			Isolated danger of depth less than the safety contour
						Safe clearance shoaler than safety contour
						Safe clearance deeper than safety contour 12₈
						Safe clearance deeper than 20 meters 25₆
47		Shellfish beds	Oys			Marine farm as a point
48.1		Marine farm (on large scale charts)		Marine Farm		
48.2		Marine farm (on small scale charts)		Obstn (Marine Farm) Marine Farm		Marine farm as an area

56

Appendix C

Rocks, Wrecks, Obstructions, Aquaculture   K

No.	INT	Description	NOAA	NGA	Other NGA	ECDIS
Supplementary National Symbols						
a		Rock awash (height unknown)	*			
b		Shoal sounding on isolated rock or rocks	5 Rk 21 Rks		9 R 2 r 2 P + (8)	
c		Sunken wreck covered 20 to 30 meters	‡		🜨	
d		Submarine volcano	Sub vol			
e		Discolored water	Discol water			
f		Sunken danger with depth cleared (swept) by wire drag	46 21 Rk	4 Obstn 35 Rk		
g		Reef of unknown extent	Reef			
h		Coral reef, detached (uncovers at sounding datum)	Co	Coral Co Co Co		
i		Submerged crib	Subm Crib	Crib	☐	
j		Crib, duck blind (above water)	■ Duck Blind	☐ Crib		
k		Submerged duck blind	Duck Blind			
l		Submerged platform	Subm platform	Platform		
m		Coral reef which covers and uncovers		Hay Reef		
n		Sinkers		Sinkers 13 14 15		
o		Foul area, foul with rocks or wreckage, dangerous to navigation	Foul Wks Wreckage			
p		Unexploded ordnance	Unexploded Ordnance	Unexploded Ordnance		
q		Float	☐ Float			
r		Stumps of posts or piles, which cover and uncover	Subm piles			

57

L   Offshore Installations

No.	INT	Description	NOAA	NGA	Other NGA	ECDIS
General						
Areas, Limits → N						
1	*Ekofisk Oilfield*	Name of oilfield or gasfield		CORRIB GAS FIELD		Area to be navigated with caution, name is obtained by cursor pick
2	Z-44	Platform with designation/name		"Name"		Offshore platform, name is obtained by cursor pick
3		Limit of safety zone around offshore installation				Area where entry is prohibited or restricted or to be avoided, with other cautions
4		Limit of development area				Cautionary area, navigate with caution
5.1		Wind turbine, floating wind turbine, vertical clearance under blade			FLY	Wind motor visually conspicuous
5.2		Offshore wind farm				Wind farm (offshore)
		Offshore wind farm (floating)				
6		Wave farm				Wave farm
Platforms and Moorings						
Mooring Buoys → Q						
10		Production platform, Platform, Oil derrick	■	▣		Offshore platform
11	Fla	Flare stack (at sea)				Conspicuous flare stack on offshore platform

Offshore Installations L

No.	INT	Description	NOAA	NGA	Other NGA	ECDIS
12	⊞ SPM	Single Point Mooring (SPM), including Single Anchor Leg Mooring (SALM), Articulated Loading Column (ALC)				
13	⊞ Ru ⊞ Z-44 (ru)	Observation/research platform (with name)	■ "Name"	⊞ "Name"	⊞ "Name"	Offshore platform, name and status of disused is obtained by cursor pick
14		Disused platform with superstructure removed			⊞ (disused)	
15		Artificial island	Artificial Island (Mukluk)		"Name"	
16		Single Buoy Mooring (SBM), Oil or gas installation buoy including Catenary Anchor Leg Mooring (CALM)				Installation buoy and mooring buoy, simplified Installation buoy, paper chart
17		Moored storage tanker		Tanker		Offshore platform
18		Mooring ground tackle				Ground tackle

Underwater Installations

Plane of Reference for Depths → H   Obstructions → K

Supplementary national symbol: a

No.	INT	Description	NOAA	NGA	Other NGA	ECDIS
20	Well	Submerged production well	Well (cov 21ft) Well (cov 83ft)	Well	(15) Prod Well Prod Well	5 (Underwater hazard with depth of 20 meters or less) 25 (Underwater hazard with depth greater than 20 meters) ⊗ (Isolated danger of depth less than the safety contour) ⊗ (Isolated danger of depth less than the safety contour)
21.1	Well	Suspended well, depth over wellhead unknown	Pipe			
21.2	(4) Well (15) Well	Suspended well, with depth over wellhead	Pipe (cov 24ft) Pipe (cov 92ft)			5 (Underwater hazard with depth of 20 meters or less) 25 (Underwater hazard with depth greater than 20 meters) ⊗ (Isolated danger of depth less than the safety contour) ⊗ (Isolated danger of depth less than the safety contour)
21.3		Wellhead with height above the sea floor			Well (5.7)	

L Offshore Installations

No.	INT	Description	NOAA	NGA	Other NGA	ECDIS
22	‡	Site of cleared platform				Foul area of seabed safe for navigation but not for anchoring
23	⊙ Pipe, ⊙ Pipe (1₈)	Above-water wellhead (lit or unit)	⊙ Pipe		⊙ Pipe (2₄)	Obstruction in the water which is always above water level
24	⊙ Turbine, ☀ Fl(2) Underwater Turbine	Underwater turbine				Underwater turbine or subsurface ODAS
25	⊙ ODAS	Subsurface Ocean(ographic) Data Acquisition System (ODAS)				

Submarine Cables

30.1		Submarine cable				Submarine cable
30.2		Submarine cable area	Cable Area			Submarine cable area
31.1		Submarine power cable				
31.2		Submarine power cable area				
32		Disused submarine cable				Status of disused is obtained by cursor pick

Submarine Pipelines

40.1	Oil, Gas (see Note), Chem, Water	Supply pipeline: unspecified, oil, gas, chemicals, water				Oil, gas pipeline, submerged or on land
40.2	Oil, Gas (see Note), Chem, Water	Supply pipeline area: unspecified, oil, gas, chemicals, water	Pipeline Area			Submarine pipeline area with potentially dangerous contents

60

193

Offshore Installations   L

No.	INT	Description	NOAA	NGA	Other NGA	ECDIS
41.1	Water Sewer Outfall Intake	Outfall and intake: unspecified, water, sewer, outfall, intake				Water pipeline, sewer, etc.
41.2	Water Sewer Outfall Intake	Outfall and intake area: unspecified, water, sewer, outfall, intake	Pipeline Area			Submarine pipeline area with generally non-dangerous contents
42.1	Buried 1.6m	Buried pipeline/pipe (with nominal depth to which buried)				Nominal depth of buried pipeline is obtained by cursor pick
42.2	(→→→)	Pipeline tunnel				Pipeline tunnel
43	(32) Obstn	Diffuser, Crib				Underwater hazard with depth of 20 meters or less Isolated danger of depth less than the safety contour
44		Disused pipeline/pipe				Status of disused is obtained by cursor pick
Supplementary National Symbols						
a		Submerged well (buoyed)	Well Well	Well		
b		Potable water intake	PWI Depth over Crib 17 ft	Crib		

M   Tracks, Routes

Tracks

Leading Beacons → Q

No.	INT	Description	NOAA	NGA	Other NGA	ECDIS
		Tracks Marked by Lights → P				Supplementary national symbols: a–c
1	270.5° / 2 Bns ǂ 270.5°	Leading line (solid line is the track to be followed, ǂ means "in line")		Lights in line 090°		Leading line bearing a non-regulated, recommended track — ‹?› — ‹ Direction not encoded / 270 deg One-way / 270 deg Two-way
2	270.5° / Island open of Headland 270.5°	Transit (other than leading line), clearing line		Beacons in line 090°	Bns in line 270.5°	270 deg Clearing line; transit line
3	090.5°–270.5°	Recommended track based on a system of fixed marks		Lights in line 090°	— › — › — › —	Non-regulated, recommended track based on fixed marks ‹?› — ‹ Direction not encoded / 90 deg One-way / 270 deg Two-way
4	090.5°–270.5°	Recommended track not based on a system of fixed marks	— ‹ — › —	— ‹ — › —		Non-regulated, recommended track not based on fixed marks ‹?› — ‹ Direction not encoded / 90 deg One-way / 270 deg Two-way
5.1	DW (see Note)	One-way track and DW track based on a system of fixed marks		— › — › —		Based on fixed marks, one-way 90 deg Non-regulated recommended track / DW Deep water route
5.2	270° / DW	One-way track and DW track not based on a system of fixed marks				Not based on fixed marks, one-way 90 deg Non-regulated recommended track / — DW — Deep water route centerline
6	‹7.0m› / ‹7.3m›	Recommended track with maximum authorized (or recommended) draft stated		‹ 7 m › / ‹ 7₃ m ›		If encoded, the shoalest depth range value along the track is obtained by cursor pick

62

195

Tracks, Routes M

Supplementary national symbols: d–e

Routing Measures

Basic Symbols

No.	INT	Description	NOAA	NGA	Other NGA	ECDIS
10		Established (mandatory) direction of traffic flow				Traffic direction in a one-way lane of a traffic separation scheme
11		Recommended direction of traffic flow				Single traffic direction in a two-way route part of a traffic-separation scheme
12		Separation line (large scale, small scale)				Traffic separation line
13		Separation zone				Traffic separation zone
14		Limit of restricted routing measure (e.g. Inshore Traffic Zone (ITZ), Area to be Avoided (ATBA))	RESTRICTED AREA			
15		Limit of routing measure				Traffic separation scheme boundary
16	Precautionary Area	Precautionary area				Traffic precautionary area as a point / Traffic precautionary area as an area
17	ASL (see Note)	Archipelagic Sea Lane (ASL); axis line and limit beyond which vessels shall not navigate				Axis and boundary of archipelagic sea lane
18	FAIRWAY 7.3m / FAIRWAY <7.3m>	Fairway designated by regulatory authority with minimum depth / Fairway designated by regulatory authority with maximum authorized draft	SAFETY FAIRWAY 166.200 (see note A)			Fairway, depth is obtained by cursor pick

63

M Tracks, Routes

Examples of Routing Measures on Paper/Raster Charts

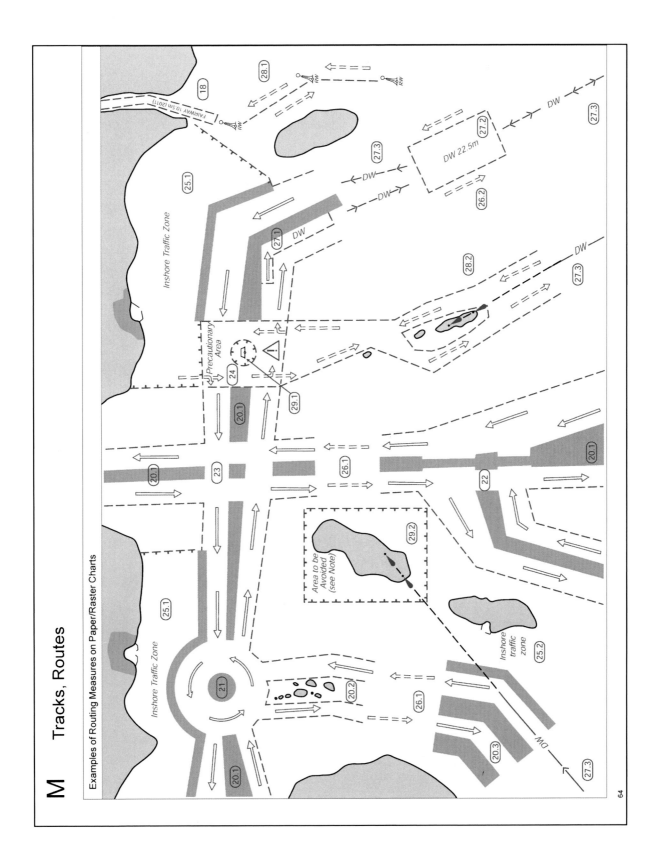

197

64

Appendix C

Tracks, Routes M

No.	
	Examples of Routing Measures
(18)	Safety fairway
(20.1)	Traffic Separation Scheme (TSS), traffic separated by separation zone
(20.2)	Traffic Separation Scheme, traffic separated by natural obstructions
(20.3)	Traffic Separation Scheme, with outer separation zone separating traffic using scheme from traffic not using it
(21)	Traffic Separation Scheme, roundabout with separation zone
(22)	Traffic Separation Scheme, with "crossing gates"
(23)	Traffic Separation Scheme crossing, without designated precautionary area
(24)	Precautionary area
(25.1)	Inshore Traffic Zone (ITZ), with defined end limits
(25.2)	Inshore Traffic Zone, without defined end limits
(26.1)	Recommended direction of traffic flow, between traffic separation schemes
(26.2)	Recommended direction of traffic flow, for ships not needing a deep water route
(27.1)	Deep water route (DW), as part of one-way traffic lane
(27.2)	Two-way deep water route, with minimum depth stated
(27.3)	Deep water route, centerline as recommended one-way or two-way track
(28.1)	Recommended route, one-way and two-way (often marked by centerline buoys)
(28.2)	Two-way route, with one-way sections
(29.1)	Area to be Avoided (ATBA), around navigational aid
(29.2)	Area to be Avoided, e.g. because of danger of stranding

65

198

M   Tracks, Routes

Examples of Routing Measures in ECDIS

Tracks, Routes　M

Radar Surveillance Systems

No.	INT	Description	NOAA	NGA	Other NGA	ECDIS
30	Radar Surveillance Station	Radar surveillance station	Ra ⊙			Radar station
31	Ra Cuxhaven	Radar range				Radar range
32.1	Ra	Radar reference line			—Ra——Ra—	Radar line
32.2	Ra　090°–270°	Radar reference line coinciding with a leading line				270 deg — Radar line; Non-regulated recommended track based on fixed marks; Direction not encoded; 90 deg One-way; 270 deg Two-way

Radio Reporting Points

No.	INT	Description	NOAA	NGA	Other NGA	ECDIS
40.1	Ⓑ ⑦ VHF 80	Radio reporting (calling-in or way) points showing direction(s) of vessel movement with designation (if any) and VHF-channel				Nr 13 ch s74 — Radio calling-in point for traffic in one direction only; Nr 13 ch s74 — Radio calling-in point for traffic in both directions; Nr 13 ch s74 — Radio calling-in point, direction not encoded
40.2	◇	Radio reporting line				Nr 13 ch s74 — Radio calling-in point for traffic in one direction only; Nr 13 ch s74 — Radio calling-in point for traffic in both directions; Nr 13 ch s74 — Radio calling-in point, direction not encoded

67

M Tracks, Routes

No.	INT	Description	NOAA	NGA	Other NGA	ECDIS
Ferries						
50		Ferry	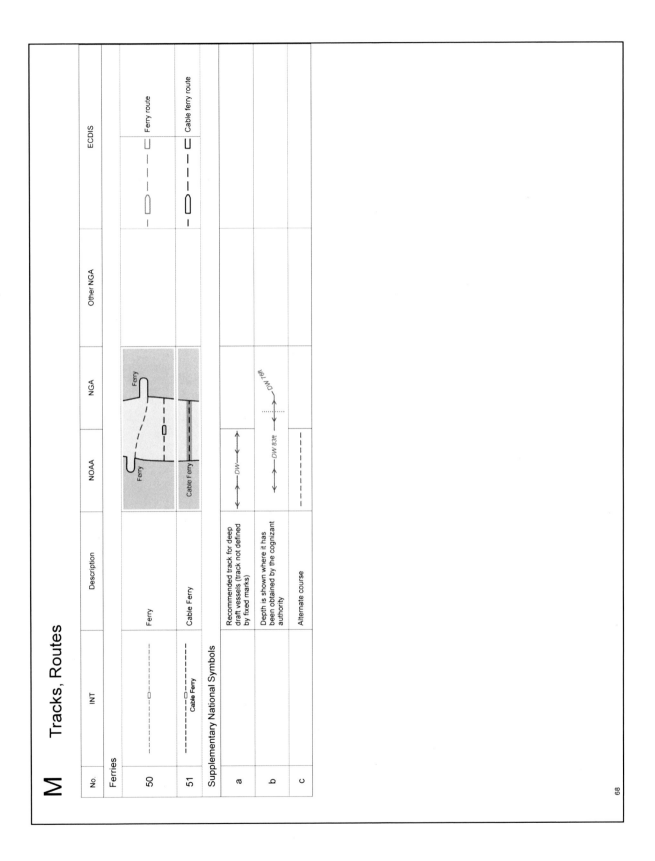 Ferry	Ferry		Ferry route
51	Cable Ferry	Cable Ferry	Cable Ferry			Cable ferry route
Supplementary National Symbols						
a		Recommended track for deep draft vessels (track not defined by fixed marks)	DW			
b		Depth is shown where it has been obtained by the cognizant authority	DW 83ft	DW 16ft		
c		Alternate course				

N
Areas, Limits

No.	INT	Description	NOAA	NGA	Other NGA	ECDIS
General *						
	Dredged and Swept Areas → I	Submarine Cables, Submarine Pipelines → L	Tracks, Routes → M			
1.1		Maritime limit in general, usually implying permanent physical obstructions (tint band for emphasis)				Caution area, a specific caution note applies
1.2		Maritime limit in general, usually implying no permanent physical obstructions (tint band for emphasis)				
2.1		Limit of restricted area	RESTRICTED AREA			Area where entry is prohibited or restricted or to be avoided
		Limit of restricted area, with tint band for emphasis				
2.2		Limit of area into which entry is prohibited	PROHIBITED AREA			Area where entry is prohibited or restricted or to be avoided, with other cautions
	Entry Prohibited		PROHIBITED AREA			Area where entry is prohibited or restricted or to be avoided, with other information
Anchorages, Anchorage Areas						
10		Reported anchorage (no defined limits)				
11.1		Anchor berths		14		Anchorage area as a point at small scale, or anchor points of mooring trot at large scale
11.2		Anchor berths with swinging circle	3	D17	6 / No 1	Anchor berth — Nr 6 — Radius of swing circle is obtained by cursor pick

* ECDIS represents many types of area limits with just a few different symbols. Information about the type of area and its associated restrictions or prohibitions may be obtained by cursor pick.

69

N   Areas, Limits

No.	INT	Description	NOAA	NGA	Other NGA	ECDIS
12.1		Anchorage area in general		Anchorage		
12.2	No 1	Numbered anchorage area		Anchorage No 1		Type of anchorage area is obtained by cursor pick
12.3	Name	Named anchorage area		Neufeld Anchorage		
12.4	DW	Deep water anchorage area, Anchorage area for deep draft vessels		DW Anchorage		
12.5	Tanker	Tanker anchorage area		Tanker Anchorage		
12.6	24 h	Anchorage area for periods up to 24 hours				
12.7		Explosives anchorage area	EXPLOSIVES ANCHORAGE			
12.8		Quarantine anchorage area	QUAR ANCH / QUARANTINE ANCHORAGE	Quarantine Anchorage		
12.9	Reserved (see Note)	Reserved anchorage area				

Note. Anchors as part of the limit symbol are not shown for small areas. Other types of anchorage areas may be shown.

No.	INT	Description	NOAA	NGA	Other NGA	ECDIS
13		Seaplane operating area	SEAPLANE LANDING AREA			Seaplane landing area
14		Anchorage for seaplanes				Type of anchorage area is obtained by cursor pick

70

203

Areas, Limits   N

Supplementary national symbols: d, e, g

No.	Description	INT	NOAA	NGA	Other NGA	ECDIS
Restricted Areas						
20	Anchoring prohibited		ANCH PROHIBITED	ANCH PROHIB		Area where anchoring is prohibited or restricted Area where anchoring is prohibited or restricted, with other cautions Area where anchoring is prohibited or restricted, with other information
21.1	Fishing prohibited		FISH PROHIBITED	FISH PROHIB		Area where fishing or trawling is prohibited or restricted Area where fishing or trawling is prohibited or restricted, with other cautions Area where fishing or trawling is prohibited or restricted, with other information

71

N Areas, Limits

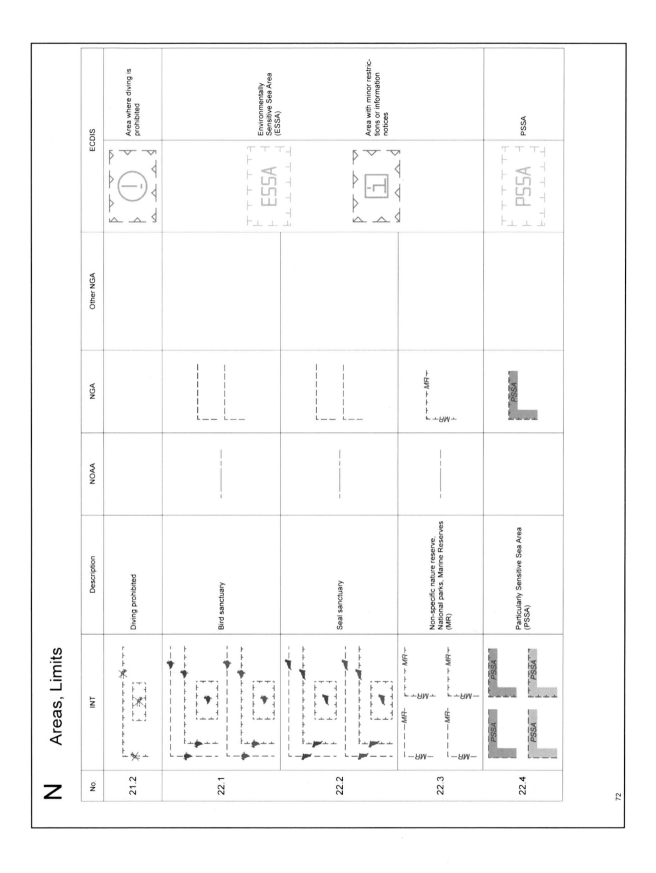

No.	INT	Description	NOAA	NGA	Other NGA	ECDIS
21.2		Diving prohibited				Area where diving is prohibited
22.1		Bird sanctuary				Environmentally Sensitive Sea Area (ESSA)
22.2		Seal sanctuary				Area with minor restrictions or information notices
22.3		Non-specific nature reserve, National parks, Marine Reserves (MR)		MR		
22.4		Particularly Sensitive Sea Area (PSSA)		PSSA		PSSA

72

Areas, Limits N

No.	INT	Description	NOAA	NGA	Other NGA	ECDIS
23.1	Explosives Dumping Ground	Explosives dumping ground, individual mine or explosive	EXPLOSIVES DUMPING AREA			Explosives or chemical dumping ground as a point
23.2	Explosives Dumping Ground (disused)	Explosives dumping ground (disused), Foul (explosives)	EXPLOSIVES DUMPING AREA DISUSED			Explosives or chemical dumping ground as an area
24	Dumping Ground for Chemicals	Dumping ground for chemical waste	Dump Site	Dumping Ground		
25	Degaussing Range	Degaussing range (DG range)	DEGAUSSING RANGE	DEGAUSSING RANGE		Degaussing area
27	5kn	Maximum speed				If a speed restriction exists, the speed limit is obtained by cursor pick
Military Practice Areas						
30		Firing practice area				Restricted area
31	Entry Prohibited	Military restricted area, entry prohibited	PROHIBITED AREA	Prohibited Area		Area where entry is prohibited or restricted or to be avoided, with other cautions
32		Mine-laying (and counter-measures) practice area				Restricted area
33		Submarine transit lane and exercise area			SUBMARINE EXERCISE AREA	Restricted area
34	Minefield (see note)	Minefield				Minefield
International Boundaries and National Limits					Supplementary national symbols: a, f, h	
40	CANADA UNITED STATES	International boundary on land				Jurisdiction boundary

N Areas, Limits

No.	INT	Description	NOAA	NGA	Other NGA	ECDIS
41	CANADA / UNITED STATES	International maritime boundary				Jurisdiction boundary
42	Log Pond (base point symbol)	Straight territorial sea baseline with base point				Straight territorial sea baseline
43		Seaward limit of territorial sea			TERRITORIAL SEA	Territorial sea
44		Seaward limit of contiguous zone				Contiguous zone
45		Limits of fishery zones				Limits of fishery zone
46	Continental Shelf	Limit of continental shelf				Continental shelf area
47	EEZ	Limit of Exclusive Economic Zone (EEZ)				Exclusive economic zone
48		Customs limit				Custom regulations zone
49	Harbor Limit	Harbor limit		Harbor Limit		Harbor area, symbolized

Various Limits

No.	INT	Description	NOAA	NGA	Other NGA	ECDIS
60.1	(2012)	Limit of fast ice, ice front (with date)				Continuous pattern for an ice area (glacier, etc.)
60.2	(2012)	Limit of sea ice (pack ice) seasonal (with date)				
61	Log Pond	Floating barrier, including log ponds, security barriers, ice booms, shark nets	Log boom			Floating hazard
						Boom, ice boom
						Boom, ice boom, floating obstruction, log pond
62.1	Spoil Ground	Spoil ground	Spoil Area			HO information note
62.2	Spoil Ground (disused)	Spoil ground (disused)	Spoil Area Discontinued			

Areas, Limits N

No.	INT	Description	NOAA	NGA	Other NGA	ECDIS
63	Extraction Area	Extraction (dredging) area				Dredging area
64	Cargo Transhipment Area	Cargo transhipment area				
65	Incineration Area	Incineration area				HO information note

Supplementary National Symbols

No.	INT	Description	NOAA	NGA	Other NGA	ECDIS
a		COLREGS demarcation line				
b		Limit of fishing area (fish trap areas)				
c		Dumping ground	Dumping Ground			
d		Dumping area (Dump site)	Disposal Area 92 / Depths from survey of 2010 85			
f		Reservation line (Options)				
g		Dump site	Dump Site			
h		Three Nautical Mile Line	THREE NAUTICAL MILE LINE			
i		No Discharge Zone	NO-DISCHARGE ZONE			

75

P   Lights

Light Structures and Major Floating Lights

Minor Light Floats → Q30, 31

No.	INT	Description	NOAA	NGA	Other NGA	ECDIS
1	Lt LtHo	Major light, minor light, light, lighthouse				Light, lighthouse, paper chart
2		Lighted offshore platform	PLATFORM (lighted)			Lighted offshore platform, paper chart
3	☆ BnTr	Lighted beacon tower	Marker o (lighted)			Lighted beacon tower, paper chart
4	☆ Bn	Lighted beacon				Lighted beacon, paper chart
5	☆ Bn	Articulated light, buoyant beacon, resilient beacon	o Art			
6		Major floating light (light vessel, major light float, LANBY)				Light vessel, paper chart

Note: Minor lights, fixed and floating, usually conform to IALA Maritime Buoyage System characteristics.

No.	INT	Description
7		Navigational lights on landmarks or other structures
8	310° ... Horns iso W 6s 32m 13M ... 320°	Important light off chart limits

Lights — P

Light Characters

Light Characters on Light Buoys → Q

No.	Abbreviation INT	Abbreviation NOAA	Class of light	Illustration		ECDIS
10.1	F	F	Fixed			
			Occulting (total duration of light longer than total duration of darkness)			
10.2	Oc	Oc	Single-occulting			
	Oc(2) Example	Oc(2)	Group-occulting			
	Oc(2+3) Example	Oc(2+3)	Composite group-occulting			
			Isophase (duration of light and darkness equal)			
10.3	Iso	Iso	Isophase			
			Flashing (total duration of light shorter than total duration of darkness)			
10.4	Fl	Fl	Single-flashing			When text for lights is displayed, ECDIS uses INT abbreviations.
	Fl(3) Example	Fl(3)	Group-flashing			
	Fl(2+1) Example	Fl(2+1)	Composite group-flashing			
10.5	LFl	LFl	Long-flashing (flash 2s or longer)			
			Quick (repetition rate of 50 to 79 - usually either 50 or 60 - flashes per minute)			
10.6	Q	Q	Continuous quick			
	Q(3) Example	Q(3)	Group quick			
	IQ	IQ	Interrupted quick			
			Very quick (repetition rate of 80 to 159 - usually either 100 or 120 - flashes per minute)			
10.7	VQ	VQ	Continuous very quick			
	VQ(3) Example	VQ(3)	Group very quick			
	IVQ	IVQ	Interrupted very quick			
			Ultra quick (repetition rate of 160 or more - usually 240 to 300 - flashes per minute)			
10.8	UQ	UQ	Continuous ultra quick			
	IUQ	IUQ	Interrupted ultra quick			

P   Lights

No.	Abbreviation INT	Abbreviation NOAA	Class of light	Illustration — Period shown	ECDIS
10.9	Mo(K) Example	Mo (K)	Morse Code	Mo (K)	When text for lights is displayed, ECDIS uses INT abbreviations.
10.10	FFl	F Fl	Fixed and flashing	F Fl	
10.11	Al.WR	AlWR	Alternating	Al WR	

No.	INT	Description	Illustration NOAA / NGA	Illustration Other NGA	ECDIS
11.1	W	White (only on sector and alternating lights)	Colors of lights shown on standard charts		Default light symbol if no color is encoded or color is other than red, green, white, yellow, amber, or orange
11.2	R	Red			Red
11.3	G	Green	on multicolored charts		Green
11.4	Bu	Blue			White, yellow, amber or orange
11.5	Vi	Violet			
11.6	Y	Yellow	on multicolored charts at sector lights		Sector lights
11.7	Or	Orange			
11.8	Am	Amber			

Period

No.					
12	2.5s 90s	Period in seconds and tenths of a second			

Elevation

Plane of reference for Heights → H   Tidal Levels → H

No.					
13	12m	Elevation of light given in meters or feet	36ft		

Range

No.					
14	15M	Light with single range			
	15/10M	Light with two different ranges	10M *only lesser of two ranges is charted*	15/10M	
	15-7M	Light with three or more ranges	7M *only least of three ranges is charted*		

Note: Charted ranges are nominal ranges given in Nautical Miles.

78

No.	INT	Description	NOAA	NGA	Other NGA	ECDIS
Disposition						
15	(hor)	Horizontally disposed				☀⚡ Disposition of light is obtained by cursor pick
	(vert)	Vertically disposed				
	(△ ▽)	3 lights disposed in the shape of a triangle				

Example of a Full Light Description

	INT	Description	NOAA / NGA	ECDIS
16	INT Example Name ☆ Fl(3)WRG.15s 21m15-11M		NOAA Example Name • Fl(3) WRG 15s 21ft 11M NGA Example Name • Fl(3) WRG 15s 21m15-11M	❯ FlR15s21m11M
	Fl(3)	Class of light: group flashing repeating a group of three flashes	Fl(3) Class of light: group flashing repeating a group of three flashes	The descriptions of non-sector lights are shown in ECDIS when the display of text is turned on, as shown above. (The aid to navigation or other structure that is always shown attached to a light flare in ECDIS is not depicted here.)
	WRG	Colors: white, red, green, exhibiting the different colors in defined sections	WRG Colors: white, red, green, exhibiting the different colors in defined sections	Sector lights (as described in the INT, NOAA and NGA examples at left) are depicted graphically in ECDIS, as shown below and in P40.
	15s	Period: the time taken to exhibit one full sequence of three flashes and eclipses: 15 seconds	15s Period: the time taken to exhibit one full sequence of three flashes and eclipses: 15 seconds	☀⚡ The description of a sector light or any other type of light may always be obtained by cursor pick.
	21m	Elevation of focal plane above datum: 21 meters	Elevation of light: 21ft 21 feet 21m 21 meters	
	15-11M	Nominal range: white 15M, green 11M, red between 15 and 11M	Nominal range: 11M shortest range of all the lights is 11M 15-11M white 15M, green 11M, red between 15 and 11M	

P   Lights

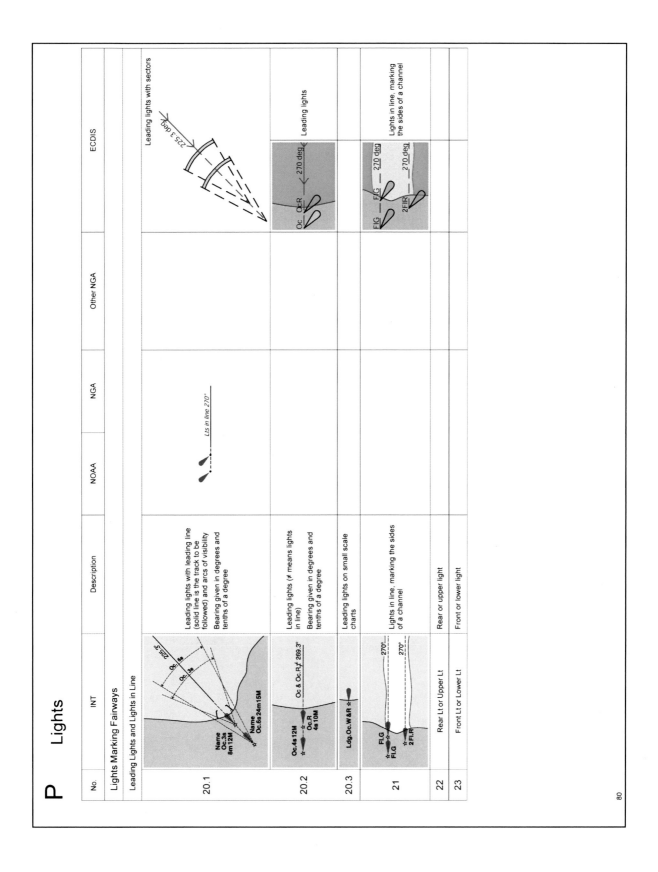

Lights Marking Fairways

Leading Lights and Lights in Line

No.	INT	Description	NOAA	NGA	Other NGA	ECDIS
20.1		Leading lights with leading line (solid line is the track to be followed) and arcs of visibility. Bearing given in degrees and tenths of a degree				Leading lights with sectors
20.2		Leading lights (≠ means lights in line). Bearing given in degrees and tenths of a degree				Leading lights
20.3		Leading lights on small scale charts				
21		Lights in line, marking the sides of a channel				Lights in line, marking the sides of a channel
22	Rear Lt or Upper Lt	Rear or upper light				
23	Front Lt or Lower Lt	Front or lower light				

Lights P

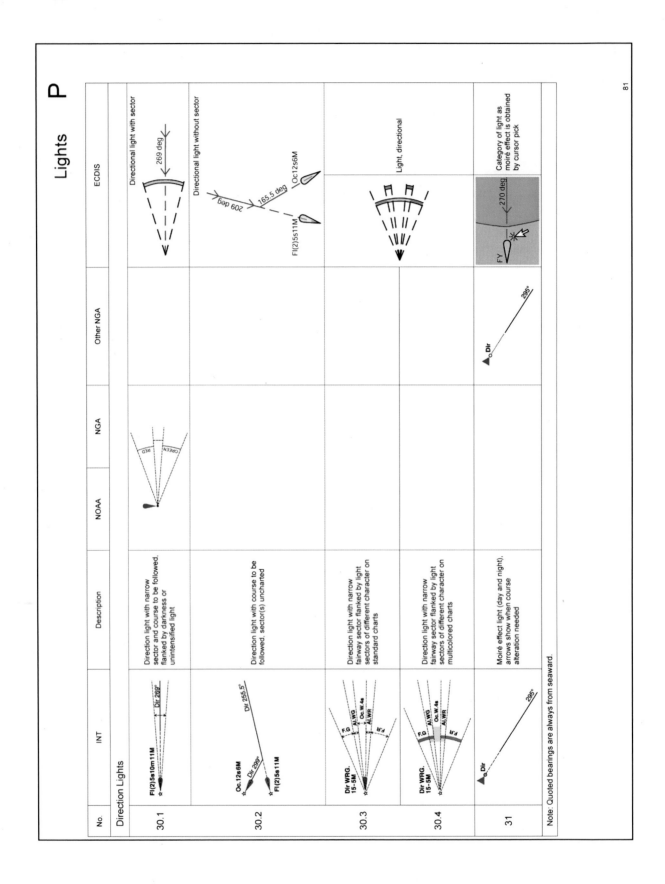

Direction Lights

No.	INT	Description	NOAA	NGA	Other NGA	ECDIS

Note: Quoted bearings are always from seaward.

81

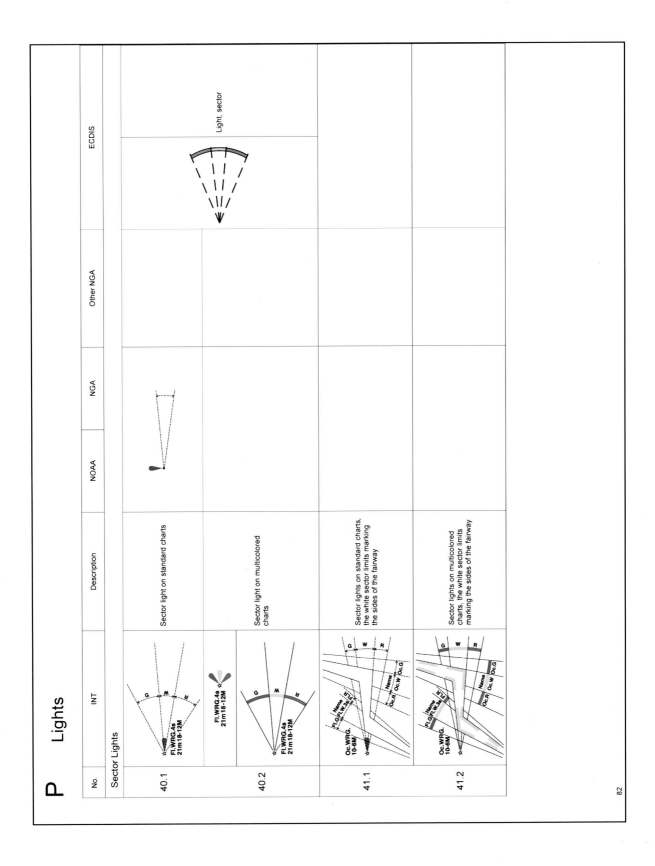

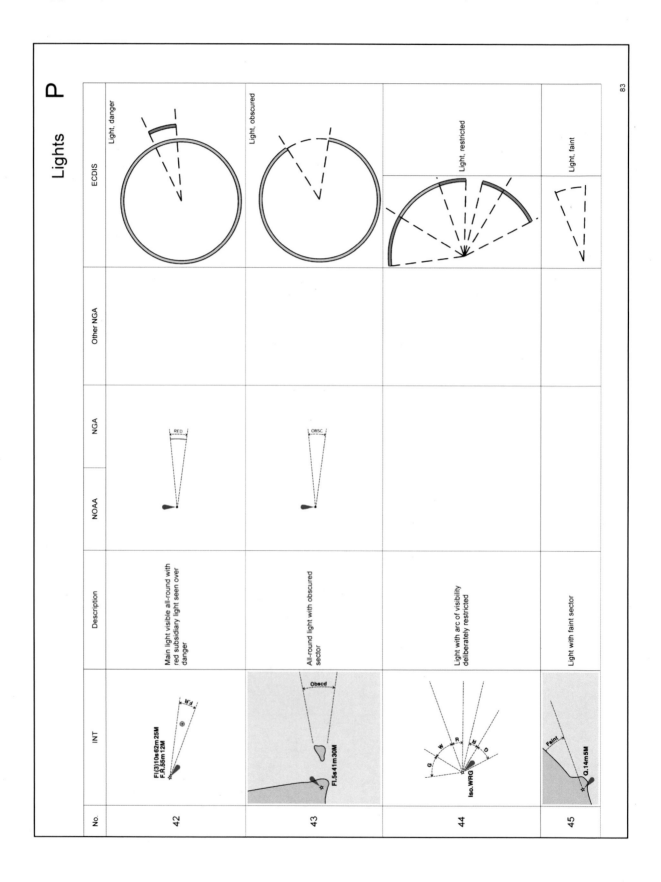

P Lights

No.	INT	Description	NOAA	NGA	Other NGA	ECDIS
46	Oc.R.8s7M / Oc.R.8s (R.5M R.9M)	Light with intensified sector				Intensified light visibility is obtained by cursor pick / Light, intensified

Lights with Limited Times of Exhibition

No.	INT	Description	NOAA	NGA	Other NGA	ECDIS
50	F.R.(occas)	Lights exhibited only when specially needed (for fishing vessels, ferries) and some private lights	Occas	F R (occas)		
51	Fl.10s40m27M (F.37m11M Day)	Daytime light (charted only where the character shown by day differs from that shown at night)		F Bu 9m 6M (F by day)		
52	Name Q.WRG.5m 10-3M (Fl.5s Fog)	Fog light (exhibited only in fog, or character changes in fog)				Status and condition of light is obtained by cursor pick
53	Fl.5s (U)	Unwatched (unmanned) light with no standby or emergency arrangements				
54	(temp)	Temporary				
55	(exting)	Extinguished				

Special Lights

Flare Stack (as sea) → L   Flare Stack (on land) → E   Signal Stations → T

No.	INT	Description	NOAA	NGA	Other NGA	ECDIS
60	Aero Al.Fl.WG.7.5s11M	Aero light (may be unreliable)	AERO	AERO Al WG 7.5s 108m 13M	AERO	AeroAlFlWG7.5s11M
61.1	Aero F.R.313m11M RADIO MAST (353)	Air obstruction light of high intensity (e.g. on radio mast)		AERO F R 77m 11M		AeroFR313m11M / Light
61.2	(89) (R Lts)	Air obstruction light of low intensity (e.g. on radio mast)		TR (RLts)		Conspicuous mast with light
62	Fog Det Lt	Fog detector light				Category of light is obtained by cursor pick
63	(Illuminated)	Floodlit, floodlighting of a structure				Floodlight

Lights P

No.	INT	Description	NOAA	NGA	Other NGA	ECDIS
64		Strip light				Strip light
65	(priv)	Private light other than one exhibited occasionally	! Priv	! F R (priv)	◇ ● Priv maintd	Status of private is obtained by cursor pick
66	(sync)	Synchronized light				
Supplementary National Symbols						
a		Riprap surrounding light				
b		Short-Long Flashing			S-L Fl	
c		Group-Short Flashing			G-S Fl	
d		Fixed and Group Flashing			F Gp Fl	
e		Unmanned light-vessel; light float			FLOAT	
f		LANBY, superbuoy as navigational aid				

ECDIS

Simplified and Traditional "Paper Chart" Symbols

ECDIS can be set to display aids to navigation with either traditional "paper chart" or simplified symbols. The two symbol sets are shown below. Some ECDIS color fill the paper chart buoy shapes, but this is not required by IHO ECDIS portrayal specifications.

Floating Marks

Paper Chart	Simplified	Simplified Symbol Name
		Cardinal buoy, north
		Cardinal buoy, east
		Cardinal buoy, south
		Cardinal buoy, west
		Default symbol for buoy (used when no defining attributes have been encoded in the ENC)
		Isolated danger buoy
		Conical lateral buoy, green
		Conical lateral buoy, red
		Can shape lateral buoy, green
		Can shape lateral buoy, red
		Installation buoy and mooring buoy
		Safe water buoy
		Special purpose buoy, spherical or barrel shaped, or default symbol for special purpose buoy
		Special purpose TSS buoy marking the starboard side of the traffic lane
		Special purpose TSS buoy marking the port side of the traffic lane
		Special purpose ice buoy or spar or pillar shaped buoy
		Super-buoy ODAS & LANBY
		Light float
		Light vessel

Fixed Marks

Paper Chart	Simplified	Simplified Symbol Name
		Cardinal beacon, north
		Cardinal beacon, east
		Cardinal beacon, south
		Cardinal beacon, west
		Default symbol for a beacon (used when no defining attributes have been encoded in the ENC)
		Isolated danger beacon
		Major lateral beacon, red
		Major lateral beacon, green
		Minor lateral beacon, green
		Major safe water beacon
		Minor safe water beacon
		Major special purpose beacon
		Minor special purpose beacon

* Paper chart symbols display various buoy or beacon shape symbols in conjunction with the topmark. Simplified portrayal only displays the topmark.

** Several different paper chart symbols correspond to this simplified symbol.

Day Marks

Paper Chart	Simplified	Simplified Symbol Name
		Square or rectangular daymark
		Triangular daymark, point up
		Triangular daymark, point down
		Retro reflector

86

Buoys, Beacons Q

No.	INT	Description	NOAA	NGA	Other NGA	ECDIS
Buoys and Beacons						
IALA Maritime Buoyage System, which includes Beacons → Q 130						
		Default buoy symbol if no other defining attribution is provided				Default symbol for buoy, paper chart / Default symbol for buoy, simplified
		Default beacon symbol if no other defining attribution is provided				Default symbol for a beacon, paper chart / Default symbol for a beacon, simplified
1		Position of buoy or beacon	°			ECDIS shows the position of buoys and beacons with a circle at the bottom of paper chart symbols. For simplified symbols, the position of the aid corresponds with the center of the symbol.
Colors of Buoys and Beacon Topmarks						Supplementary national symbols: p
Abbreviations for Colors → P						
2		Green and black (symbols filled black)				
3		Single color other than green and black				
4		Multiple colors in horizontal bands, the color sequence is from top to bottom				
5		Multiple colors in vertical or diagonal stripes, the darker color is given first				
6		Retroreflecting material				⠿ Retro reflector

Note: Retroreflecting material may be fitted to some unlit marks. Charts do not usually show it. Under IALA Recommendations, black bands will appear blue under a spotlight.

Lighted Marks

Marks with Fog Signals → R

No.	INT	Description	NOAA	NGA	Other NGA	ECDIS
7		Lighted marks on standard charts				
8		Lighted marks on multicolored charts				

Q Buoys, Beacons

No.	INT	Description	NOAA	NGA	Other NGA	ECDIS
		Topmarks and Radar Reflectors				
		For Application of Topmarks within the IALA System → Q 130	For other topmarks (special purpose buoys and beacons) → Q			
						Paper chart symbols for topmarks (on the left, below) are always displayed above a buoy or beacon shape symbol, as in Q 10 and Q 11.
						Simplified symbols (on the right, below) for cardinal marks, isolated dangers and safe water consist of only the topmark without the buoy shape symbol. Simplified symbology for marks with any other type of topmark will display only the simplified buoy or beacon shape symbol without a topmark.
						2 cones point upward
						2 cones point downward
						2 cones base to base
						2 cones point to point
						2 spheres
						Sphere
						Cone point up
						Cone point down
						Cylinder, square, vertical rectangle
						X-shape
						Flag or other shape
						Board, horizontal rectangle
						Cube point up
						Upright cross over a circle
						T-shape
9		IALA System buoy topmarks (beacon topmarks shown upright)				
10	No2	Beacon with topmark, color, radar reflector and designation	G "3" Ra Ref			bn No 2
11	No3	Buoy with topmark, color, radar reflector and designation		No 3		by No 3

Note: Radar reflectors on floating marks usually are not charted. ECDIS does not display radar reflectors on fixed or floating aids; this information is obtained by cursor pick.

88

221

Buoys, Beacons   Q

Buoys

Shapes of Buoys

Features Common to Buoys and Beacons → Q 1–11

No.	INT	Description	NOAA	NGA	Other NGA	ECDIS Paper Chart	ECDIS Simplified	
20		Conical buoy, nun buoy, ogival buoy	N					Conical buoy
21		Can buoy or cylindrical buoy	C					Can buoy
22		Spherical buoy	SP					Spherical buoy
23		Pillar buoy	P					Pillar buoy
24		Spar buoy, spindle buoy	S					Spar buoy
25		Barrel buoy, tun buoy						Barrel buoy
26		Superbuoy						Super-buoy / Lanby, super-buoy / Super-buoy odas & lanby

Minor Light Floats

No.	INT	Description	NOAA	NGA	Other NGA	ECDIS Paper Chart	ECDIS Simplified	
30	Fl.G.3s Name	Light float as part of IALA System						Light float
31	Fl.10s	Light float not part of IALA System						Light float

89

Q Buoys, Beacons

Mooring Buoys

Supplementary national symbols: m, n

Oil or Gas Installation Buoy → L

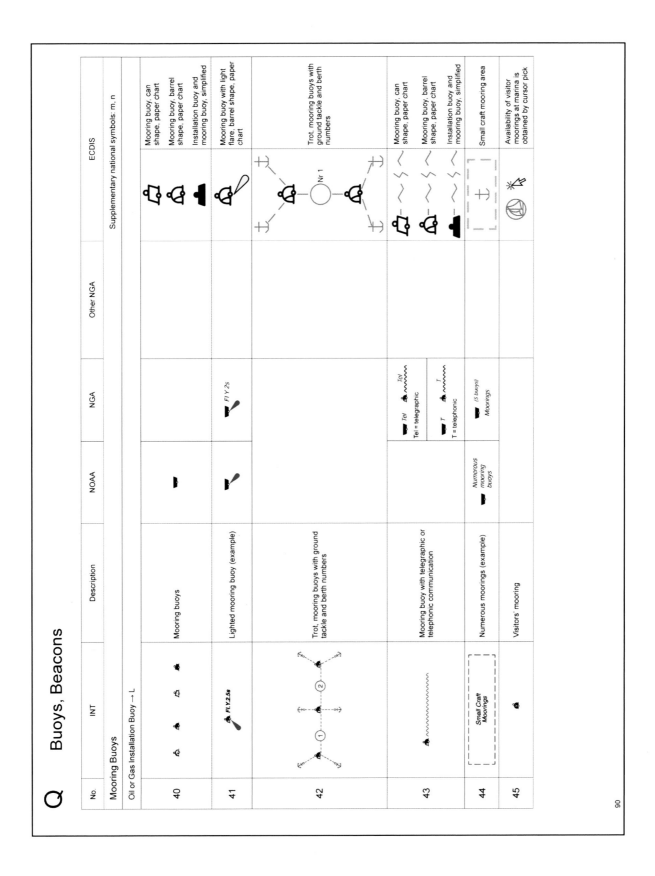

No.	INT	Description	NOAA	NGA	Other NGA	ECDIS
40		Mooring buoys				Mooring buoy, can shape, paper chart / Mooring buoy, barrel shape, paper chart / Installation buoy and mooring buoy, simplified
41	Fl.Y.2.5s	Lighted mooring buoy (example)		Fl Y 2s		Mooring buoy with light flare, barrel shape, paper chart
42		Trot, mooring buoys with ground tackle and berth numbers				Trot, mooring buoys with ground tackle and berth numbers Nr 1
43		Mooring buoy with telegraphic or telephonic communication		Tel Tel = telegraphic / T T = telephonic		Mooring buoy, can shape, paper chart / Mooring buoy, barrel shape, paper chart / Installation buoy and mooring buoy, simplified
44	Small Craft Moorings	Numerous moorings (example)	Numerous mooring buoys	(5 buoys) Moorings		Small craft mooring area
45		Visitors' mooring				Availability of visitor moorings at marina is obtained by cursor pick

Buoys, Beacons Q

Special Purpose Buoys

Note: Shapes of buoys are variable. Lateral or Cardinal buoys may be used in some situations.

No.	INT	Description	NOAA	NGA	Other NGA	ECDIS
						Purpose of buoy and other information is obtained by cursor pick
50	DZ	Firing danger area (Danger Zone) buoy				
51	Target	Target				
52	Marker Ship	Marker Ship				Conical buoy with topmark, paper chart
53	Barge	Barge				
54	DG	Degaussing Range buoy				
55	Cable	Cable buoy	Tel			Special purpose buoy, spherical or barrel shaped, or default symbol for special purpose buoy, simplified
56		Spoil ground buoy				
57		Buoy marking outfall				
58	ODAS ODAS	ODAS buoy (Ocean Data Acquisition System), data collecting buoy	ODAS	ODAS ODAS		Super-buoy, paper chart; Super-buoy odas & lanby, simplified; Spherical buoy, paper chart; Spherical buoy, simplified
59		Buoy marking wave recorder or current meter				Conical buoy with topmark, paper chart; Special purpose buoy, spherical or barrel shaped, or default symbol for special purpose buoy, simplified
60		Seaplane anchorage buoy	AERO			Conical buoy, paper chart
61		Buoy marking traffic separation scheme				
62		Buoy marking recreation zone				Conical buoy with topmark, paper chart
63	BUY BUY Al.Oc.BuY.3s	Emergency wreck marking buoy (EVMB)				

Q   Buoys, Beacons

No.	Description	INT	NOAA	NGA	Other NGA	ECDIS
Seasonal Buoys						
70	Buoy privately maintained (example)	⚑ (priv)	⚑ Priv		⚑ (occas) / ⚑ (01.04 – 31.10)	✳ Status as private is obtained by cursor pick
71	Seasonal buoy (example)	⚑ (Apr–Oct)				✳ Status as periodic and period start and stop dates are obtained by cursor pick
Beacons						Supplementary national symbols: o
Lighted Beacons → P	Features Common to Beacons and Buoys → Q1–11					
80	Beacon in general, characteristics unknown or chart scale too small to show	⊙ Bn	□ Bn	★ Bn G / ⊙ Bn R		Default symbol for a beacon, paper chart / Default symbol for a beacon, simplified / Beacon in general, paper chart
81	Beacon with color, no distinctive topmark	□ R BW	▲ R □ RW / ■ G □ Bn			✳ Beacon color is obtained by cursor pick / ✳ Beacon color is obtained by cursor pick
						See note at Q 9 for information about topmarks and ECDIS simplified symbology
82	Beacons with colors and topmarks (examples)	◄◄ BY / ●● BRB				Beacon in general with topmark, paper chart / Major red lateral beacon, simplified / Beacon in general with topmark, paper chart / Cardinal beacon, north, simplified / Beacon in general with topmark, paper chart / Isolated danger beacon, simplified
83	Beacon on submerged rock with colors (topmark as appropriate)	BRB		●● BRB		Beacon in general with topmark, paper chart / Isolated danger beacon, simplified

92

Buoys, Beacons — Q

No.	INT	Description	NOAA	NGA	Other NGA	ECDIS
Minor Impermanent Marks Usually in Drying Areas (Lateral Marks of Minor Channels)						
Minor Pile → F						
90		Stake, pole	Stake / Pole			Minor, stake or pole beacon, paper chart
91	Port Hand / Starboard Hand	Perch, withy				Minor, stake or pole beacon, paper chart
						Minor red lateral beacon, simplified
92		Withy				Minor green lateral beacon, simplified
Minor Marks, Usually on Land						
Landmarks → E						
100		Cairn	Cairn / CAIRN			Conspicuous cairn
						Square or rectangular day mark, paper chart
						Square or rectangular day mark, simplified
101		Colored or white mark				Triangular day mark, point up, paper chart
						Triangular day mark, point up, simplified
						Triangular day mark, point down, paper chart
						Triangular day mark, point down, simplified
102.1		Colored topmark (color known or unknown) with function of a beacon				
102.2		Painted boards with function of leading beacons				

93

226

Q Buoys, Beacons

Beacon Towers

No.	INT	Description	NOAA	NGA	Other NGA	ECDIS
110		Beacon towers without and with topmarks and colors (examples)				Beacon tower, paper chart Beacon tower with topmarks, paper chart Major red lateral beacon, simplified Major green lateral beacon, simplified
111		Lattice beacon				Lattice beacon, paper chart

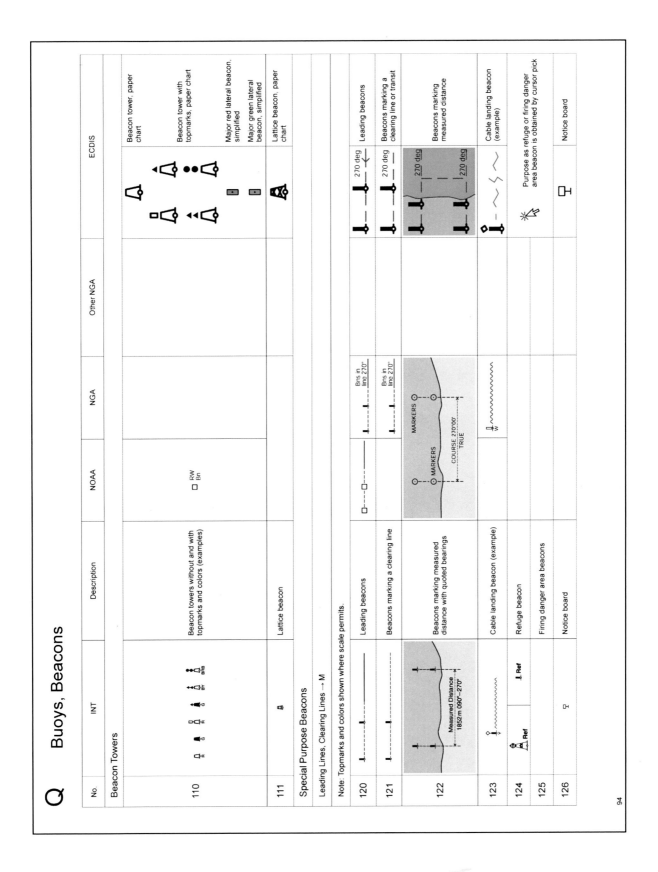

Special Purpose Beacons

Leading Lines, Clearing Lines → M

Note: Topmarks and colors shown where scale permits.

No.	INT	Description	NOAA	NGA	Other NGA	ECDIS
120		Leading beacons		Bns in line 270°		Leading beacons 270 deg
121		Beacons marking a clearing line		Bns in line 270°		Beacons marking a clearing line or transit 270 deg
122	Measured Distance 1852 m 090°–270°	Beacons marking measured distance with quoted bearings	MARKERS COURSE 270°00' TRUE MARKERS			Beacons marking measured distance 270 deg 270 deg
123		Cable landing beacon (example)		W		Cable landing beacon (example)
124	Ref Ref	Refuge beacon				Purpose as refuge or firing danger area beacon is obtained by cursor pick
125		Firing danger area beacons				
126		Notice board				Notice board

Appendix C

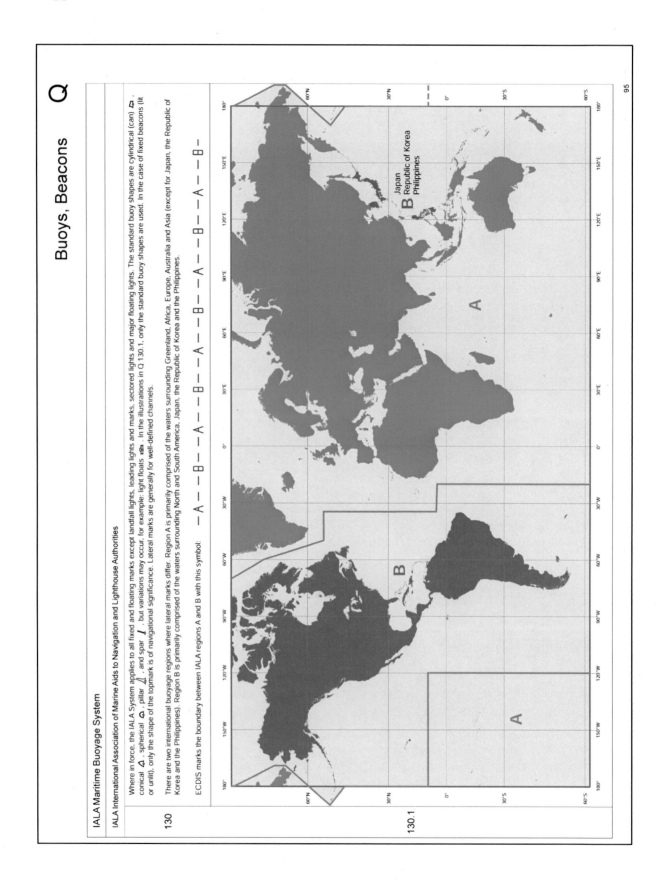

Q   Buoys, Beacons

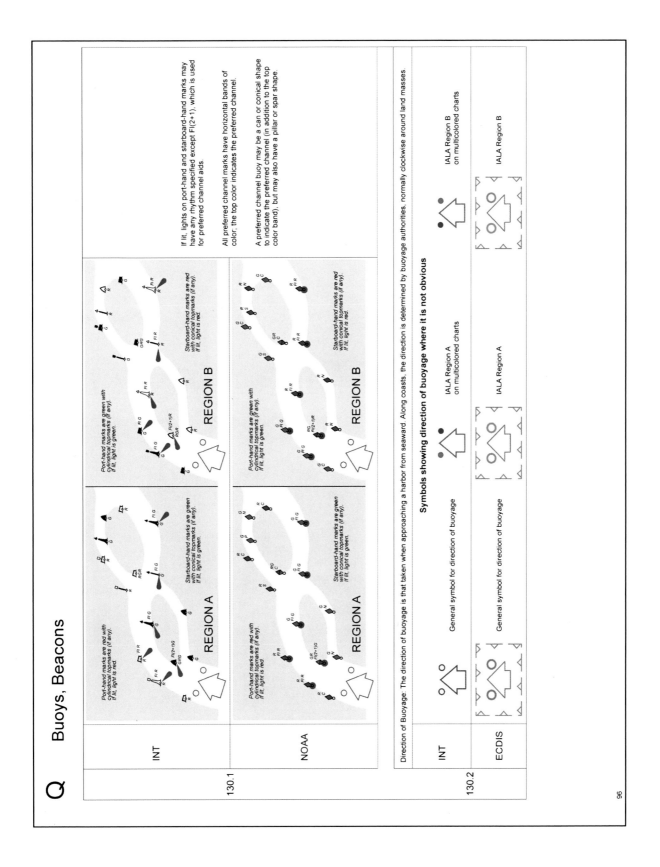

If lit, lights on port-hand and starboard-hand marks may have any rhythm specified except Fl(2+1), which is used for preferred channel aids.

All preferred channel marks have horizontal bands of color; the top color indicates the preferred channel.

A preferred channel buoy may be a can or conical shape to indicate the preferred channel (in addition to the top color band), but may also have a pillar or spar shape.

Direction of Buoyage: The direction of buoyage is that taken when approaching a harbor from seaward. Along coasts, the direction is determined by buoyage authorities, normally clockwise around land masses.

Symbols showing direction of buoyage where it is not obvious

Buoys, Beacons

Q

No.	INT	ECDIS

Cardinal Marks: indicating navigable water to the named side of the marks. In the illustration below all marks are the same in Regions A and B.

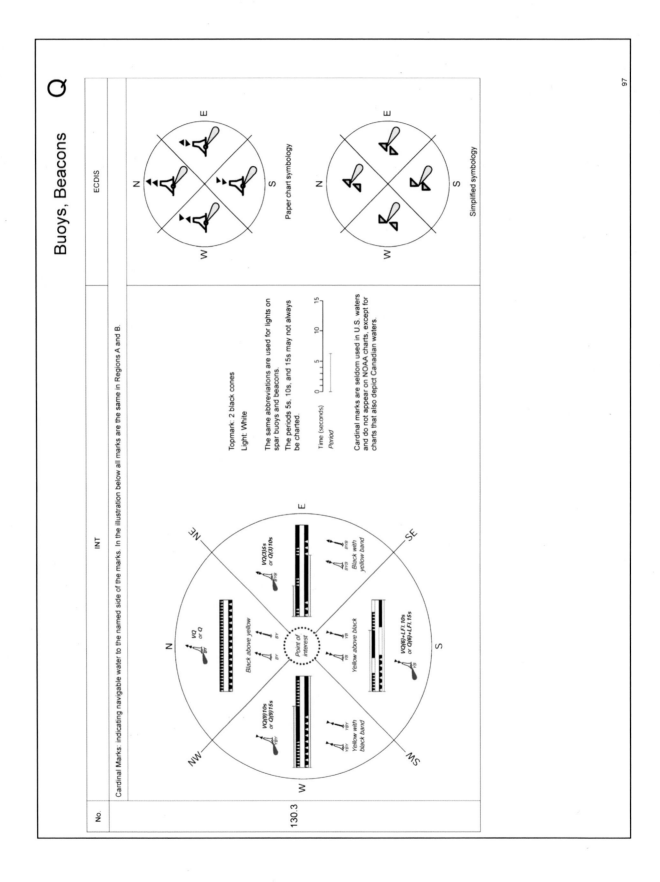

Topmark: 2 black cones
Light: White

The same abbreviations are used for lights on spar buoys and beacons.

The periods 5s, 10s, and 15s may not always be charted.

Cardinal marks are seldom used in U.S. waters and do not appear on NOAA charts, except for charts that also depict Canadian waters.

130.3

97

Q Buoys, Beacons

No.	INT	Description	NOAA	NGA	Other NGA	ECDIS
130.4		Isolated Danger Marks stationed over dangers with navigable water around them Body: black with red horizontal band(s) Topmark: 2 black spheres Light: white	BR			Pillar buoy with 2 spheres topmark Spar buoy with 2 spheres topmark Isolated danger buoy, simplified
130.5		Safe Water Marks such as mid-channel and landfall marks Body: red and white vertical stripes Topmark (if any): red sphere Light: white	RW			Spherical buoy, paper chart Pillar buoy with sphere topmark Spar buoy with sphere topmark Safe water buoy, simplified
130.6		Special Marks not primarily to assist navigation but to indicate special features Body (shape optional): yellow* Topmark (if any): yellow x or upright cross Lights: yellow, rhythm optional* *In special cases yellow may be in conjunction with another color	Y			Spherical buoy, paper chart Can buoy Conical buoy Spar buoy with x-shape topmark Special purpose buoy, simplified

Buoys, Beacons Q

No.	INT	Description	NOAA	NGA	Other NGA	ECDIS
Supplementary National Symbols						
a		Bell buoy	♦ BELL	⨍ BELL		
b		Gong buoy	♦ GONG	⨍ GONG		
c		Whistle buoy	♦ WHIS	⨍ WHIS		
d		Fairway buoy (red and white vertical stripe)	♦ RW			
e		Mid-channel buoy (red and white vertical stripe)	♦ RW			
f		Starboard-hand buoy (entering from seaward - US waters)	♦ R "2"			
g		Port-hand buoy (entering from seaward - US waters)	♦ G "1"	♦ "1"		
h		Bifurcation/Junction buoys	♦ RG ♦ GR			
		Isolated danger, Wreck or Obstruction buoy	♦ BR			
i		Fish trap (area) buoy	♦ Y			
j		Anchorage buoy (marks limits)	♦ Y			
l		Triangular shaped beacons	▲ R	△ RG Bn		
		Square shaped beacons	■ G □ GR Bn □ W Bn □ B Bn			
		Beacon, color unknown	□ Bn			
o		Lighted beacon	♦•	⬩	⬩ Bn	
q		Security barrier	─ ♦ Security barrier ♦ ─	─ ─ ♦ ─		
r		Scientific mooring buoy	♦			
s		Float (unlighted)	♦			
t		White and blue buoy		⨍ WBuW		

R   Fog Signals

General

No.	INT	Description	NOAA	NGA	Other NGA	ECDIS
	Fog Detector Light → P	Fog Light → P				
1	AIS	Position of fog signal, type of fog signal not stated	Fog Sig			Position of a conspicuous point feature with fog signal
						Lighted pillar buoy, paper chart with fog signal
						Lighted super-buoy, paper chart with fog signal

Types of Fog Signals, with Abbreviations

No.	INT	Description	NOAA	NGA	Other NGA	ECDIS
						Supplementary national symbol: a
10	Explos	Explosive	GUN			
11	Dia	Diaphone	DIA			
12	Siren	Siren	SIREN			Type of fog signal and its characteristics are obtained by cursor pick
13	Horn	Horn (nautophone, reed, tyfon)	HORN			
14	Bell	Bell	BELL			
15	Whis	Whistle	WHISTLE			
16	Gong	Gong	GONG			

Examples of Fog Signal Descriptions

Note: The the fog signal symbol will usually be omitted when a description of the signal is given.

No.	INT	Description	NOAA	NGA	Other NGA	ECDIS
20	Fl.3s70m29M ☆ Siren Mo(N)60s	Siren at a lighthouse, giving a long blast followed by a short one (N), repeated every 60 seconds	Fl 3s 70m 29M SIREN Mo(N) 60s	Fl 3s 70m 29M SIREN		Light with fog signal
21	Bell	Wave-actuated bell buoy	BELL	BELL		Pillar buoy, paper chart with fog signal
22	Q(6)+LFl.15s Horn(1)15sWhis	Light buoy, with horn giving a single blast every 15 seconds, in conjunction with a wave-actuated whistle	Q(6)+LFl 15s HORN(1) 15s WHIS	Q(6)+LFl 15s HORN WHIS		Paper Chart / Simplified — Lighted pillar buoy, paper chart with fog signal

Supplementary National Symbol

No.	INT	Description	NOAA	NGA	Other NGA	ECDIS
a		Morse Code fog signal	Mo			

100

Radar, Radio, Satellite Navigation Systems S

Radar

Radar Structures Forming Landmarks → E   Radar Surveillance Systems → M

No.	INT	Description	NOAA	NGA	Other NGA	ECDIS
1	Ra	Coast radar station, providing range and bearing service on request	Ra			◯ Radio station
2	Ramark	Ramark, radar beacon transmitting continuously	Ramark			
3.1	Racon(Z)(3cm)	Radar transponder beacon, with morse identification, responding within the 3 cm (X) band	RACON			
3.2	Racon(Z)(10cm)	Radar transponder beacon, with morse identification, responding within the 10 cm (S) band				
3.3	Racon(Z)	Radar transponder beacon, with morse identification			Racon (Z) (3 & 10 cm)	(dashed circle) Radar transponder beacon
3.4	Racon(Z) (sector diagrams: Racon Obscd / Racons ‡ 270°)	Radar transponder beacon with sector of obscured reception / Radar transponder beacon with sector of reception				
3.5	Racon / Racons ‡ 270° / Lts ‡ 270° Racons ‡ 270°	Leading radar transponder beacons (‡: objects in line) / Leading radar transponder beacons coincident with leading lights				
3.6	Racon	Radar transponder beacons on floating marks	RACON (-) R "2" Fl R 4s	Racon		Paper Chart / Simplified — Radar transponder on floating mark
4		Radar reflector	Ra Ref			
5		Radar conspicuous feature	Ra (conspic)			☼ Symbol indicating this object is radar conspicuous

101

S Radar, Radio, Satellite Navigation Systems

Radio

Radio Structures Forming Landmarks → E

Radio Reporting (Calling-in or Way) points → M

No.	INT	Description	NOAA	NGA	Other NGA	ECDIS
10	Name RC	Circular (non-directional) marine or aeromarine radiobeacon	RC	R Bn		Radio station
11	RD 269.5° / RD / Lts ≠ 270° RD 270° / RD	Directional radiobeacon with bearing line / Directional radiobeacon coincident with leading lights	RD	RD 270°		
12	RW	Rotating pattern radiobeacon	RW	RW		Additional information regarding radio, such as category of radio station, signal frequency, communication channel, call sign, estimated signal range, periodicity and status may be included in the cursor pick.
13	Consol	Consol beacon	CONSOL Bn 190 kHz MMF ⁻·⁻	CONSOL		The presence of an AIS transmitted signal intended for use as an aid to navigation associated with a physical aid, including the AIS MMSI Number, can be obtained by cursor pick on the physical aid.
14	RG	Radio direction-finding station	RDF	RDF		
15	R	Coast radio station providing QTG service	R Sta	R		
16	Aero RC	Aeronautical radiobeacon		AERO R Bn		
17.1	AIS	Automatic Identification System transmitter				
17.2	AIS	Automatic Identification System transmitter on floating marks (examples)				
18.1	V-AIS	Virtual AIS (with unknown IALA-defined function)				
18.2	V-AIS	Virtual AIS (with known IALA-defined function)			V-AIS	North cardinal virtual aid

Satellite Navigation Systems

No.	INT	Description	NOAA	NGA	Other NGA	ECDIS
50	WGS WGS72 WGS84	World Geodetic System, 1972 or 1984				
		Note: A note may be shown to indicate the shifts of latitude and longitude, to one, two or three decimal places of a minute, depending on the chart scale, which should be made to satellite-derived positions (which are referred to WGS 84) to relate them to the chart.				
51	DGPS	Station providing DGPS corrections				DGPS reference station

102

Services T

No.	INT	Description	NOAA	NGA	Other NGA	ECDIS
Pilotage						
1.1	⬥	Boarding place, position of a pilot cruising vessel	⬥ *Pilots*			Pilot boarding place
1.2	⬥ *Name*	Boarding place, position of a pilot cruising vessel, with name (e.g. District, Port)		⬥ *Name*		
1.3	⬥ *Note*	Boarding place, position of a pilot cruising vessel, with note (e.g. Tanker, Disembarkation)		⬥ (see note)		Pilot boarding area
1.4	⬥ *H*	Pilots transferred by helicopter				
2	⌐ Pilot Lookout	Pilot office with pilot lookout, Pilot lookout station				
3	■ Pilots	Pilot office	⊙ PIL STA	■ Pilots		
4	Port name (Pilots)	Port with pilotage service (boarding place not shown)				
Coast Guard, Rescue						
10	■ CG ⊙ CG ᵖ CG	Coast Guard station		✦ C G		Coast guard station
11	■ CG ✦ ⊙ CG ✦ ᵖ CG ✦	Coast Guard station with Rescue station		⊙ R T R C G WALLIS SANDS		Coast guard station / Rescue station
12	✦	Rescue station, Lifeboat station, Rocket station		✦ LS S		Rescue station
13	⚓ ✦	Lifeboat lying at a mooring				
14	Ref	Refuge for shipwrecked mariners				
Signal Stations						
20	⊙ SS	Signal station in general	⊙ SS		⊗ Sig Sta	Signal station
21	⊙ SS (INT)	Signal station, showing international port traffic signals				
22	⊙ SS (Traffic)	Traffic signal station, Port entry and departure signals				
23	⊙ SS (Port Control)	Port control signal station	⊙ HECP			

T Services

No.	INT	Description	NOAA	NGA	Other NGA	ECDIS
24	SS (Lock)	Lock signal station				
25.1	SS (Bridge)	Bridge passage signal station				
25.2	Traffic-Sig	Bridge lights including traffic signals				
26	SS	Distress signal station				
27	SS	Telegraph station				
28	SS (Storm)	Storm signal station	S Sig Sta			
29	SS (Weather)	Weather signal station, Wind signal station, National Weather Service (NWS) signal station	NWS SIG STA			SS Signal station
30	SS (Ice)	Ice signal station				
31	SS (Time)	Time signal station				
32.1		Tide scale or gauge		o Tide Gauge		
32.2	Tide Gauge	Automatically recording tide gauge				
33	SS (Tide)	Tide signal station				
34	SS (Stream)	Tidal stream signal station				
35	SS (Danger)	Danger signal station				
36	SS (Firing)	Firing practice signal station				

Supplementary National Symbols

a		Bell (on land)	o BELL			
b		Marine police station	o MARINE POLICE			
c		Fireboat station	o FIREBOAT STATION			
d		Notice board				
e		Lookout station; Watch tower		⊙ LOOK TR		
f		Semaphore	Sem			
g		Park Ranger station				

104

237

Appendix C

Small Craft (Leisure) Facilities   U

No.	INT	Description	NOAA	NGA	Other NGA	ECDIS

Small Craft (Leisure) Facilities

Traffic Features, Bridges → D   Public Buildings, Cranes → F   Pilots, Coast Guard, Rescue, Signal Stations → T

Marina facilities

a

NO	LOCATION	APPROACH-FEET (REPORTED)	ALONGSIDE-FEET (REPORTED)	ELECTRICITY-MOORINGS-BERTHS (TRANSIENTS)	RAMP SURFACED-NATURAL	REPAIRS HULL-MOTOR-RADIO	MARINE RAILWAY-FEET	LIFT CAPACITY-TONS	CANOE-ROW-MOTOR	CHARTER-HOUSE-SAIL	FOOD-LODGING-CAMPING	TOILETS-SHOWERS-LAUNDRY	PUMP-OUT STATION	WINTER STORAGE WET-DRY	NAUTICAL CHART SALES	WATER-ICE	GROCERIES-HARDWARE	BAIT-TACKLE	DIESEL OIL-GASOLINE
1	LAS VEGAS BOAT	80	20		S	HM			M		F C	T	P	WD	C	WI	GH	BT	G
2	LAKE MEAD MAR	80	15	B E	S	HM			M		FL	T	P	WD	C	WI			DG
3	HEMENWAY HARBOR	80			S	SN													
4	TEMPLE BAR HAR	80	15		SN	M			M	H	FLC	TSL	P	WD	C	WI	GH	BT	G
5	ECHO BAY RESORT	35	35	BM		M			M	H	FLC	TSL		WD	C	WI	GH		G
6	OVERTON BEACH	100			S	M			M	H	F C	TSL		WD		WI	G	BT	G
7	CALLVILLE BAY M	100	40		S	M			M	H	F C	TS	P	WD		WI	G	B	G

(-) DENOTES HOURS LATER   (+) DENOTES HOURS EARLIER
THE LOCATIONS OF THE ABOVE PUBLIC MARINE FACILITIES ARE SHOWN ON THE CHART BY LARGE PURPLE NUMBERS.
THE TABULATED "APPROACH-FEET (REPORTED)" IS THE DEPTH AVAILABLE FROM THE NEAREST NATURAL OR DREDGED CHANNEL TO THE FACILITY.
THE TABULATED "PUMPING STATION" IS DEFINED AS FACILITIES AVAILABLE FOR PUMPING OUT BOAT HOLDING TANKS.
(H) APPROACH DEPTH FLUCTUATES WITH LAKE LEVELS.

†

Index of Abbreviations

Note: INT abbreviations are in bold type

106

239

Index of Abbreviations

Note: INT abbreviations are in bold type

Abbreviation	Term	Ref.
D		
D.	Destroyed	
dec.	Decayed	
Dec.	December	J an
Deg.	Degree(s)	
Destr.	Destroyed	B n
dev	Deviation	B 67
DF	Direction Finder	
DG	**Degaussing Range**	N 25, Q 54
DGPS	**Differential Global Positioning System**	S 51
Di	Diatoms	J aa
DIA, Dia	Diaphone	R 11
Dir.	Direction light	P 30-31
Discol	Discolored	K e
dist	Distant	
dk	Dark	J bd
dm	**Decimeter(s)**	B 42
Dn, Dns	**Dolphin(s)**	F 20
Dol	Dolphin(s)	F 20
DW	**Deep Water route**	M 27.1, N 12.4
DZ	**Danger Zone**	Q 50
E		
E	**East**	B 10
ED	**Existence Doubtful**	I 1
EEZ	**Exclusive Economic Zone**	N 47
Entr.	Entrance	
ESSA	**Environmentally Sensitive Sea Area**	N 22
Est	Estuary	
exper.	Experimental	
Explos	**Explosive**	R 10
Exting, exting	Extinguished	P 55
F		
F	**Fixed**	P 10.1
f	Fine	J 30
F Fl	**Fixed and flashing**	P 10.10
F Gp Fl	Fixed and Group Flashing	P f
Facty	Factory	E d
FAD	**Fish Aggregating Device**	
Fd	Fjord	
Feb.	February	
FISH	**Fishing**	N 21
Fl	**Flashing**	P 10.4
fl	Flood	H q
Fla	**Flare stack**	L 11
fly	Flinty	J ao
fm, fms	Fathom(s)	B 48
fne	Fine	J 30
Fog Det Lt	**Fog detector light**	P 62
Fog Sig	Fog Signal	R 1
FP	Flagpole	E 27
FPSO	**Floating Production, Storage and Offloading Vessel**	L 17
Fr	Foraminifera	J y
Fs, FS	**Flagstaff**	E 27
Fsh stks	Fishing stakes	K 44.1
FT, ft	**Foot, Feet**	B 47, D 20
Fu	Fucus	J af
G		
G	**Gravel**	J 6
G	**Green**	P 11.3, Q 2
G.	Gulf	
GAB, Gab	Gable	E i
GCLWD	Gulf Coast Low Water Datum	H k
Gl	Globigerina	J z
glac.	Glacial	J ap
gn	Green	J av
Govt Ho	Government House	E m
Gp Fl	Group flashing	P 10.4
Gp Oc	Group occulting	P 10.2
GPS	**Global Positioning System**	
Grd	Ground	J a
Grs	Grass	J v
grt	**Gross Register Tonnage**	
GT	**Gross Tonnage**	
gty	Gritty	J am
gy	Gray	J bb
H		
H	**Helicopter**	T 1.4
h	Hard	J 39
h	Hour	B 49
HAT	Highest Astronomical Tide	H 3
Hbr Mr	Harbormaster	F 60
HHW	Higher High Water	H b
Hk	Hulk	F 34, K 21, 22
Ho	House	
hor	**Horizontally disposed**	P 15
Hor CL	Horizontal clearance	D 21
Hosp.	Hospital	E g, F 62.2
hr	Hour	B 49

107

Index of Abbreviations

Note: INT abbreviations are in bold type

hrd	Hard	J 39
ht.	Height	H p
HW	High Water	H a
HWF&C	High Water Full & Change	H h
Hz.	Hertz	B g

I

IALA	International Association of Lighthouse Authorities*	Q 130
IHO.	International Hydrographic Organization	
illum	Illuminated	P 63
IMO.	International Maritime Organization	
In.	Inlet.	
in, ins	Inch(es)	B c
Inst	Institute	E n
INT	**International**	A 2, T 21
Intens	Intensified	P 46
IQ	Interrupted quick	P 10.6
ISLW	Indian Spring Low Water	H g
Iso	Isophase	P 10.3
ITZ	Inshore Traffic Zone	M 25.1
IUQ	Interrupted ultra quick	P 10.8
IVQ	Interrupted very quick	P 10.7

J

Jan	January	
Jul	July	
Jun	June	

K

K	Kelp	J u
kc	Kilocycle	B k
kHz	Kilohertz	B h
km	**Kilometer(s)**	B 40
kn	**Knot(s)**	B 52

L

L	Lake, loch, lough	
L Fl	**Long-flashing**	P 10.5
La	Lava	J l
Lag	Lagoon	
LANBY	**Large Automatic Navigational Buoy**	P 6
LASH	Lighter Aboard Ship	
LAT	Lowest Astronomical Tide	H 2
Lat	Latitude	B 1
Ldg	Landing	F 17
Ldg	**Leading Lights**	P 20.3

Le	Ledge	H e
LLW	Lower Low Water	F 17
Lndg.	**Landing for boats**	
LNG	**Liquefied Natural Gas**	
LoLo	Load-on, Load-off	
Long.	Longitude	B 2
LPG	**Liquefied Petroleum Gas**	
Lrg	Large	J ai
LS S	Life saving station	T 12
lt	Light	J bc
Lt Ho.	Light house	P 1
Lt, Lt(s)	**Light(s)**	P 1
Ltd.	Limited	E r
LW	Low Water	H c
LWD	Low Water Datum.	H d
LWF&C	Low Water Full and Change	H i

M

M.	**Mud, muddy**	J 2
M.	Nautical mile(s).	B 45
m	Medium (in relation to sand)	J 31
m	**Meter(s)**	B 41
m	Minute(s) of time	B 50
Ma.	Mattes	J ag
mag.	Magnetic	B 61
Magz.	Magazine	E l
Maintd	Maintained	P 65
Mar	March	
Mc.	Megacycles	B l
Mds	Madrepores	J j
MHHW	Mean Higher High Water	H 13
MHLW	Mean Higher Low Water.	H 14
MHW.	Mean High Water	H 5
MHWN	Mean High Water Neaps	H 11
MHWS	Mean High Water Springs	H 9
Mi.	Nautical mile(s).	B 45
min	Minimum.	K 46.2
min	Minute(s) of time.	B 50
Mk.	**Mark**	Q 101
Ml	Marl.	J c
MLHW.	Mean Lower High Water.	H 15
MLLW	Mean Lower Low Water	H 12
MLW.	Mean Low Water	H 4

*Now known as the International Association of Marine Aids to Navigation and Lighthouse Authorities, the organization formerly called the International Association of Lighthouse Authorities/Association Internationale de Signalisation Maritime (IALA/AISM) continues to use IALA as an abbreviation for its full name.

108

Index of Abbreviations

Note: INT abbreviations are in bold type

MLWN	Mean Low Water Neaps	H 10
MLWS	Mean Low Water Springs	H 8
mm	**Millimeter(s)**	B 44
Mn	Manganese	J q
Mo	Morse Code	P 10.9, R 20
MON. Mon	**Monument**	E 24
MR	**Marine Reserve**	N 22
MRCC	**Maritime Rescue and Coordination Center**	
Ms	Mussels	J s
MSL	Mean Sea Level	H 6
Mt	Mountain, Mount.	
Mth	Mouth	
MTL	Mean Tide Level	H f

N

N	**North**	B 9
N.	Nun	Q 20
NE	**Northeast**	B 13
NGA	National Geospatial-Intelligence Agency	
NM	Nautical mile(s)	B 45
NMi	Nautical miles(s)	B 45
No	**Number**	N 12.2
NOAA	National Oceanic and Atmospheric Administration.	
NOS	National Ocean Service	
Nov	November	
Np	Neap tide	H 17
NT	**Net Tonnage**	
NTM	Notice to Mariners	
NW	**Northwest**	B 15
NWS SIG STA	National weather service signal station	T 29

O

Obs Spot	Observation spot	B 21
OBSC. Obscd	**Obscured**	P 43
Obstn	Obstruction	K 41
Oc	Occulting	P 10.2
Occas	Occasional	P 50
Oct	October	
ODAS	**Ocean Data Acquisition System**	Q 58
Or	**Orange**	P 11.7
OVHD	Overhead	D 28
Oys	Oysters	J r

P

P	**Pebbles**	J 7
P	Pillar	Q 23
(P)	Preliminary (NTM)	

PA	**Position approximate**	B 7
Pass	Passage, Pass	
Pav	Pavilion	E p
PD	**Position doubtful**	B 8
Pk	Peak	
PLT STA	Pilot station	T 3
Pm	Pumice	J m
PO	Post office	F 63
Po	Polyzoa	J ad
pos. posn	Position	
Post Off	Post office	F 63
Priv, priv	**Private**	P 65, Q 70
Prod well	**Production well**	L 20
PROHIB	Prohibited	N 2.2
PSSA	**Particularly Sensitive Sea Area**	N 22
Pt	Pteropods	J ac
Pyl	**Pylon**	D 26

Q

Q	**Quick**	P 10.6
QTG	Service providing DF signals	S 15
Quar	Quarantine	F e
Qz	Quartz	J g

R

R	**Coast radio station providing QTG service**	S 15
R	Radio Station	S 15
R	**Red**	P 11.2
R, r	**Rock, Rocky**	J 9.1, K b
R Bn	Circular radiobeacon	S 10
R Lts	Air obstruction lights	P 61.2
R Mast	Radio mast	E 28
R Sta	Radio Station	S 15
R Tower	Radio tower	E 29
R TR, R Tr	Radio tower	E 29
Ra	**Radar**	M 31-32, S 1
Ra	Radar reference line	M 32.1
Ra (conspic)	Radar conspicuous object	S 5
Ra Ref	Radar reflector	S 4
Racon	**Radar transponder beacon**	S 3
Radar Sc.	Radar scanner	E 30.3
Radar Tr, RADAR TR	Radar tower	E 30.2
Ramark	Radar marker beacon	S 2
RC	**Circular radiobeacon**	S 10
RD	**Directional radiobeacon**	S 11
Rd	Radiolaria	J ab

Index of Abbreviations

Note: INT abbreviations are in bold type

Rd.	Road, roadstead	J ay
rd	Red	S 14
RDF	Radio direction finding station	Q 124
Ref	**Refuge**	I 3
Rep	Reported	
Rf	Reef	S 14
RG	**Radio direction finding station**	J 9.1, K b
Rk.	Rocks	J 9.1
Rky	Rocky	F 50
RoRo	Roll-on, Roll-off Ferry (RoRo Terminal)	J aj
rt	Rotten	D 8, E 25.2, F33
Ru, (ru)	**Ruin, ruined**	S 12
RW	Rotating-pattern radiobeacon	
S	**Sand**	J 1
S	**South**	B 11
S	Spar, spindle	Q 24
s	**Second(s) of time**	B 51, P 12
SALM	**Single Anchor Leg Mooring**	L 16
SBM	**Single Buoy Mooring**	L 16
Sc	Scanner	E 30.3
Sc	Scoriae	J o
Sch	Schist	J h
Sch	School	E f
SD	Sailing Directions	
Sd	Sound	I 2
SD.	Sounding doubtful	I 2
SE	**Southeast**	B 14
sec	Seconds of time	B 51
Sep	September	
sf	**Stiff**	J 36
sft	Soft	J 35
Sh	**Shells**	J 11
Shl	Shoal	
Si	Silt	J 4
Sig	**Signal**	R 1, T 25.2
Sig Sta	Signal station	T 20
S-L Fl	Short-Long Flashing	P b
S/M	Sand over mud	J 12.1
sml	Small	J ah
SMt.	**Seamount**	J d
Sn	Shingle	J 35
so	**Soft**	J 35
Sp.	Church spire	E 10.3

SP.	Spherical	Q 22
Sp.	spire	E 10.3
Sp.	Spring tide	H 16
Spg	Sponge	J t
Spi	Spicules	J x
Spipe, S'pipe	Standpipe	E 21
spk	Speckled	J al
SPM	**Single Point Mooring**	L 12
SS	**Signal station**	T 20-36
St	**Stones**	J 5
St M, St Mi	Statute mile(s)	B e
STA, Sta	Station	F 41.1, S 15, T 3
stf	Stiff	J 36
Stg	Sea-tangle	J w
stk	Sticky	J 34
Str	Strait	H l
Str	Stream	
str	Streaky	J ak
sub	Submarine	K d
Subm	Submerged	K 43.1
SW	**Southwest**	B 16
sy	**Sticky**	J 34
T	Short ton(s)	B m
T	Telephone	E q
T	TRUE	B 63
T	Tufa	J n
t	**Ton(s), Tonnage (weight)**	B 53, F 53
Tel	Telegraph	D 27
Tel off	Telegraph office	E k
Temp, temp	**Temporary**	P 54
ten.	Tenacious	J aq
Tk	Tank	E 32
TR, Tr, Trs	**Tower(s)**	E 10.2, E 20
TSS	Traffic Separation Scheme	M 20.1
TT	Tree tops	C 14
TV Mast	Television mast	E 28
TV Tower	Television tower	E 29
ULCC	**Ultra Large Crude Carrier**	K 11
Uncov	Uncovers	J bf
unev	Uneven	E h
Univ	University	
UQ	**Ultra quick**	P 10.8

110

Index of Abbreviations

Note: INT abbreviations are in bold type

| UTC | Coordinated Universal Time | |
| UTM | Universal Transverse Mercator | |

V

v.	Volcanic	J 37
var, VAR	Variation	B 60
vard	Varied	J be
vel.	Velocity	H n
vert	**Vertically disposed**	P 15
Vert CL	Vertical clearance	D20, 28
Vi	**Violet**	P 11.5
Vil	Village	D 4
VLCC	**Very Large Crude Carrier**	G 187
vol	Volcanic, Volcano	J 37
Vol Ash	Volcanic ash	J k
VQ	Very quick	P 10.7
VTS	**Vessel Traffic Service**	

W

W	**West**	B 12
W	**White**	P 11.1
Wd	**Weed**	J 13.1
Well	Wellhead	L 21
WGS	**World Geodetic System**	S 50
Wh	White	J ar
Whf	Wharf	F 13
WHIS, Whis	Whistle	R 15
Wk, Wks	**Wreck(s)**	K 20
Wtr Tr, WTR TR	Water tower	E 21

Y

Y	**Yellow, Orange, Amber**	P 11.6-11.8
yd, yds	Yard(s)	B d
yl	Yellow	J aw

μ

| μs, μsec | Microsecond(s) | B f |

Index

Index

Index

Index

116

Index

Index

119

Index

120

Index

Index

122

Appendix 1 IALA Maritime Buoyage System

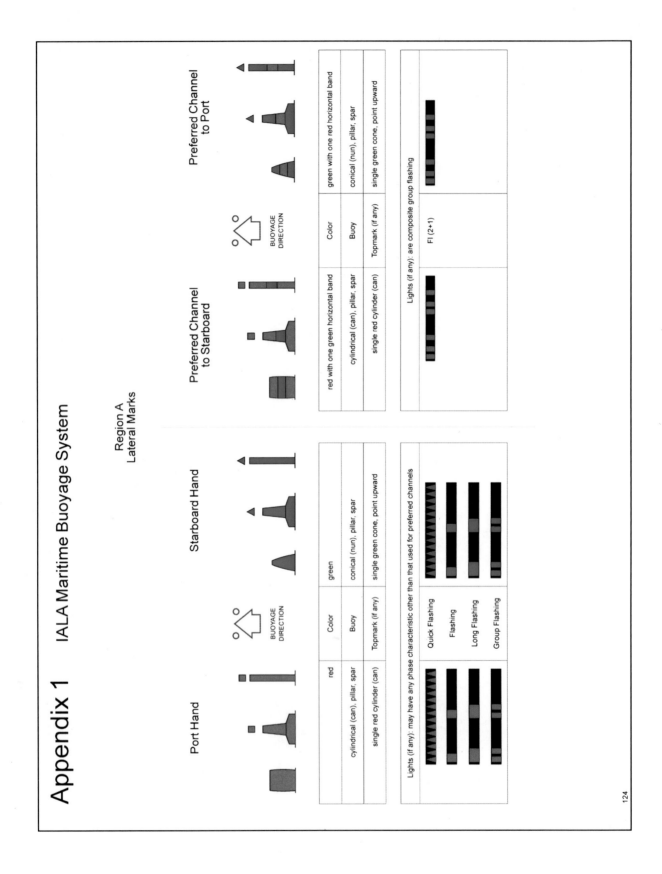

Region A
Lateral Marks

Port Hand

red		
Color	Buoy	Topmark (if any)
cylindrical (can), pillar, spar	single red cylinder (can)	

Starboard Hand

green		
Color	Buoy	Topmark (if any)
conical (nun), pillar, spar	single green cone, point upward	

Lights (if any): may have any phase characteristic other than that used for preferred channels

Quick Flashing

Flashing

Long Flashing

Group Flashing

Preferred Channel to Starboard

red with one green horizontal band		
Color	Buoy	Topmark (if any)
cylindrical (can), pillar, spar	single red cylinder (can)	

Preferred Channel to Port

green with one red horizontal band		
Color	Buoy	Topmark (if any)
conical (nun), pillar, spar	single green cone, point upward	

Lights (if any): are composite group flashing

Fl (2+1)

BUOYAGE DIRECTION

BUOYAGE DIRECTION

124

256

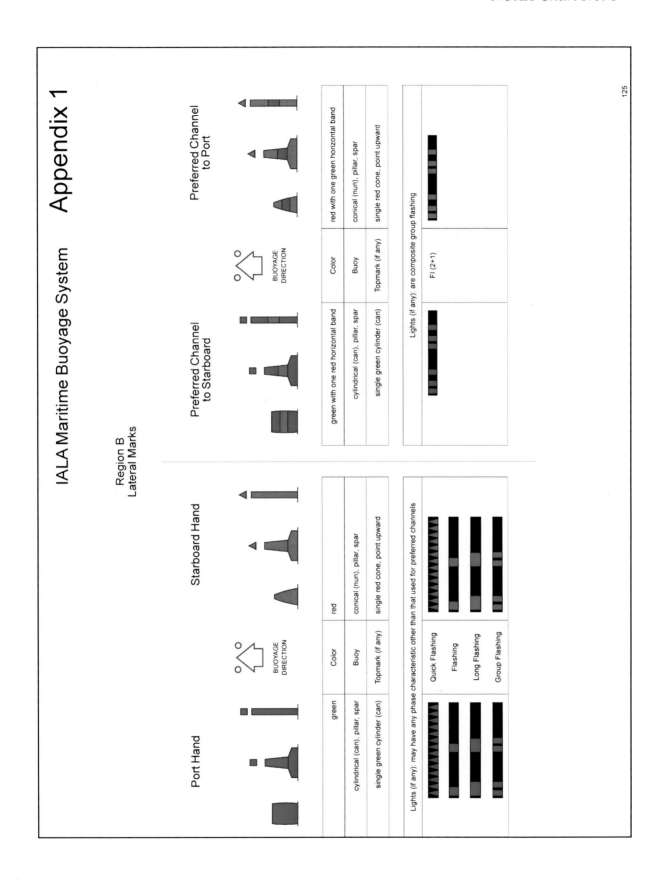

257

Appendix 1   IALA Maritime Buoyage System

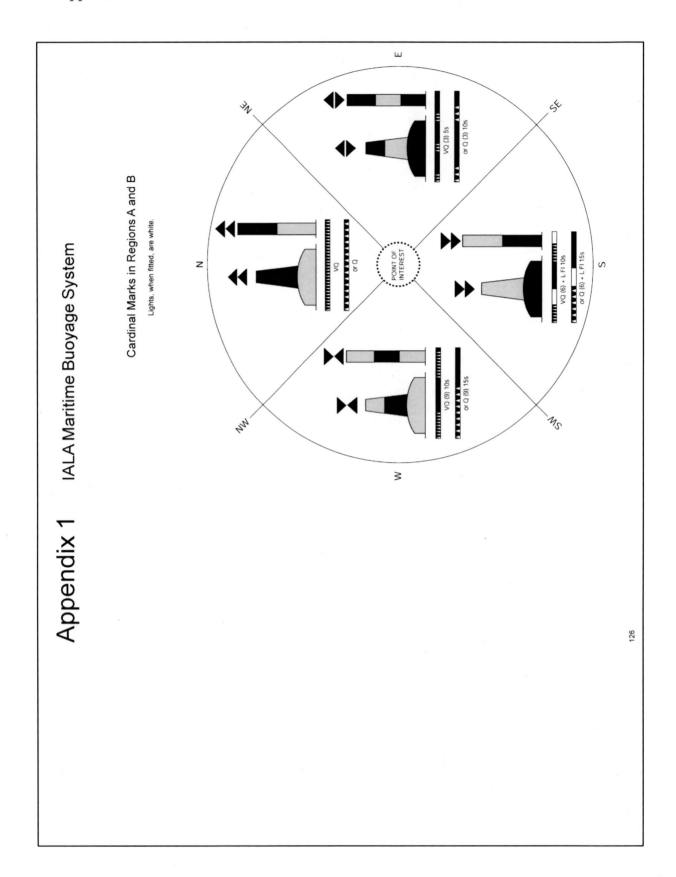

Cardinal Marks in Regions A and B

Lights, when fitted, are white.

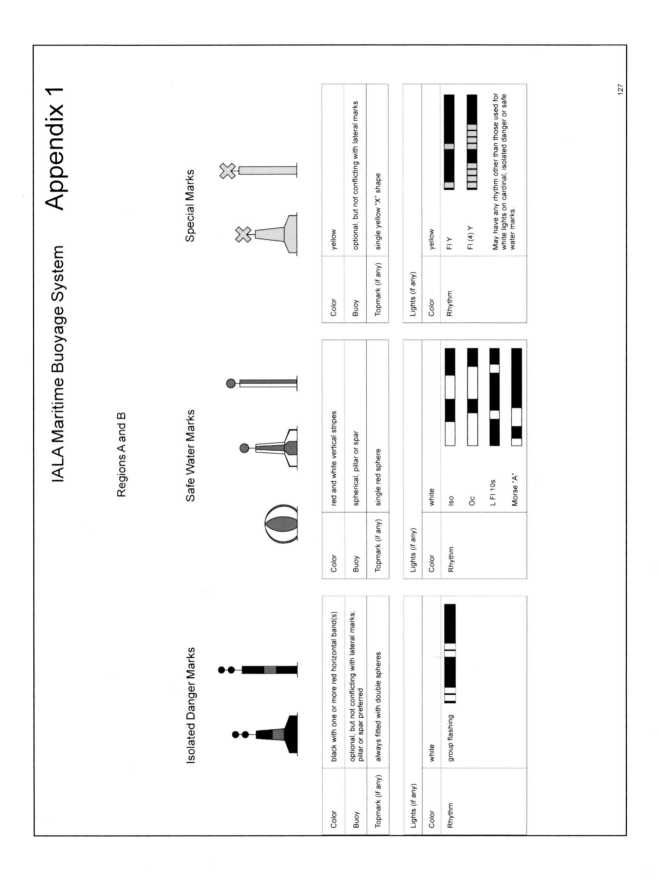

IALA Maritime Buoyage System — Appendix 1

Regions A and B

Isolated Danger Marks

Color	black with one or more red horizontal band(s)
Buoy	optional, but not conflicting with lateral marks; pillar or spar preferred
Topmark (if any)	always fitted with double spheres

Lights (if any)	
Color	white
Rhythm	group flashing

Safe Water Marks

Color	red and white vertical stripes
Buoy	spherical, pillar or spar
Topmark (if any)	single red sphere

Lights (if any)	
Color	white
Rhythm	Iso Oc L Fl 10s Morse "A"

Special Marks

Color	yellow
Buoy	optional, but not conflicting with lateral marks
Topmark (if any)	single yellow "X" shape

Lights (if any)	
Color	yellow
Rhythm	Fl Y Fl (4) Y May have any rhythm other than those used for white lights on cardinal, isolated danger or safe water marks.

127

Record of Corrections

Notice No.	Corrected on	Corrected by

Notice No.	Corrected on	Corrected by

Notice No.	Corrected on	Corrected by

129

Section Key

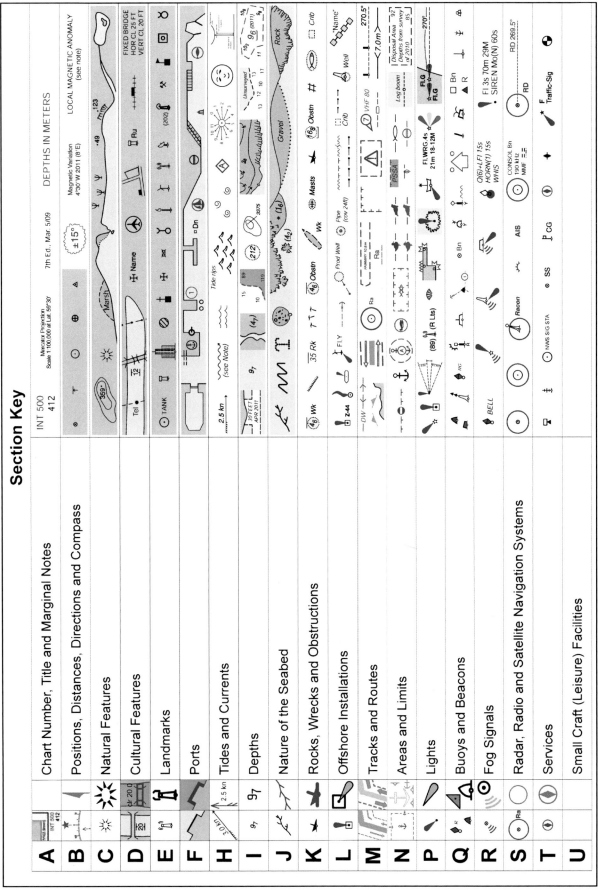

A	Chart Number, Title and Marginal Notes
B	Positions, Distances, Directions and Compass
C	Natural Features
D	Cultural Features
E	Landmarks
F	Ports
H	Tides and Currents
I	Depths
J	Nature of the Seabed
K	Rocks, Wrecks and Obstructions
L	Offshore Installations
M	Tracks and Routes
N	Areas and Limits
P	Lights
Q	Buoys and Beacons
R	Fog Signals
S	Radar, Radio and Satellite Navigation Systems
T	Services
U	Small Craft (Leisure) Facilities

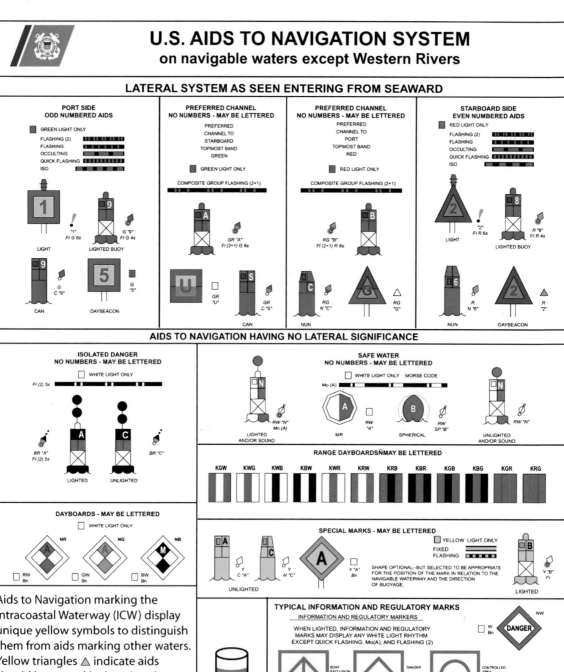

Aids to Navigation marking the Intracoastal Waterway (ICW) display unique yellow symbols to distinguish them from aids marking other waters. Yellow triangles △ indicate aids should be passed by keeping them on the starboard (right) hand of the vessel. Yellow squares ▢ indicate aids should be passed by keeping them on the port (left) hand of the vessel. A yellow horizontal band ▭ provides no lateral information, but simply identifies aids as marking the ICW.

U.S. AIDS TO NAVIGATION SYSTEM
on the Western River System

AS SEEN ENTERING FROM SEAWARD

PORT SIDE
OR RIGHT DESCENDING BANK

■ GREEN OR □ WHITE LIGHTS

FLASHING
ISO

LIGHT   LIGHTED BUOY   CAN

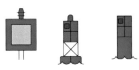

CNG

SG

PASSING DAYBEACON   CROSSING DAYBEACON

176.9
MILE BOARD

PREFERRED CHANNEL
MARK JUNCTIONS AND OBSTRUCTIONS
COMPOSITE GROUP FLASHING (2+1)

PREFERRED CHANNEL TO STARBOARD TOPMOST BAND GREEN Fl (2+1) G	PREFERRED CHANNEL TO PORT TOPMOST BAND RED Fl (2+1) R

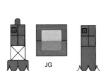

JG

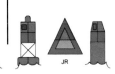

JR

DAYBOARDS HAVING NO LATERAL SIGNIFICANCE

MAY BE LETTERED   □ WHITE LIGHT ONLY

NB

STARBOARD SIDE
OR LEFT DESCENDING BANK

■ RED OR □ WHITE LIGHTS

FLASHING (2)
ISO

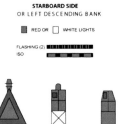

LIGHT   LIGHTED BUOY   NUN

MAY BE LIGHTED   TR   CNR

PASSING DAYBEACON   CROSSING DAYBEACON

123.5
MILE BOARD

SPECIAL MARKS--MAYBE LETTERED

SHAPE: OPTIONAL--BUT SELECTED TO BE APPROPRIATE FOR THE POSITION OF THE MARK IN RELATION TO THE NAVIGABLE WATERWAY AND THE DIRECTION OF BUOYAGE.

NY

□ YELLOW LIGHT ONLY
FIXED
FLASHING

UNLIGHTED   LIGHTED

MOORING BUOY
WHITE WITH BLUE BAND

MAY SHOW WHITE REFLECTOR OR LIGHT

TYPICAL INFORMATION AND REGULATORY MARKS
INFORMATION AND REGULATORY MARKERS
WHEN LIGHTED, INFORMATION AND REGULATORY MARKS MAY DISPLAY ANY LIGHT RHYTHM EXCEPT QUICK FLASHING, Mo(a) AND FLASHING (2)

NW □ WHITE LIGHT ONLY

DANGER

BOAT EXCLUSION AREA

SWIM AREA

EXPLAINATION MAY BE PLACED OUTSIDE THE CROSSED DIAMOND SHAPE, SUCH AS DAM, RAPIDS, SWIM AREA, ETC.

DANGER

ROCK

THE NATURE OF DANGER MAY BE INDICATED INSIDE THE DIAMOND SHAPE, SUCH AS ROCK, WRECK, SHOAL, DAM, ETC.

CONTROLLED AREA

SLOW
NO WAKE

TYPE OF CONTROL IS INDICATED IN THE CIRCLE, SUCH AS SLOW, NO WAKE, ANCHORING, ETC.

MULLET LAKE
BLACK RIVER

INFORMATION

FOR DISPLAYING INFORMATION SUCH AS DIRECTIONS, DISTANCES, LOCATIONS, ETC.

BUOY USED TO DISPLAY REGULATORY MARKERS

5

MAY SHOW WHITE LIGHT MAY BE LETTERED

STATE WATERS

3   2

INLAND (STATE) WATERS OBSTRUCTION MARK
MAY SHOW WHITE REFLECTOR OR QUICK FLASHING WHITE LIGHT

BLACK-STRIPED WHITE BUOY

Used to indicate an obstruction to navigation, extends from the nearest shore to the buoy. This means "do not pass between the buoy and the nearest shore." This aid is replacing the red and white striped buoy within the USWMS, but cannot be used until all red and white striped buoys on a waterway have been replaced.

PLATE 4

v 1.3

Made in United States
North Haven, CT
29 August 2022

23411616R00148